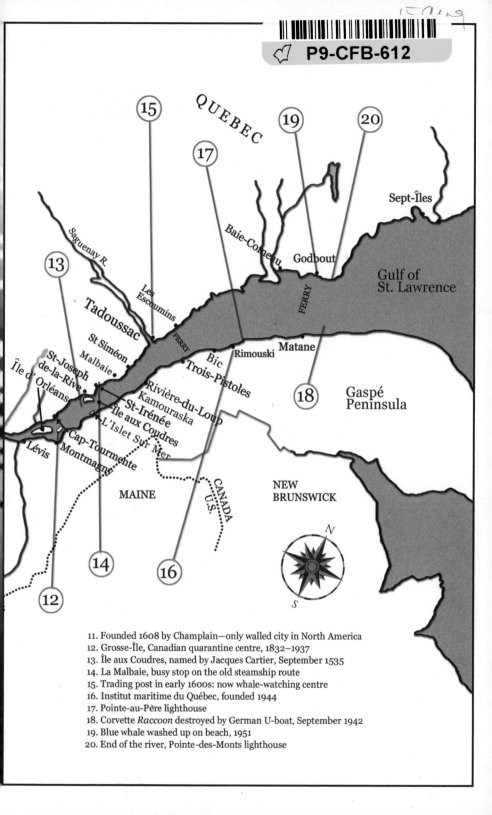

P9-CFB-612

11. Founded 1608 by Champlain—only walled city in North America
12. Grosse-Île, Canadian quarantine centre, 1832–1937
13. Île aux Coudres, named by Jacques Cartier, September 1535
14. La Malbaie, busy stop on the old steamship route
15. Trading post in early 1600s: now whale-watching centre
16. Institut maritime du Québec, founded 1944
17. Pointe-au-Père lighthouse
18. Corvette *Raccoon* destroyed by German U-boat, September 1942
19. Blue whale washed up on beach, 1951
20. End of the river, Pointe-des-Monts lighthouse

River Song

Sailing the History of the St. Lawrence

To brother Alan, my first mate on the good ship *Jenkins*,
and Sue, Johnny and Kate the Great
from the Armstrong line

Our lives are the rivers
Which flow into the sea.

—José Manrique, 1440–79

RIVER SONG
Sailing the History of the St. Lawrence

PHIL JENKINS

PENGUIN

VIKING

VIKING
Published by the Penguin Group
Penguin Books Canada Ltd, 10 Alcorn Avenue, Toronto, Ontario,
Canada M4V 3B2
Penguin Books Ltd, 27 Wrights Lane, London W8 5TZ, England
Penguin Putnam Inc., 375 Hudson Street, New York, New York 10014, U.S.A.
Penguin Books Australia Ltd, Ringwood, Victoria, Australia
Penguin Books (NZ) Ltd, cnr Rosedale and Airborne Roads, Albany,
Auckland 1310, New Zealand

Penguin Books Ltd, Registered Offices: Harmondsworth, Middlesex,
England

First published 2001

1 3 5 7 9 10 8 6 4 2

Copyright © Phil Jenkins, 2001

The author would like to acknowledge the support of the Canada Council.

The quotation on page 298 is from Hugh MacLennan's *Rivers of Canada*,
published in 1974 by Macmillan of Canada and appears
with the permission of the copyright owner, McGill University.

Printed and bound in Canada on acid free paper ∞
Text design and typesetting by Ruthe Swern

CANADIAN CATALOGUING IN PUBLICATION DATA
Jenkins, Phil, 1951–
River song: sailing the history of the St. Lawrence

ISBN 0-670-88009-4

1. Saint Lawrence River–History I. Title.
FC2756.J46 2000   971.4   C00-931041-X
F1050.J46 2000

Visit Penguin Canada's website at **www.penguin.ca**

CONTENTS

All chapter titles are taken from song titles.

Second Watch: Riding the Waves

MESSAGE IN A BOTTLE

*The ferry over to Wolfe Island goes from Kingston,
a kindly town of safe harbour.*

Although it continues to bear a saint's name, the St. Lawrence
is not holy water, as the Ganges still is. Tens of thousands of
Canadians do not take ritual daily dips in it, or light fires
alongside it in honour of the river's spirit. In the hearts of its
congregation, the Ganges holds on to its status, even as its
vigour is desecrated; but the St. Lawrence, drop by tainted
drop, has fallen from grace. It is indentured for life as a highway, a sewer, a larder and a playground. For the vast majority of
the six million Canadians and Americans who live on the St.
Lawrence, it is Hapi, the fat-bellied Egyptian god of the Nile
who stands between two goddesses—the riverbanks—dressed

as a fisherman, offering his endless gifts to the people huddled around him.

The St. Lawrence is the longest river running east-west in North America, an eight-hundred-mile umbilical cord conveying the tremendous pressure of the Great Lakes, the greatest freshwater kingdom on earth, into the saline reservoir of the Atlantic. It has fulfilled this destiny for ten thousand years, along the path it adopted after the last ice age.

On the surface the river flows one way; underneath there are two currents, one of economy and one of poetry. Food for the table, and food for the soul. Four hundred beluga whales and ten thousand ships a year ply the same waters, and rituals of business are performed on the same altar as rituals of beauty. Nine different species of whale, living in smoggy, toxic water, have become profitable tourist destinations, while birchbark canoes have grown into sixty-thousand-ton freighters. This matriarchal river, the headwater of the country's flowing past, has borne the bulk of Canada's history—and history, as a historian once said, is just one damn thing after another.

At the entrance to Lake Ontario, where it yields to the St. Lawrence, lies Wolfe Island, the most westerly of thousands of islands embedded in the river. Some are no more than humble rocks, supporting a few terns. The biggest, Montréal, is home to three million people.

Originally called Ganoukouesnot ("long island standing up") by the Ojibwa who hunted there, Grande Île by the French and, briefly, Hog Island by the British after an incident involving escaped pigs, Wolfe Island is big enough to support the small town of Marysville, some homes dotted along the shoreline and a bunch of farms. It does not possess a single traffic light.

The ferry over to Wolfe Island goes from Kingston, a kindly town of safe harbour that was briefly the capital of Canada and nowadays bulges with students, soldiers and prisoners. Today, May Day, the three o'clock ferry is filling with islanders who, like their fellow islanders up and down the river, are heading home at the end of a working week. Cars from various provinces and states, a couple of pickups with American plates towing boats, and one from Ontario loaded with small trees make up the manifest.

The *Wolfe Islander III* is one of twenty ferries that shuttle back and forth across the St. Lawrence. Essentially, it's a moving piece of the Ontario provincial highway, a floating slab of road with a gantry on it like a giant staple. Captain Woodman, a dark-haired, relaxed man in a short-sleeved shirt, is at the helm. He was born on Wolfe Island, as was his father, who was also the ferry captain in his time. In his first year out of marine college Captain Woodman sailed along the St. Lawrence, doing the cargo run from the Great Lakes to the Gulf. But he is a man who likes to see his family every day, and for the last nine years he has only sailed back and forth on the river's western border, painting the same slow arc of metallic white across a blue-brown canvas. At the end of each journey, thirty times a day, he simply turns around and is ready to go back.

Twenty minutes after taking her out of Kingston, Captain Woodman nuzzles the highly manoeuvrable *Wolfe Islander III* up to the dock at Marysville without mishap, the choreography studied to its conclusion by resident experts on the wharf. The ferry empties and reloads; Marysville breathes in some people and breathes out others, then settles down for a half-hour respite before the ferry departs.

Reaching the western tip of Wolfe Island, Long Point requires a five-minute drive and an hour's walk. The point is indeed long: it's a grassy, almost treeless barrow with a cow path running along its back and a stony beach on each side, a finger of land reaching out to touch the cheek of the Great Lakes. Usually, its only visitors this time of year are cattle, foxes, some mergansers, nervous coots, cormorants, flocks of clarineting Canada geese and millions and millions of mayflies. The flies rise in a solid mass when they are disturbed and settle on an intruder like living paint.

A mile or so along the path, past the roofless ruin of a stone farmhouse, past an abandoned duck hunters' hide lying drunkenly on its side, is the very tip of the tip. On this day a few spent shotgun shells are the only human signs, but not so long ago twelve-gallon bottles of hash oil were washed up here, the fallout of a smuggling run gone wrong; the American border is only a mile south of here. This modern treasure chest was discovered by a twelve-year-old boy, who dutifully reported it to his father, the island policeman—something an older person might not have bothered to do. Drugs are just one of several profitable stimulants smuggled across the St. Lawrence. Booze and cigarettes flow from the States into Canada, and illegal immigrants go the other way.

Running out from the point into oblivion in an eerily straight line is one end of a vast chain. The links are Olympian in size. It was once a tether for giant rafts of square timber on their way to shipyards downriver; runaway logs a hundred years old and more occasionally pop up around the island. Now the chain seems to anchor the island itself to the riverbed against the mighty flow of water coming from the third, fifth, sixth, ninth and twelfth largest lakes by volume on earth, enough of it passing Wolfe Island in one minute to fill every bath in Canada.

I believe in small rituals. They take time and planning, and thus indicate respect. The ritual of casting things onto the water is an old and honourable one. The Vikings launched burning boats on rivers as funeral pyres, and the Algonquin Indians threw tobacco into waterfalls. The Japanese remember Hiroshima by floating small paper lanterns downriver. To walk along both sides of the Narmada, India's most sacred river, is an act of spiritual enlightenment that takes months and is known as *parikrama*.

I've chosen the offering of a bottle as my ritual because sailors traditionally put model ships and distress notes in them, and once afloat they carry both meanings of the word vessel. One of the most famous examples of a bottle as dual vessel occurred in 1784, when a Japanese sailor called Matsuyama was shipwrecked on a reef. Before he died, the doomed man put a note scratched on wood in a bottle, describing his situation. The bottle was found one hundred and fifty years later, washed up at *the same village where Matsuyama was born*.

The only bottle I have here with me is a small green one, shaped like a torpedo. It was retrieved at the bottom of the St. Lawrence by a diver, and I bought it on the way to Long Point at an antique store in Maitland, a nearby village on the Canadian side. Now my bottle will go back to the river whence it came and, if luck holds, make its way through three thousand islands, two countries and two provinces to the ocean. A long journey, but bottles have been known to cover great distances. In 1929, German scientists began tracking a bottle released in the South Indian Ocean, and by 1935 it had travelled sixteen thousand miles.

Pants off, I wade into water cold enough to halt circulation of the blood. A nearby troop of gulls rises and wheels off the water, chortling at my clumsiness. I blow a note across the neck of the bottle, then insert a note into it explaining its mission and hoping whoever finds it will contact me. Finally, I wish the little object *bonne chance*, cork it, and set it on the moving water. Perversely, it begins to head upriver, out into Lake Ontario; the easterly wind is stronger than the current. But, once out in deeper water, the undertow asserts itself. Gradually the bottle comes about and heads for the shipping lane on the American side. Through binoculars I watch it shrink to a dot, and then it is no longer my vessel; it is the river's.

For a while after the bottle is gone from sight, I just stare at the water. Then I dip my head in it for a moment with my eyes closed, listening to the underwater sounds, imagining I can hear everything from the river's crowded history. The swish of the canoe paddle, the snap of the sail, the exhale of the diver, the whine of the outboard and the low thunder of the heavy-laden tanker—the river song, the song cycle of its history.

A river, more than an ocean or a lake, is a stand-in for Time, for the relentless vector of history. We push into the world from broken water, and when we die it washes our sins away. Standing in a river like this, staring into its flowing past, moves the mind from the objective to the subjective. It weathers away the everyday and leaves exposed the imagination. And so I take up my pen, dip it in the water, and begin to write the song cycle of the St. Lawrence River, a river of stories, of things that float and settle, of beauty and the bottom line.

First Watch

The Tides of Time

*And
now, through the present expedition under-
taken at your royal command for the discovery of the lands
in the west formerly unknown to you and to us, lying in the same cli-
mates and parallels as your territories and kingdom, you will learn and
hear of their richness and fertility, of the immense number of people living
there, of their kindness and peacefulness, and likewise of the richness of
the great river which flows through and waters the midst of these
lands of yours, which is without comparison the largest river
that is known to have ever been seen.*

—from the dedication to Francis I of France in
Jacques Cartier's account of his second voyage to Canada, 1535–36

1

ONLY OUR RIVERS RUN FREE

*The main freeway, the St. Lawrence, flowed ever eastward,
inhaling and exhaling to the pulse of the moon.*

It is a wonder that something as steadfast as a tree, so tenacious in its embrace of the earth, floats when laid on water. The problem facing early North American woodlanders—tightly packed forests extending right down to the riverbank that snookered travelling in a straight line—also happily contained the solution. The people of the woods got around by taking to the rivers on trees. Starting with crude, serviceable rafts, they went on to design vehicles of such glorious purpose, reconfiguring the raw matter of the forest into watertight arks perfectly matched to their requirements, that the concept is immortal. The canoe sits, quite rightly, at the base of the Canadian coat of arms, and in any list of symbols of the country's culture it floats naturally to the top.

So the working life of the St. Lawrence, its term of employment, began with the skinning of a birch trunk. Birch has the farthest northern reach of any deciduous tree, and the woodlands along the banks of the rivers were stiff with them. The bark came away in rolls twice as long as a man, and, thick as a thumb, it was strongest in spring, when canoe building and repair were top of the list of extended family chores in the longhouses. As the ice on the river yielded to the warming sun, the tribes living on the riverbanks, the ones academics refer to as the proto-Iroquois and Algonquians, shifted into the new season, greasing snowshoes for summer storage out of reach of grease-loving bears, tapping the maple trees for their syrup, and readying the fishing fleet for launch in the river they called Magtogoek, meaning "the road that walks."

Panelled with the side of the bark that had been facing out on the tree now looking inwards, the birchbark canoe resisted water and remained strong and light. Supple braces made of ash and bindings of spruce root, as well as gum of charcoal and resin, held it together. (To the south and west of the St. Lawrence birch was scarce, and canoeists there were forced to use the inferior elm.) Punctures and tears were redeemed after a quick forage in the woods. Customizing of the completed vehicles, a deep-seated urge in canoe and car owners alike, was evident in the prow's silhouette, tall and sharp on the St. Lawrence, with sun signs or eyes etched directly onto the birch panels.

There is evidence of the daily lives of the proto-Iroquois all along the upper St. Lawrence River, including the recent discovery of a fishing camp under Vieux-Montréal. Three-thousand-year-old artifacts are embedded like slivers in the skin of the earth all over Montréal Island. The St. Lawrence Iroquois, as they are also known, hunted the migratory eel in their canoes and smoked them. At Hochelaga, the Iroquois settlement superseded by French Montréal, the eel smokehouse may have been close to where Ben's, a famous restaurant, now sells smoked meat. Outsized cucumbers and berries rounded out the eel diet. An unblemished, elegant clay cooking pot with a concentric rope pattern just above its hip was discovered on the river bottom near Wolfe Island by a diver in the mid-1900s. It was wisely handed over to a local archaeologist, who identified it as being made at least twelve hundred years ago, when it probably fell there in a canoeing accident.

Wild rice was also on the menu, growing in stands in the wetlands. Harvesting the rice was as simple for the women as paddling into the rice stand and carpet-beating the grains into the belly of the boat. Fish, a more mobile prey than rice, required a different tactic. A torch of tightly wrapped birchbark, mounted on the prow of the canoe, drew fish to the light, there to be speared.

The network of rivers was the highway system of the northeastern woodlands. The canoe was its truck, tractor, runabout and Jeep. The main freeway, the St. Lawrence, flowed ever eastward, inhaling and exhaling to the pulse of the moon, and her sister rivers, her Shiva-like arms, reached far into the territory. If you were travelling down a river and the way ahead was impassable, you simply picked your vehicle up and looped along the shoreline to the next reasonable stretch of water. Finding a parking spot was never a problem, and canoes sat on the shore in front of the longhouses like giant milkweed pods, clumsy as seals until they regained their element. In winter, when the roads were closed, it was time to tend the traplines.

You are what you drive, and the pace of life for the St. Lawrence Iroquois was dictated by their canoes. When they rushed through a set of rapids—at Lachine or in the Long Sault—that was the fastest the woodlanders ever got to move; it was their speed limit.

This rhythm of water traffic made possible the great Aboriginal trade alliances—and wars—that redressed the uneven distribution of copper, obsidian, quahog clams and fur-bearing animals throughout the eastern waterways. Sealed and maintained with gifts, these alliances were built up over at least five thousand years in the St. Lawrence valley. In the bottom of a birchbark canoe, making its way along the river a thousand years ago, there were items of trade from all over the continent: cold-hammered copper spearheads from the Great Lakes, stone flights like arrow feathers for spears, decorative beads made of mother-of-pearl, and silver amulets.

The pattern of trade in the eastern woodlands was extensive—tobacco from what is now Florida was available a millennium ago in what is now Quebec—but there was an insurmountable trade barrier that the St. Lawrence canoeists were, as far as is known, unable to cross: the Atlantic Ocean. It's a wise rule in history never to say never, but the woodlanders never paddled to Europe; their navigational technology could not get them there from here. The flow of trade expansion, like a prevailing wind, came from the other direction; it ran from east to west, not west to east.

2

UP A LAZY RIVER

Cartier took his ships into the St. Lawrence valley, anchoring at Bic on the south shore on the twenty-ninth.

According to a man called Napoleon Martin, who wrote a book about it not too long ago, there were Vikings in the St. Lawrence valley around AD 1000. They stayed for one year, in a colony they called Hop. Martin figures Hop was where Baie-Comeau is now—on the north shore near the mouth of the river—and he bases his hypothesis on clues in the saga of Eric the Red, a Norse rebel who was thrown out of Iceland and settled in Greenland. Martin, reading between the lines of Eric's story, deduces that the Norsemen abandoned Hop because they didn't get along with the people already living there, or vice versa.

Setting Martin aside, the only hard evidence of settlement available to date points to the Vikings first landing on the Labrador coast in the year 986, when Bjarni Herjulfsson was blown off course. Fourteen years later one of Eric the Red's sons, Leif Ericsson, set up camp at L'Anse aux Meadows on the tip of Newfoundland, and a little while later his brother Thorvald took over. Outnumbered and having no dramatically superior weapons, the Vikings either ran out or fell out with the people they called skraelings. There ensued a gap of almost five centuries while the Europeans gradually acquired the will and the way to cross the Atlantic.

In the space of a few short decades the naval architecture of the late Middle Ages moved through a series of improvements that reduced the risk of sinking on a long sea journey. Each model of ship, coincidentally, began with the letter C. First came the north European cog, then the southern carrack. After that was the beautiful caravel (exploration ship of choice of the Portuguese in the late fifteenth century) and finally the majestic clipper ships, the airliners of their day.

The race to locate fresh resources of spices, timber, fish, precious metals and slave labour on behalf of the various European heads of state became the preoccupation of European sea captains. They went madly off in all directions, including to the west. The result of all those busy ships was a rewriting of the world map in the rush for colonies. They were Christians who believed they were travelling the lines of God's palm, and that the lines were veins of wealth.

Just before the end of the fifteenth century Columbus returned to Spain under the misconception that he had reached India, when in fact he had got no more than halfway. He landed at the island now shared by two of the world's poorest nations, Haiti and the Dominican Republic, and there met the Arawak peoples, long since exterminated. At that meeting, as explorers are wont to do, Columbus asked the Arawak the name of their vessels. The Arawaks replied *canoas*, and the Italian explorer took the word back with him as part of his haul of New World vocabulary. The little five-letter word *canoa* travelled from mouth to mouth around Europe, becoming *canot* in French, while the English replaced the *a* with one of their much loved *es*.

Five years after Columbus, John Cabot returned from a touchdown on the Newfoundland coast with a report of inexhaustible cod stocks in the waters off Newfoundland, and by the beginning of the sixteenth century both explorers and fishermen were making their way across the ocean in leagues and bounds, into the fertile Grand Banks and beyond, to the very cliffs and beaches at the edge of the western continent. The southerly trade winds took them there, and the northern ones took them back with more detailed reports of the coastline as a possible new marketing region. The maps and journals that ensued from these voyages were brochures pushing ships to the new lands in search of an answer to the question that was filling their sails: is this the way to Asia?

It was the Basque fishermen, then as now determined sailors in pursuit of their catch, who most likely introduced the Native peoples of the St. Lawrence to the primary piece of European technology, the sailing ship, in the early sixteenth century. There is speculation that the Basques went as far as Tadoussac, which is a good two hundred miles upriver, and certainly several of the explorers who came later were surprised to hear a smattering of Basque words when trying to converse with the locals. The fishermen, as well as loading their boats with cod, traded goods with the Mi'kmaq in the Gulf of St. Lawrence. The Mi'kmaq in their turn made deals with the river peoples: the Montagnais on the north shore, and the Maliseet, Passamaquoddy and Penobscot on the more crowded south. Included in the deals were samples of another European technology the fishermen had brought with them: iron, stronger than fire or flesh, worked into bowls or the barrels of guns.

The precise moment when canoe met sailing ship on the St. Lawrence River, and daily life there began an irreversible exponential change, is unknown. The first recorded meeting of St. Lawrence Native people with a European happened when a sailor from Brittany, Jacques Cartier, made his first westward crossing of the Atlantic in a convoy of two ships with a crew of sixty-one. They left St-Malo, as though heading off to work, on a Monday morning in April, and the journey took them a mere twenty days. The year was 1534.

Cartier shinnied down the coast of Labrador, saw the Beothuk hunting seal and later used gunfire to turn away a trading party of forty Mi'kmaq canoes. Riding towards shore in a longboat—the large rowboats carried on sailing ships to shuttle about in—he had interpreted the Mi'kmaq approach as hostile, and displayed his technological superiority. By now he had realized for himself that, as in Europe, he was dealing with a large territory inhabited by several distinct tribes. When the Mi'kmaq, unintimidated, tried again, this time using sign language to indicate that they wanted to barter not brawl, the two tribes, French and Native, did business. The Mi'kmaq even threw in the furs they were wearing, initiating the Canadian second-hand clothing business.

By mid-July, taking his time, Cartier had crossed a large gulf and was in a natural harbour. It was Gaspé, and he was only a couple of days east of the mouth of the St. Lawrence. Ashore, and in need of marking this new territory, Cartier supervised the erection of a large cross on the mainland, a billboard decorated with a fleur-de-lys and the words VIVE LE ROI DE FRANCE (Long Live the King of France, then Francis I), advertising France's colonial intentions.

This ritual was watched offshore by several canoes. In them were Iroquois from the St. Lawrence River, from Stadacona (the future site of Québec), making their annual eastern fishing trip. In one canoe containing several young men and an older one, the latter stood up and began pointing at the Frenchmen and the cross and then sweeping his arm out across the water. The chief, or *sachem*, of the village, Donnacona, wearing a black bearskin, clearly understood the broader territorial implications of the cross, and was dressing the Frenchmen down for trespassing. A sailor offered Donnacona an axe, probably in return for the bearskin, and the canoes moved closer in to the French ships. Cartier, whose nerves may have been a little stretched at this point, had the canoe boarded and the five men in it forcibly brought on board, the first recorded incident of St. Lawrence Indians being on a sailing ship.

On deck, the men of the two worlds attempted to converse. Cartier signalled that three of the men could go back to their canoes, with hatchets and knives as prizes, but that two, Domagaya and Taignoagny, Donnacona's sons, would be travelling on the ship for a while and then would return. The two men, who had exchanged their clothes for shirts, ribbons, red caps and a brass necklace, would return to St-Malo for training as interpreters and to be displayed as specimens of the local species, much as the Victorians, in a fit of taxonomy, would later collect rare plants in the South Seas.

Cartier does not record the reaction of any of the Iroquois, and Donnacona left no permanent account of his first meeting with European colonialists. Six Native canoes paddled back to the ship in the afternoon, with some fish for Domagaya and

Taignoagny. Certainly the two brothers couldn't have understood that nine months would pass before they saw their home again, but several years later in France, when dictating his record of his Canadian trips, Cartier gave his reaction to meeting the St. Lawrence Iroquois for the first time: "This people may well be called savage, for they are the sorriest folk there can be in the world, and the whole lot of them had not anything above the value of five sous, their canoes and fishing nets excepted." (Notice that the Frenchman mentions money right away, and that he equates lack of wealth with being in a sorry state.)

Cartier pulled away from Gaspé the next day, the twenty-fifth of July, came within about twenty miles of the St. Lawrence, then made for Newfoundland, which he left on the fifteenth of August. The two Iroquois brothers who went with him to St-Malo and *terra incognita* were thus the first people from the St. Lawrence valley to make the trip to Europe. Would that they could have written what befell them that winter.

Cartier spent the nine months in Paris and St-Malo quizzing the two Stadaconans, and now knew that the gulf he had mapped on his first voyage was connected to a sizable river. The river, he had been informed, was divided into three regions: the Saguenay territory around the great, deep river on the north shore; Canada down as far as Lac St-Pierre; and beyond that Hochelaga, which took in the pair of large islands that would become Montréal. (There is an old sailing myth that *Canada* is not a Native word but rather corrupted Spanish. A pre-Cartier explorer apparently saw the snow-capped mountains of Notre-Dame, which form Cap Rosiers at the entrance to the river, and decided to name it *Capo de Nada*, or Cape Nothing. According to the myth, saying *Capo de Nada* quickly metamorphosed into *Canada*. I think not.)

Domagaya and Taignoagny, after two seasons away from the St. Lawrence, returned with Cartier on his second voyage, which left St-Malo in mid-May 1535. This time there were three ships of differing sizes. The *Grande Hermine* was a hundred and twenty tons and had a crew of sixty. Her little sister, the *Petite Hermine*, was half that, and the très petite *Émérillon* (French for *Merlin*) was only forty tons. (There is a replica of the *Grande Hermine* in a park in Quebec City. It sits on dry land, resting on a wood crib, forever ten feet from regaining the water. It seems such a tiny thing to be crossing oceans in.)

For the crew it was a cramped life, the men bedding down near the stove they called the firehole, in among the barrels and bales of stores. Only Cartier would have had a bedroom to himself, probably quite an ornate one compared with the chicken coops the sailors slept in. At the change of each watch, after a ship's boy had turned over the half-hour glass for the eighth time, there was a blast on a trumpet and a saying of prayers. Fierce winds in the Atlantic separated the ships, and they weren't reunited until they reached Newfoundland eleven weeks later.

As the ships, together again, made their way westwards along the north shore of the gulf, their progress was followed by the coast guard system the eastern tribes had in place and the news passed along by messengers. During the month of July, Cartier carefully picked his way among the coastlines, shoals and reefs—the word *dangereux* crops up frequently in his log—and spent the first week of August in harbour at Natashkwan Point.

Then, on the tenth of August 1535, Cartier set sail again and paused at a small bay just east of Havre St-Pierre. Elsewhere the world was busy setting up the London Stock Exchange, the English were getting ready to break with the Pope, and the Jesuit order was enjoying its first anniversary.

Consulting his missive, Cartier named the bay after the saint whose day this was: Lawrence of Rome, a man who had died for his faith in a Roman pogrom against Christians 1,277 years earlier. (St. Lawrence had been asked by the heathen Romans to produce the riches of his church. The Romans expected a treasure chest of gold chalices, silver crosses and the like. Instead, the fledgling saint produced a lineup of the blind, lepers, widows and orphans. For this lack of respect Lawrence was waffled on a heated gridiron and, legend has it, asked to be turned over when sufficiently roasted on one side.)

It wasn't until the twenty-fourth of August, a few days after seeing his first walrus, which he described as a "fish in appearance like horses which go on land at night," that Cartier took his ships into the St. Lawrence valley, anchoring at Bic on the south shore on the twenty-ninth.

Cartier continued upriver on September 1 as far as the mouth of the Saguenay River and there met some St. Lawrence Native people in birchbark canoes, the first he encountered on the river itself. "We found four canoes from Canada," Cartier noted, "that had come there to fish for seals and other fish. Two of the canoes came towards our ships but in such great fear and trembling that one of them finally went back, but the other approached near enough to hear one of our savages, who gave his name and told who he was and made them come alongside in all confidence."

Proceeding upriver, Cartier saw his first beluga whales, which he likened to greyhounds, and was told they were good to eat. The next day he made the Île aux Coudres, and named it for its hazelnuts, which he considered tastier than the French variety. Island hopping, he reached the Île d'Orléans, where the locals, made aware of his trading habits by Domagaya and Taignoagny, brought him eels, melons and cornmeal fashioned into cakes.

Cartier took his first canoe trip on Wednesday, the eighth of September, when Donnacona caught up with him at Île d'Orléans, and he describes the moment at length. Note that Cartier refers to himself in the third person as "the Captain"—he may have been dictating years later to a ghost writer—and the way he puts a rosy, cocktail-party spin on events.

> On the morrow the Lord of Canada, named Donnacona, came to our ships accompanied by many people in twelve canoes. He then sent back ten of these and came alongside our ships with only two canoes carrying sixteen men. And when he was opposite to the smallest of our three ships this Donnacona started to make a speech and harangue us, moving his body and limbs in a marvellous manner, as is their custom when showing joy and contentment. And when he came opposite to the Captain's vessel, on board of which were Taignoagny and Domagaya, the leader spoke to them and they to him, telling him what they had seen in France, and the good treatment meted out to them there. At this the leader was much pleased and begged the Captain to stretch out his arms to him that he might hug and kiss them, which is the way they welcome one in that country. After this the Captain stepped down into this Donnacona's canoe, and ordered bread and wine to be brought that the chief and his followers might partake thereof.

Abandoning the canoe for a longboat, Cartier went into Donnacona's village, Stadacona, the future Québec. His sailor's eyes fell on the great variety of trees thereabouts—oak, elm, ash, walnut, plum, yew, cedar, hawthorn, vines with fruit as big as damsons—and he spotted hemp, used in the making of rope, growing wild. He thought the place very fine, and went back to fetch his ships.

On his return, Cartier noted a distinct change in attitude by Taignoagny and Domagaya, and over the next few days they used all manner of attempts, including pantomime in costume, cries of *Jesus!*, *Maria!* and *Jacques Cartier!*, and bribery, to dissuade Cartier from going upriver, out of Canada and into Hochelaga. Most probably, although only one side of the story is available to us now, the Stadaconans wanted an exclusive contract with this apparently wealthy man, whose large ships were full of knives, kettles, broaches and glass beads. At one point in the negotiations, at Donnacona's request, Cartier fired a salvo of cannon balls into the woods, a shot that was to have many an echo in the centuries to come. The Stadaconans were impressed, as generals might be at an arms show.

Leaving the two bigger ships in harbour at Stadacona and loading several longboats and fifty men onto the *Émérillon*, Cartier set out for Hochelaga. Along the way he noted fourteen villages on the north shore, and he had plenty of time to observe the village of the Abenakis on the south shore, at the eastern end of Lac St-Pierre, when he ran aground in a longboat in extremely shallow water. Realizing he could not risk going any farther in the *Émérillon*, Cartier took to the longboats and later that day landed in St. Lawrence Iroquois territory, on Île de Montréal. The fortified village of longhouses with a population of around a thousand offered him a festive welcome. (The village's exact whereabouts are still under discussion.) He toured the village, taking a stroll up an extinct volcano to a lookout point. The light of day was such that the river to his left, the Ottawa, appeared silver, while the one to his right, the St. Lawrence, appeared golden.

Cartier set sail downriver back to Stadacona from Hochelaga in early October. Winter was setting in, and the Stadaconans extended their hospitality over the cruel season. The sailing ships, Cartier noted, were covered in a winter coat of ice "four fingers' breadth," and all their "beverages" on board were frozen solid.

By the spring of 1536, twenty-five of Cartier's crew were dead of scurvy, the first Europeans to be buried in the St. Lawrence valley. It was only because of a distillation of cedar sap administered by the Stadaconans—Cartier says they "received knowledge of a tree"—that the rest were saved. The cure had already worked on Domagaya, whom Cartier saw one day with blackened teeth and a knee swollen "to the size of a two-year-old baby"; ten days later all traces of the disease were gone. (In the interpretation centre near the model of the *Grande Hermine* there is a keg of this concoction available for testing. It has a bitter, coniferous flavour; definitely an acquired taste.)

Cartier was anxious to get back to France and, a year after he left St-Malo, he sailed out of Stadacona. However, the *Petite Hermine* never left Canada. His crew depleted by a quarter, Cartier had only enough able-bodied sailors to man two ships for the return to France. He ran the *Petite Hermine* ashore and left it there. Pieces of the abandoned ship were discovered three centuries later, and some were stored in Québec, where they were later destroyed in a fire. Other timbers from the *Petite Hermine* were sent back to St-Malo, Cartier's hometown, where they were incorporated into a monument to the first man to sail into the St. Lawrence.

As he had on his first voyage, Cartier returned to France with hostages, but this time, instead of two, he upped the number to ten, and among them was Donnacona himself. Cartier leaves no doubt that the men were kidnapped, and gifts of wampum, "the most valuable articles they possess in the world," did not make him change his mind. None of the ten ever went back to the river or the land of their birth. When Cartier returned with five ships to Stadacona, fully four years later, as the advance party for a French nobleman called Roberval, he lied to the Natives' extended family, saying that they had become Parisian persons of note. In fact, nine of them were dead. The history books have no record of who the sole survivor was or what happened to him.

Cartier's final visit, in 1541, did not go well, although he did return to Hochelaga and saw the Lachine Rapids. By now the Stadaconans had developed a reasonable mistrust for the men in the winged ships, and there was not much chance for establishing trade, which was the point of his mission. He does report planting some French seeds in an acre and a half of ploughed field at Cap-Rouge; these cabbages, turnips and lettuce quickly germinated—Canada's first imported crop. In some cliffs above Cap-Rouge he allowed himself to believe that embedded in the limestone was a goodly supply of diamonds and gold; in fact, it was quartz, iron pyrites and mica. Of what happened after that there is no record, and we do not know why the record ends there, although Cartier did make it back to France and died in 1557.

Though Cartier's third and final, year-long stay in Canada, from spring 1541 to 1542, is not fully written up in the history books, we do know that the man he was scouting for, the nobleman de Roberval, sailed over to the Gulf of St. Lawrence, where the two expeditions met up and Cartier informed his commander, *fait accompli*, that he was heading for home. Roberval made ready to carry on to Stadacona and take a shot at establishing a colony.

While preparing to sail into the St. Lawrence, Roberval discovered that his niece, Marguerite de la Roque, who was travelling with him as a potential colonist, was having an affair with one of the crew. Roberval went into a fit of Catholic outrage, and jettisoned Marguerite and her maidservant on a small island the French had named Île des Diables, the Island of Demons. (The island is just off the present very small town of Harrington Harbour on the gulf's north shore, reachable only by boat.) The lover opted to join the two women, and with only an axe, a gun and some food the outcast trio prepared to live out their lives. Marguerite was by now pregnant.

In the fall, the servant died, and neither the baby nor the man survived the first winter. Marguerite refused to die, however, and made it through another winter alone before being rescued by some Breton fishermen. She was taken back to France, where another Marguerite, the Queen of Navarre, took her under her wing. Marguerite de la Roque told her story to a historian and became notorious. Roberval, meanwhile, had failed after one winter to establish a colony at Stadacona and returned to France a year before Marguerite's rescue. She is therefore Canada's first colonist to stay more than a year.

In 1543, the French essentially shut down their Canada office, but word of the great river nevertheless travelled, via maps, from seaport to seaport. In the 1540s, pilot Jean Alphose and mapmaker Nicolas Vallard referred to the section of the river around Québec as "River of Canada" and "The Great Hochelaga River," and the land above it as "France Prime." In 1583, a navigator with the very English name of Humphrey Gilbert dubbed it "the great river called St. Laurence in Canada," and that was the name that caught on. Like a rumour that expands and then hardens into an established truth, the name Cartier gave to that one small bay gradually came to signify the entire river, as well as the enormous gulf into which it drained. Cartier could have had no idea that his simple naming ceremony in August 1535 would spawn such future diversities as the St. Lawrence String Quartet, the St-Laurent Walk-In Clinic, the St. Lawrence Pizzeria, St. Lawrence Tae-Kwan-Do, St-Laurent Suspension, St. Lawrence Cement and St. Lawrence and Hudson Railway.

Jacques Cartier had a grandnephew, Jacques Noël, whose father had been with Cartier on his third voyage. Noël was a strand off the same rope as his uncle, and in 1585 he sailed into the St. Lawrence and made the same walk up Mont Royal at Hochelaga that Cartier had undertaken fifty years earlier. This time, however, there was no one there. Hochelaga was a ghost town. Something had happened to the St. Lawrence Iroquois.

Twenty-three years later, when the French were in the mood to try again to reach China through Canada, another French-man, Samuel de Champlain, entered the St. Lawrence, his emphatic sails a signal to the St. Lawrence Native peoples that the kidnappers had returned. When Champlain's expedition retraced Cartier's route, they discovered that the fourteen villages Cartier had noted on the north shore were also gone.

What had happened? No one knows, but the educated guesses are internecine war or any one of several imported European diseases. Maybe the culprit was smallpox, whose effect on the roughly one hundred thousand people living in eastern Canada then was anything but small.

The war theory has some historical support. A battle-weary Mohawk mentioned to Champlain that he was tired of a pro-tracted feud with another Aboriginal band. If war did see off the St. Lawrence Iroquois, it was probably based on a trade imbalance, as most wars are. The woodlanders nearest to the European trading posts naturally got first pick of superior European artifacts, such as iron axes, and jealously blocked them from going upriver. The frustrated Indians to the south of the upper river—the Abenaki, Mohican, Mohawk, Oneida and Onondaga—may have violently assimilated the Iroquois or excommunicated them from their holy waterway. This would explain the deserted villages that Champlain sailed by.

Assimilated, driven off or wiped out, the St. Lawrence Iroquois left history through the side door around 1575, but the name Iroquois lived on, when the second wave of French colonizers applied it to the people living in the western half of the St. Lawrence.

3

CAN I CANOE YOU UP THE RIVER?

*That city, along with trading posts and Tadoussac (above)
on the north shore and Matane on the south, became an export centre.*

Although the Europeans arrived in boats capable of crossing
an ocean, they quickly saw that sailing ships were not suited to
heading inland past rapids and between tightly packed islands.
The locals already had the technology, and the French, who
were inclined to adapt to life in the woodlands, climbed
aboard canoes.

It was Champlain, a confirmed admirer of the canoe's
virtues, who fostered the adoption of canoes by the French. The
explorer got an object lesson in the canoe's suitability when he
tried to mount the Lachine Rapids in a longboat in 1611, three
years after founding Québec. He sat there, immobile, while the

Native canoeists, stripped naked and in close formation, went past him as though they had four-wheel drive. After test-driving a Maliseet canoe in the lower St. Lawrence (similar to the splendid hundred-year-old model on view in the Canadian Canoe Museum in Peterborough, Ontario), Champlain always kept one on board ship. He went sightseeing in his canoe, travelling from Bangor, Maine, up to the St. Lawrence and making only one short portage. In an Algonquin canoe, with field rations of corn-based sagamite, a baked cake, he went to war against the Iroquois, took an arrow in the neck and made thirty leagues in a day. (A league is not a fixed distance, and explorers took poetic licence with it, but the average league is about three and a half miles.)

In 1613, canoeing up the Ottawa River, Champlain kept one eye on the treacherous water—he had almost lost a hand in some rapids—and the other on opportunities for purchasing beaver pelts. On that trip, as he proceeded upriver, he sent some forty canoes manned by Native crews back down the Ottawa and along the St. Lawrence to the now-thriving trading post at Tadoussac. By the time the convoy reached harbour at the mouth of the Saguenay, it had doubled. Word had spread of the strangers who would exchange useful artifacts for furs, and there were plenty of furs to be had: the beaver population in Canada at that time was around one hundred million.

Champlain spent the next sixteen years building up the fur trade, surviving an assassination attempt masterminded by the Spanish (for which one of the conspirators was executed and his head stuck on the wall of the fort at Québec), pleading with France to give him the resources to colonize the St. Lawrence properly, and building a town where Stadacona had stood. Many of his pleas for an immigration policy that would anchor his colony went unheeded, and his fledgling empire paid the price. In 1629, two English brothers, Thomas and Louis Kirke, who had been itching to oust Champlain and take over his fur monopoly, and who had told him so a year earlier, stood off Québec with three ships sprouting twenty cannon between them. France and England were at war, and they had brought the conflict to the St. Lawrence. Under white flags, the Kirkes went ashore and the gentlemen exchanged letters. The end result was Champlain's capitulation, which he acknowledged with a doff of his beaver hat. The English flag went up over the bastion of the French fort on July 20, the first time it had flown in a St. Lawrence breeze.

Champlain retreated to England in October in the Kirkes' ships with most of the colony, leaving only five families, and thence he proceeded to France. Thomas Kirke stayed on in what was now New England. Before he left, Champlain made sure that Hope and Charity, two young Native girls he had taken under his wing and renamed, were looked after by one of the remaining families, the Héberts. (There had been a Faith too, but she opted to return to her own people.) In England, the Kirkes learned that England and France had been at peace for six months and that their occupation was therefore illegal. But that did not prevent them from shipping as many furs as they could to England in the next three years.

The politics of the return of New France to the French are complicated, involving the dowry of King Charles of England and a payment of four hundred thousand crowns, but the treaty restoring the St. Lawrence to France was finally signed on March 29, 1632. Champlain, who had taken the time out to write his fourth book, a treatise on seamanship and navigation, was back in Québec by late May the following year, and he rolled up his sleeves and began to rebuild. Hope and Charity, he learnt, had rejoined Faith in the woods soon after he left.

Champlain died in Canada a year later, on Christmas Day, of a stroke, having crossed the Atlantic twenty-nine times. He died a happy man, master of all he could see, and he had succeeded where Cartier failed, establishing a fort at Québec that grew into a city. That city, along with trading posts at Tadoussac on the north shore and Matane on the south, became an export centre whence Canada's resources were shipped back to old France. Prime among the exports was the dark, thick, rich fur of the beaver. The carriage set in Europe—the people who could afford to travel behind a horse instead of on it—developed a fancy for beaver hats and coats, and millions of beavers died in the cause of millinery.

The centre of French canoe building for a century was the town of Trois-Rivières. The three rivers that give the town its name are actually three channels: the St-Maurice forms a trident where it jabs into the St. Lawrence, and Trois-Rivières has grown on the sides of the channels. There was a fort there as early as 1634, the year before Champlain died, and seventy people lived around the walls. At that time there were only a couple of hundred Frenchmen living on the entire river. The trading post that became Trois-Rivières was then the western limit of the European push across North America. Indians anxious to trade preferred coming down the Ottawa, Gatineau and St-Maurice rivers to do business in Trois-Rivières rather than trekking to the more distant Quebec.

The fort saw a flurry of activity in 1641 when a party of twenty Iroquois canoes turned up with a couple of settlers they had kidnapped during the winter. The Iroquois demanded a ransom of guns to fuel their resistance movement against the bias of the French towards the Huron and the Algonquin. A French canoe was dispatched to Québec to obtain, so the Iroquois were told, the Governor's approval of the deal. In fact, the Governor sent back an armed sloop, and the kidnappers handed back the relieved Frenchmen free of charge.

A decade later, relations with the Iroquois were still itchy, and two of them were dragged into the fort and burned as an example to the others. The tactic worked, but shortly afterwards Montréal, which was better protected, got going, and a lot of the fur business transferred there. By then the skill of making large birchbark canoes had transferred from Algonquins to French craftsmen living in Trois-Rivières, so the town was able to retain that expertise and export it along the river.

The majority of the transport fleet was built in family canoe yards, and canoe service stations sprang up all along the fur trade routes. The Le Maître family of Trois-Rivières gave their name to a grand style of canoe—the *canot du maître*—that was the vessel of choice for seasoned canoeists. Each spring, the ice break-up underway, the new fleet of Le Maître canoes would skim down to Montréal to pick up their crews. Loaded with several tons of freight and copious spare red-bladed paddles wedged between the *avant*, the *guide*, the *milieu*, the *gouvernail* and several additional paddlers, the canoes pulled away from the waving crowds on the Montreal dock, to return low in the water with furs before the ice bound up the river again. The French authorities actually regulated the market by having a canoe quota, rather like the modern licensing system for city taxis. With a restricted number of canoes available to satisfy a rising demand for furs, the obvious happened: the canoes got bigger, until they were as long as a city bus and as wide as a man's outstretched arms.

A whole culture grew up around the fur business along the

St. Lawrence, the sect of the coureurs de bois, the working men of the woods. They learned their skills from the Native people and worked alongside them. Young French canoeists, when they came of age, left the villages and strip farms of the St. Lawrence and ran away to the river to work on the Great Trace, the name given to the route ever westward taken by the big canoes. Some canoeists, like the restless La Salle, dreamt of paddling all the way to the pepper mountains of China. La Salle's dream left its mark on the river: he called his Montréal estate La Chine (China).

The best of the coureurs were small and very strong, canoe jockeys paddling and portaging along the veins and capillaries of the country. They returned with furs bundled into bales of around ninety pounds, each known as a "piece," fitted with straps for backpacking the weight at a canter along a portage.

En route, the canoeists would slow down several times a day for a snack, perhaps of roasted beaver tail. Pipes popped in and out like detachable beaks, and the smoke gave the men the appearance of human engines. The distance between smoke breaks was known as a "pipe," and a canoeist could picture in his mind a journey of "sept pipes," a seven-pipe trip. Occasionally, they grabbed their canoe cups and scooped out a quenching drink of unpolluted water. These lipped cups, whittled from wood at night or cast in pewter, were elaborately etched and shaped to fit snugly in a palm, and they became the canoeist's trademark. They were talismans of labour, similar to the cowhand's water canteen.

It was during the fur trade that the venerable St. Lawrence profession of smuggling began. As rivers often do, the St. Lawrence became a border between two colonial franchises, the New French and the New English. It was illegal for the New French to traffic in fur with the English, but of course when the return-versus-risk ratio became favourable, they did it anyway. The Desanniers sisters, two older women who lived on the south shore of the St. Lawrence below Montreal Island, were well-known fur smugglers in the early 1700s. The Mohawks were happy to canoe the booty down to Albany for the sisters and return with the money, less a percentage.

The French also used the canoe, a silent weapon, as a military landing craft, often in campaigns against the very people who had introduced them to birchbark technology. A thousand veterans of the French war with Turkey were shipped to New France in 1665, where they were deployed in canoes to attack Iroquois villages south of the St. Lawrence and patrol the river. In 1673, Comte Louis de Frontenac, the military head of New France, sent a flotilla of canoes up the St. Lawrence to the fort at Kingston. It was a flexing of the French nautical biceps. Some one hundred and twenty canoes and a couple of flatboats were aggressively arranged on Lake Ontario. When the Iroquois viewed the size of the fleet, they conferred among themselves and decided to negotiate a peace deal.

As well as money and rifles, the French carried the Christian word into the woodlands in canoes. The black-robed priests travelled on waves of conviction, through hardships for which they were physically unprepared. Before they set off, the missionaries painted a guardian saint's name on the side of the canoe, and these "decals" endured frequent baptism in the Canadian rivers.

In the 1630s, Father Paul Le Jeune, a senior Jesuit stationed in Québec, instigated a campaign for the conversion of souls in the woodlands. He founded schools for Native boys, which he stocked by bribing their parents. Father Paul also went out and lived among the Indians, at a time when there were fewer than two hundred French men and women in the whole of Canada.

He wrote up his experiences, and included in his journals are handy travel tips for priests taking long canoe trips. Do not wear wide-brimmed hats, Father Paul advised, as they block the view of those behind. The berth you take on the first day will remain yours for the entire journey, so choose carefully. Once the paddle has been taken up, it is considered bad form to put it down again. Be willing to pull all day, and be aware that savages eat only at sunrise and sunset. More than one missionary set off, mindful of these rules and careful of canoe etiquette, only to arrive at some distant village, blistered and part insane from the mosquitoes and blackflies, and there be killed, as Father Jean de Brébeuf was in 1648 for the arrogance of his quest.

The priests were not deterred, however, and the concept of a Catholic New France poured down the St. Lawrence valley and into Canada. By 1650, around three thousand settlers along the valley were farming on church-owned land. In the trio of north shore towns— Montréal, Trois-Rivières and Québec—both the merchants and the priests, as representatives of large Paris-based companies, attempted to establish the framework for a working relationship with the Native peoples.

That wild man spoke to me in the Algonquin language. I wondered to hear this stranger. He asked me concerning Three Rivers and Quebec. He wished himself there, and I said the same, though I did not intend it.

—Pierre-Esprit Radisson,
The Explorations, 1668

Although the French were small in number, their presence was very disruptive to the Native trade balance established over centuries, particularly between the Iroquois and the Huron. Both tribes were clear-cut by imported European diseases, especially smallpox—half of the entire Huron nation may have been wiped out—and this must have been socially devastating. Both tribes knew who was to blame for the disruption, but they handled it in different ways. The Iroquois, who did not become infected with Christianity to the same extent as the Huron, saw the French as enemies, and mounted a series of ambushes in canoes on the Huron fur flotillas making their way to Québec and Montréal to trade with the French. Eventually, the ambushes escalated into an all-out assault, and the Huron nation was broken up. The more Christian Huron camped around Québec, while the unconverted ones joined the Iroquois and began harassing Montréal, which had been founded officially in 1642.

The fur trade, despite being clipped by the Iroquois agitation, carried on. France sent shiploads of young men over to ride shotgun for the canoes, and the ports of Montréal, Trois-Rivières and Québec exported the furs back to France.

It was inevitable, as Canada became a French trading post, that sailing ships would be built on the shores of the St. Lawrence to carry the bounty home. Most, but not all, of the construction of wooden sailing ships took place in and around Québec, and a lot of the ships were built simply to carry timber back to Europe—wood carrying wood.

In its time, the river would see the rise and fall of over eighty shipyards, from Kingston to Rimouski, but Québec launched three times as many as the others combined. The Québec shipyard started as a Crown corporation, in royal fashion, with the arrival of Intendant Jean Talon in 1665 in the *Saint Sebastien*, after a cruel one hundred and seventeen days at sea. It was the same year that the first horse race was held in New York, and Molière had just finished *Don Juan*.

4

DOWN BY THE RIVERSIDE

Jean Talon was the father of Canadian shipbuilding, and the man who really got Québec going.

In 1665, most of Québec's buildings were by the water, on the flat land below the cliffs, either on the St. Lawrence, which is less than a mile wide there, or along the Rivière St-Charles, which hinges onto it. The town's population, according to Canada's first census taken that year, was less than six hundred, the houses numbered seventy, and the entire citizenry of New France would have fit into a modern high-rise apartment complex.

Jean Talon was the father of Canadian shipbuilding, and the man who really got Québec going. Shortly after his arrival, three merchant ships were built on the sand near the Intendant's palace, which was a short way up the St-Charles river, close to the modern St-Roch church. Talon experimented with the properties of the different woods in the forest around him and sent sample masts back to France. Another shipyard started up on the beach at Cap Diamant, the thin strip of land facing the St. Lawrence below the Plains of Abraham. It was at this latter yard that the French began building warships. They knew already that they were going to need them.

La Rochelle, France, was the base camp for the Canadian colony, and Talon shuttled between there and his growing settlement on the river, suffering repeated bad luck on his ocean crossings, developing the colony's market in wood and making the ships to transport it. Grade A Canadian timber was loaded into vessels called flutes in a suppository action via doors in the rear and then trundled back to France to bolster the navy, which was on a more or less permanent aggressive stance with Britain. By the time he was recalled and replaced by Comte Frontenac—who earned the same nickname, Iron, that would later go to Margaret Thatcher—Talon had overseen a trebling of the colony's population.

There is a rule in history that if you draw a line on a map and call it a border, sooner or later there will be a fight about it. Draw the line on water and, indubitably, there will be boats involved. As the European nations got on with the business of colonizing North America, they were more successful in some areas than in others. On page one of the colonizing handbook, in big letters, it says GET THERE FIRST, and the French had done so on the St. Lawrence. The British, simultaneously, were setting up fences south of the river and along the eastern seaboard. The second trick to colonizing is to hold on to what you have seized, and the border fights were not long in starting.

Because they were there first, the French had the best charts of the St. Lawrence, a river with lots of personality. The British navy were anxious to take on the French, whose fleet was not the equal of theirs, but first they had to conquer the St. Lawrence. In 1690, Sir William Phips, the governor of Massachusetts, sailed out of Boston in command of thirty-two ships and two thousand men, intent on conquering New France. Phips groped his way up the St. Lawrence like a man blindfolded. He did manage to line up his navy before the Québec citadel, and even to lob some ordnance at it, but, as one observer called it, "the hand of Heaven"—in the form of a major gust of wind—skittled his formation and the disgusted Phips called it quits. He groped his way back down the river, leaving wrecks along the way like a man leaving bits of clothing snagged on branches as he ploughs through the forest.

Next out of the gate, twenty-one years later, was Admiral Sir Hovenden Walker. A year earlier, after trading blows for a decade, the British had taken Port-Royal in Nova Scotia. Walker was now intent on seizing Québec, and he had taken the precaution of buying the services of a French smuggler named Paradis as a guide. French spies spotted Walker's fleet shortly after takeoff, and twenty-six-year-old François de Lavaltrie, who was in the French militia at Fort Pontchartrain, was ordered to sail to Québec with a warning. Lavaltrie set off in a small boat on the seven-hundred-mile journey while Walker's fleet was still coming up the coast.

Walker went to bed on the foggy night of August 22, 1711, sure that he was in mid-channel at the mouth of the St. Lawrence, heading south towards shore. In fact, he was heading north. He was awoken in the night with the report of land ahead, assumed it was the south shore, and stayed below. The next thing, he was awoken with a report of an island toothed with reefs, dead ahead. Walker ordered hard right, but it was too late. One by one his transport ships, all sixty of them, stuffed

with twelve thousand marines, a force greater than the population of Boston, began piling up on the rocks as though pushed
there by an unseen enemy. The dead shrouded the reef—eight
hundred and eighty-five of them in a single afternoon.

Meanwhile, Lavaltrie had reached Québec, passed on the
warning and sailed out again, on his way home. After several
days he started to come across wreckage, masts, timbers and
torn canvas. When he saw the number of bloated corpses, he
turned around and sailed back to Québec, where his news that
the fleet had self-destructed set the church bells ringing.

The remains of Walker's invasion force returned to Boston
without setting an eye on Québec. Lavaltrie, back home and
exhausted from his shuttle mission, was rewarded with a powerful gift: the seigneury (the French equivalent of a land grant)
at the mouth of the St. Augustine River, in Labrador, where he
traded and fished. Later he became a priest, and died in
Québec in 1750 in his sixties.

While the British pondered their next attack, the French
realized they needed more infrastructure. In 1709, people on
the north shore between Québec and Montréal, who could
travel to each other only in canoes, had been told to put mark-
ers in front of their homes; the road, when it was built, would
join the dots. As any modern ruralist will know, country roads
are often a long time coming, but in 1730, Roadmaster Jean-
Eustache de Boisclerc took up the challenge of constructing
what was essentially a tunnel through the bush. First he built
the bridges, then the twenty-four-foot-wide road, which ran
between fences, and finally established ferries where bridges
were impossible. Boisclerc left Québec on August 9, 1734, and
four and a half days later walked into Montréal and declared the
Chemin du Roy open. In doing so, he became the first person to
travel between the two cities without setting foot in a canoe.

It was also time to build more warships, and there was dredging, quay building, rock clearing and timber piling in front of the Intendant's Palace to make a serious royal shipyard that could crank out fighting vessels. A three-hundred-and-fifty-ton frigate was launched from the beach at Cap Diamant in 1712. A second royal shipyard began laying keels in 1739, and a very capable man called René Levasseur was appointed as the yard's master shipbuilder. Under Levasseur the shipyard moved away from the St-Charles, which had a tricky current, and shuffled down to the elbow of Québec, known as Pointe à Carcy. The first ship launched there, a sixty-gun frigate, slipped into the water and immediately broke its back, leaving a set of red faces on the dockside. Subsequent launches were more successful.

Levasseur's job in the shipyards was in continual danger of being scuttled by his boss, Intendant François Bigot. Bigot had decided that the essence of colonial government was self-interest, and he raided Levasseur's supplies of excellent timber for his own use, paid his friends extremely well for their contracts and generally abided by the well-varnished rules of political corruption. Despite Bigot's grasping hands, Levasseur lasted twenty years and managed to get nine ships of around five hundred tons into the water, all of them square riggers, including one called the *Canada*, which bristled with forty guns.

The kings of Europe spent much of the first half of the eighteenth century feuding. Indeed, feuding was a national sport amongst European royalty. When they went to war with themselves in the 1750s, a secondary England-versus-France conflict was again induced in North America. The river of Canada effectively became a stand-in for the English Channel.

As a bonus for the British this time, they were facing a half-hearted enemy. The writer/philosopher Voltaire had recently made his fatuous remark about Canada being no more than a few acres of snow, and the citizens of New France, now a well-managed colony several generations old, considered themselves Canadians first. The St. Lawrence valley was their homeland and they were French only by default. The colonial office back in Paris thought of them only when seeking funding for war or bodies to use as weapons; otherwise they gave the colony on the St. Lawrence the cold shoulder.

In July of 1758, the British took the fortress of Louisbourg, the citadel the French had built to protect the St. Lawrence. They were now ready to sweep down the river and lay siege to Québec. At the other end of the river, the citadel at Frontenac (later Kingston) was bracing for a British attack there, and French warships had been hastily assembled at Frontenac and at nearby Pointe au Baril. (The latter eventually became Maitland, the little place where I bought the bottle I launched off Wolfe Island. There is a plaque there indicating that the last two French barques to sail Lake Ontario were built at Pointe au Baril in 1760.)

With the hardware in place on both sides, the old enemies now selected the men who would decide the battle for New France. An old definition of a maritime battle states that the army is a bullet fired from a naval gun. For the Québec siege, the British bullet was James Wolfe, then the leading expert among British generals on amphibious landings.

Inside the walls of Québec, the French general Montcalm, his trusted, brilliant aide-de-camp Bougainville, and his distrusted boss, the Montréal-born Governor of New France, the Marquis de Vaudreuil, worried about how to stop Wolfe. Their home country had supplied them with a woefully inadequate army; as the Minister of Colonies in Paris, preoccupied with the European sector of the war, said, "When the house is on fire, one cannot worry about the stables."

Over the winter of 1758–59, one of the worst the Canadians had seen, ice corked tight the St. Lawrence. Both French and British ships sat outside the ice sheet waiting for it to crack open wide enough for them to get at Québec. Finally, in May, the ice relented. Bougainville was first through, with the British still sitting in Halifax twiddling their thumbs. With their frigates anchored and unloaded of men and supplies, the French at Québec built large rafts loaded with gunpowder and timber, floating firebombs they intended to launch at the enemy fleet they knew was not far behind.

The French had controlled both shores of the St. Lawrence for over a century at this point and nurtured a group of pilots who knew the river for what it was. They had also never published navigation charts. Bougainville (the flowering tree is indeed named after him) therefore had no trouble negotiating the river's hidden depths and currents with his fleet of twenty-five small supply ships, but when the British came down a week or so after, under the command of Admiral Saunders, they were almost in uncharted territory. This time, though, they had two aces up their frilly sleeves.

One of the aces was only thirty years old, but already his navigational skills had earned him quite a reputation. He had been brought up sailing coal ships in the North of England. In the Americas he had pestered the surveyors at the siege of Louisbourg for their techniques, then applied them to mapping the Gulf of St. Lawrence and the entrance to the river. His name was James Cook, the same Cook who would go on in life to circumnavigate the world twice, be the first European to sail into Botany Bay in Australia, bring the tattoo to the Western world, and be put to death by natives on a Hawaiian beach in 1778.

The other man, Master Killock, had grown up on the Thames. It was Killock who led the British fleet through the most difficult part of the St. Lawrence, the Traverse, a channel that started at the eastern edge of the Île aux Coudres. (As backup the British lured several pilots from the island's pilot station onto their ships by falsely flying the white Bourbon flag.) Killock, on the deck of the lead frigate, pooh-poohed his way through the Traverse using, as his captain noted in his log, "the ripple and colour of the water where there was danger, and distinguishing the places where there were ledges of rock from banks of sand, mud and gravel." By June 26, 1759, the entire British fleet was anchored off the village of St-Laurent on the Île d'Orléans. (They were minus one soldier, named Hovington, who had jumped ship at Tadoussac. There are still Hovingtons in the Tadoussac phone book.)

It was only when the city fell under siege in 1759 that work stopped in the French royal shipyard. As fate would have it, the ship that was left sitting in the stocks—the wooden rib cage within which ships were built—was a frigate with the working title *Le Québec*.

The British fleet arraigned off the Île d'Orléans was impressive. Naval sailing ships were described by the number of guns they carried; Admiral Saunders's flagship, the *Neptune*, for instance, carried ninety guns on three decks. In all, Saunders had one hundred and seventy vessels under his command, twenty-three of them bristling with cannon pointing outward like porcupine's quills. Flat-bottomed boats with lowerable fronts, similar to those used in landings on French beaches in World War II, now rowed batches of soldiers to the island, where they met no resistance. A sign on the church door asked the invaders not to desecrate the empty building and informed them, for some reason, perhaps spite, that they had just missed the vegetable harvest. The day after taking the Île d'Orléans, Wolfe stood on the northwest corner looking across at the formidable natural and man-made defences of Québec, and at the disposition of Montcalm's sixteen thousand men.

The siege of Québec started the day after, June 18, but it was interrupted by a storm that shook the stationary British fleet and dragged it on its anchors. After the storm, Saunders resolved to relocate the next day to a calmer harbour. The French kicked off their side of the conflict at midnight of that first day, launching seven fire boats—rafts piled with blazing, pitch-soaked brush—at the unsettled British ships. Fire ships work best if lit at the last minute, but a nervous officer fired them up too soon, and the British were able to detour the floating bonfires onto shore with boathooks, where they illuminated their own uselessness.

Wolfe now set up a camp at Lévis, separated from Québec by a mile-wide strip of water. For six weeks various objects of war, human and metal, crossed the river, some returning, some not. Eighteenth-century cannon and mortars could lob a shell over a mile, so there was daily exercise for the French in taking cover. In retaliation the French only managed to lightly stipple the British position. Québec's Basse Ville, the Lower Town, was slowly crushed. Boats of supplies were constantly moving between Wolfe's three positions—on Île d'Orléans, just east of Montmorency and at Lévis—and arriving from New England with nourishment for the men and the mortars.

Occasionally, this being what was oxymoronically called a gentleman's war, boats from each side would row out to midstream, under white flags, and exchange messages. "We are determined that your army shall never get a footing within these walls," read one of Montcalm's memos. "I will be master of Québec, if I stay here till the end of November," was Wolfe's rebuttal.

The siege of Québec developed a rhythm, almost like the tides that moved in and out of the harbour. Activity was followed by inertia, skirmish by retaliation, mistake by rethinking. Wolfe periodically used his ships to scurry across and up and down the river, taunting and testing Montcalm's position, looking for the weak spot. Wolfe was also appalled by the behaviour of his New England Rangers and ordered them to cease scalping anyone—except Indians, whom he detested, or Canadians dressed as Indians.

The French tried the fire ship trick again, a massive effort this time, with three ships lashed together. This too ended up on shore, a waste of timber and powder. Then, more in exasperation than cunning, Wolfe tried an amphibious landing near the Montmorency Falls, a spectacular scarf of water a mile or so downriver from Québec. The idea was to ford the Montmorency stream at the foot of the falls at low tide, while offshore ships' cannon rained down some heat and smaller, flat-bottomed ships called cats put an assault force ashore. The result, as the British say, was a cock-up. Everything that could go wrong did, including the landing boats being grounded on their flat bottoms in the mud flats.

The strain of extended failure now worked its way through the British. Wolfe took sick, and his men, short of vegetables and vitamin C, got scurvy. One folk cure for this vitamin deficiency, which the British actually tried, involved burying men up to their necks in the sand at the edge of the St. Lawrence—an extreme form of getting back to the land. Lassitude prevailed on both shores, until news came through in late August that the British had taken the western end of the river, in the Thousand Islands. They were even now heading east to grab Montréal.

Wolfe's brigadiers got together, rejected his scheme for another Montmorency attack and suggested a landing upriver, a notion that Wolfe had doubts about. However, looking through a telescope at the suggested site for an assault, he saw that something might be possible at a nasty cleft in the cliffs at a spot called Foulon. The cleft led up to an under-defended plain named after a river pilot from the mid-seventeenth century who had farmed there, Abraham Martin.

And so it was. On September 13, Wolfe slipped a convoy of landing craft upriver, about ten miles past Foulon. That night, at around two a.m., the landing craft set off back the way they had come with muffled oars. Halfway to Foulon, they were hailed by lookouts expecting some French provision boats to pass. Across the dark water came a reply in perfect French, and the sentries let the enemy sail on by. Admiral Saunders, meanwhile, was downriver at Montmorency providing a diversion.

By dawn, almost five thousand men had landed at Foulon, pulled their way up the bushes in the cleft and were in line of battle. On Wolfe's orders they lay down to rest, making it hard for Montcalm to decide how many troops he was up against. When they got up at around nine o'clock, the French were moving towards them, firing wildly. The British, with two balls in each musket, let go a volley of metal that sounded as though an almighty pair of hands had clapped. The French were scythed down like the hemp in the fields of New France that the war had left rotting. In a quarter of an hour, a battle four months in the making was over.

Wolfe, who had died of the effects of three separate bullets, was carried on board ship and his body borne back to England on the *Royal William*. Montcalm died a few hours after his rival, within the walls of Québec. It only remained for Admiral Saunders to bombard the town into submission, which he duly did. The Bourbon flag came down at four o'clock on September 18, the Union Jack went up and the town fell under the command of General James Murray.

Murray's first concern was to get him and his men through the winter, which he did. A thousand Canadiens, stranded outside the fort by the battle, were not so fortunate, and many of them starved to death.

After the hard winter, in the spring of 1760, with the ground still slushy, Murray learned from a Frenchman, who had fallen overboard and was fished out of the water, clinging to a piece of ice, that the French fleet was on its way. The schooner *Lawrence* was dispatched downriver to scream for reinforcements, while the British left the walls and met a superior force on the Plains of Abraham, this time led by the Duc de Lévis. It was a bitter sequel to the skirmish nine months before. The much-tested British general realized after a morning's bloodletting that he was losing, and he withdrew back into the walls.

Into whose hands Québec now fell would be decided by nature and seamanship. Whoever could get their reinforcing ships up the ice-clogged St. Lawrence first would win the prize. All eyes, looking through perspective glasses, as telescopes were then called, turned towards the Île d'Orléans, waiting for a sail to appear and the colour of the flag flying above it. On May 9, a ship rounded the island's corner: It wore English colours and was called the *Lowestoft*.

The British now had naval control of the St. Lawrence. They posted ships at the mouth of the river, and there discovered, hiding in a bay, a convoy of French transport ships guarded by a frigate. They destroyed them. With both ends of the river plugged with British corks, it now only remained to take Montréal. At the beginning of September, Murray left Québec in a gaggle of sloops with names that read like the lineup for a horse race—*Porcupine, Diana, Racehorse* and *Pegasus*—and joined up with an army of eleven thousand encamped outside Montréal. The French knew defeat when they faced it, and on September 8, 1760, the regiments within Montréal burnt their flags as an act of defiant capitulation.

The river is one of the noblest in the world.

—Frances Brooke, *The History of Emily Montague*, 1769, the first English Canadian novel

A week later the French soldiers boarded the ships that would take four weeks to carry the news back to France that the colony was lost. The British-born merchants of New England had their territory, and the borderline on the St. Lawrence evaporated. The river was marching to a different drummer now, to a Handel fugue (the composer had died in London during the siege of Québec) rather than a French gigue.

5
RIVERS WILL RUN

Even the Iroquois took jobs as voyageurs, guides, pilots and deckhands on the huge floating timber rafts (above: Montmagny, P2).

The British, who spent several centuries under Roman rule, knew the nuts and bolts of running an empire. They were fanatical bureaucrats and proficient drainers of the natural resources of their colonies. According to their map, British North America was now a swath of land running from Hudson Bay to Florida, with the St. Lawrence dead centre and providing access far into the interior.

The exploitation of Canada's resources by Europeans had arrived in three waves. *Fish* were the first to be harvested, by the Basques, and soon enough by everyone. They trolled the Gulf of St. Lawrence and Newfoundland's Grand Banks, where the fish were in such supply that it would take five relentless centuries to exhaust them. Next up was the *fur* trade, and phase three was the downloading of the *forests*, conveyed along the St. Lawrence in rafts and on to the shipyards of Europe in ships. Thus, by 1760, the Europeans had already thoroughly *f'ed* Canada, and the British embraced the tradition. The fur and the forests continued to fly across the Atlantic.

With a new set of flags waving in the sea breeze over Québec's roofs and at the top of masts, the shipsmiths (the fashioners of a ship's ironmongery), the sawyers (splitters of logs to make planks), the caulkers, and the block, mast, rope and sail makers went back to work in the various lofts and in the quarter-mile-long "'rope walk" sheds. The majority of French tradesmen remained in their homes and at their jobs; the factory had merely changed owners.

Now they worked in government yards or at private wharves owned by men with names like Black, Campbell, Davie, Dining, Gilmour, Gingras, Lee, Munn, Oliver and Rosa, each of whom built over forty ships. The vocabulary in the watering holes the tradesmen used after work was now dovetailed with English words such as "scarf" (a verb describing the joining together of several timbers), "futtock" (a lower part of the cross-sectional framing of a ship) and "wale" (a length of wood used to strengthen a stress point such as a join). Building ships was what Québec had done, and it was what Québec continued to do, and for a decade and a half fresh hulls slid smoothly down the slipways into the river.

But the waters off the New England coast were not calm. Just as each generation of French Canadians considered itself less and less French, the same was true of the Americans of the Thirteen Colonies facing London on the Atlantic coast. They wanted to become mercantile in their own right and stop sending their wealth back to a distant throne. A war of independence was fermenting.

In 1775, Paul Revere rode from Charleston to Lexington, and the killing began. Soon enough it spilled across the river. The Americans, sensing discontent, tried to push a wedge between the English overlords of Lower Canada, who were anxious to live in a British sort of way, and the Canadiens, who still chafed at the new language of business they were expected to use. The Americans got busy trying to inflame that discontent. They distributed subversive flyers to the Canadiens around Montréal. They put republican spies in the back streets of the harbour. Then, as the leaves of the maple trees were starting to turn, the Americans made their move.

First, they easily picked up some casually guarded forts on the south shore. Buoyed by how little resistance they were meeting, a hundred and fifty men under a keen soldier named Ethan Allen crossed the St. Lawrence during the night of September 24, and made camp outside Montréal. The British governor, Guy Carleton, in town and aware that the Americans were going to try something, dispatched troops to the camp. Allen and thirty-five of his men soon found themselves in the hold of a British schooner, the *Gaspé*, en route to the dungeon of an English castle.

Carleton knew he'd been lucky, and that Montréal was shaky and underdefended. At the last possible moment, November 11, he put eleven small ships on the river and made for the safer nest of Québec. He hadn't got far when he was attacked by Americans. Carleton took to a lifeboat with a handful of officers, the only ones among a hundred and thirty soldiers to escape capture, and they rowed quietly away, using overhanging branches to pull hand over hand along the shore. It took eight days and some more luck at Trois-Rivières before they reached Québec.

Upriver, the Americans walked into Montréal to be greeted by a delegation of fairweather Montrealers anxious to be on the right side. The rest of the city kept quiet. Some high-level members of the United States Congress, including Benjamin Franklin, rode into town to negotiate the island becoming an American colony. One by one the north shore towns sent messages to the American generals, either professing strident neutrality or offering a sure welcome.

The docile reception the American invaders received put a shine on their buckles, and they decided to go for Québec. General Montgomery, leading the American forces, teamed up with a bigger force under Benedict Arnold and they laid siege to Québec, as the British, who were now inside the walls, had done twenty-six years earlier. The British won again, and Montgomery died near the shipyards at Cap-aux-Diamants. Arnold went back to Montréal, his already very tired troops starting to come down with smallpox. Inside the walls of siegeless Québec, Carleton awaited reinforcements, which he got. Ten thousand men worked a stress-free way back to Montréal. When they arrived, the Americans had already said *au revoir*; they had gone back across the St. Lawrence in the boats they sailed in on.

With the Americans busy setting up a republic to the south, it was back to business in the St. Lawrence valley. The European thirst for beaver fur had not abated. After a brief hiccup while they assessed the situation, the British, whose knowledge of canoes was about as deep as their knowledge of camels, let the veteran men of the woods carry on. Trois-Rivières, whose seven thousand citizens toiled under Governor Ralph Burton, remained the centre for canoe building, and the French family firms that embodied the birchbark tradition laboured on under the Union Jack. In time newcomers like Scotsman Alexander Henry, after considerable trial and error, picked up the art of getting a fully laden canoe from Lachine to the head of Lake Superior and back. The large anglophone trading houses that would dominate Montréal for the next two hundred years now set up shop along Rue Saint-Paul, and their warehouses swelled with the take from the traplines along the Ottawa River, around the Great Lakes and beyond. The biggest of them, the North West Company, founded in 1779 by a coalition of Scotsmen, started shipping an average two hundred thousand pelts a year out of Montréal, half of them beaver.

Latter-day Romans, the British had learnt the efficacy of having a well-run waterway system. After staving off the half-hearted invasion by the Americans in 1775, the British military took note of how slowly the paraphernalia of strife and settlement moved up and down the turbulent St. Lawrence in their small transport vessels. The ideal river, as far as they were concerned, ran straight as a mast through low, well-populated country; it had forsworn the moon's influence and had no tides; it was smooth and rockless at the edges and blessed at regular intervals with deep harbours and arterial rivers that went far inland; every day on it was a calm one, and every night a full lunar light illuminated it; the bottom of the river was as smooth as the surface, and there was only an imperceptible, steady flow towards the sea.

The St. Lawrence, apart from its several hospitable harbours and the family of sibling rivers running into it, could offer the British none of this, and so they started to rectify the mistakes in its natural design. It was not going to be easy. Nine sets of rapids between Kingston and Montreal—a turbulent ramp that dropped the river the equivalent of a twenty-storey building over a distance of a hundred and sixty-eight miles—had to be overcome.

The first person to make a modest attempt to tame the river was actually a Frenchman, the religious strongman Dollier de Casson, a soldier and engineer turned priest. As head of the Sulpicians of Montréal in the 1680s, de Casson wanted the fickle stream that fed the order's flour mill hooked into Lac St-Louis to provide a more faithful water supply. He managed to get a trench dug over a mile long, passing by the village of Lachine. Then, on an otherwise calm night in August 1689, the Lachine settlement was all but wiped out by the Iroquois, in whose territory the gouge was being made. The building site fell quiet for a few years. Digging finally resumed in 1700, but de Casson ran out of money within the year, the canal still incomplete, and that was that. Half a century later, the people of Lachine placed some boulders in a line, parallel to the river-bank in the same general area as de Casson's trench. Their effort calmed the water slightly, but failed to pacify it.

The serious cutting and stitching of the river by the British began at Coteau-du-Lac in 1779. Between Lac St-Francis and Lac St-Louis, the two bulges in the river between Cornwall and Montréal, there is a strip of river fourteen miles long infested with islands and three sets of rapids as the river drops eighty feet. The biggest island is called, appropriately, Grande Île. Grande Île, at the east end of Lac St-Francis, forces the river to thread either side of it, and smaller satellite islands cluster at each end of the split, whipping up the water into first the Coteau and then the Cedar rapids. At the entrance to Lac St-Louis another sprinkling of islands creates the Split Rock rapids. All that froth was no deterrent to fur-bearing birchbark canoes, but when the British began moving serious amounts of supplies along the river, it became a headache.

The most common cargo boat used by the British at that time was the bateau, a basic wooden hull that was rowed and possessed a big luggage compartment, which could carry around three dozen barrels of flour. Two men loading a bateau from either side could reach across and shake hands, and so the first canals were made to that width. The canal at Coteau-du-Lac ran for nine hundred feet, had two lock gates—a so-called mitre-gate system invented by Leonardo da Vinci in 1487—and was largely hand-built. It was waist-deep.

The engineer in charge of installing da Vinci's invention at Coteau-du-Lac was a Captain Twiss. Once Twiss had his hole dug, walled and gated, he went to Montréal to drum up business among the merchants. He offered a Grand Opening special rate of ten shillings per bateau. Twiss kept a running total for commercial shipping through his canal, and in 1781, two hundred and sixty-three bateaux, a couple of canoes and one "small craft," perhaps an officer on a Sunday outing, nudged between the gates.

The river was now a fraction straighter, and things were moving, but they weren't moving quickly enough. After the end of the American War of Independence, ten thousand potential homemakers, who had chosen not to be post-revolutionary Americans, had headed north across the St. Lawrence and spread out along its shore and down to Lake Ontario. They were given parcels of land purloined from the Native peoples and promptly set up house. One definition of "house" is a place where you put stuff while you go out and get some more, and in the closing years of the eighteenth century the river became a conveyor belt for goods and chattels as the Loyalists erected walls and began to fill them.

Delivery times were slow, and there were complaints, so Twiss tackled the bottleneck at the Cascades rapids at the western end of Grande Île. Between 1781 and 1783, he built a network of three canals: the Faucille ("sickle"), the Trou-du-Moulin (a *moulin* is a mill) and the Split Rock, which was right at the mouth of Lac St-Louis. The canal at Trou-du-Moulin has not disappeared, although it's no longer in use, and you can walk along its dry, stony bed.

Twiss's canals, manifestations of the British affinity for straight lines, marked the end of an era for the river. Before Twiss, boats had been adapted from nature to suit the St. Lawrence; now the river had been reconfigured to suit the boats. The canals heralded a shift away from an indigenous approach to river transport, which had mastered all styles of waters, and towards the European model that could carry awkward and more abundant cargo. Canoes and bateaux now passed side by side at Coteau-du-Lac, one safe in calm water, the other nonchalantly riding the rapids.

The original designers of the birchbark canoe, noting the clean lines of the canals and their rotating gates, resigned themselves to the fact that the Europeans were here to stay and looked for work. Even the Iroquois took jobs as voyageurs, guides, pilots and deckhands on the huge floating timber rafts, a quarter-mile square, that passed their doorsteps. A letter written in 1858 from an elderly man to his grandson in Montréal recalls a raft the grandfather saw as a boy in the late eighteenth century, with Indians in the crew:

> We left Three Rivers at 4 o'clock in the morning and proceeded up stream against wind and current. Shortly we met one of these immense large rafts which I had heard of, but never seen before—it was about the size of one of my fields at the farm. Our Pilot told us that it covered

about four acres and would contain more than
ten thousand tons of timber. We counted about
nineteen temporary houses, saw upon it a great
number of men, women and children and pigs
and dogs and hens. They had long poles erected
at the ends of some of the houses with lan-
thorns at the top which they lit at night to
warn vessels to keep clear.

Although they rode the rafts, the Native peoples did not abandon the family canoe. Contemporary reports of the St. Lawrence
Indians and their fading relationship with birchbark in the late
1700s are not plentiful, and they are mostly told through the eyes
of passersby on, as it were, the opposite shore. In 1791, an Englishman, John Long, published an account called *Voyages and
Travels of an Indian Interpreter and Trader*. This was the same year
that, via the Canada Act, the one large province of Quebec was
bisected into two, Upper and Lower Canada, with the Ottawa
River forming the natural boundary. (The Quebec/Ontario borderline now meets the St. Lawrence between the villages of
Bainsville and St-Zotique, to be exact between number 22256 on
the South Service Road and number 8 on Chemin Frontière.
Part of the border, prettily enough, is a flowerbed.)

In his account of his adventures in late eighteenth-century
Canada, Mr. Long is not short in his estimation of his own
prowess. He boasts at one point that "not content with being
proficient at their sports, I learnt to make a canoe, bark a tree
for the purpose, and perform the whole business regular as
natives." He also gives away the Native trick for killing loons,
namely by mounting a bow on the front of the canoe like a
gunship, and he mentions that mosquitoes, which he called
fleas, could be escaped by canoeing out on the river for a

respite from bloodsucking. On land, he said, they made for a "quickness of conversation."

Long also mentions hiring a passing Native canoe as a taxi. He set out one day to walk from Montréal to Kingston but along the way saw "two Indians of my acquaintance in a canoe, and having money in my pocket to buy rum, I hired them to convey me." Whether the rum money was subverted to paying the fare or rum was the payment, Long doesn't say, but he did write down some Algonquian canoe terms. A great canoe, he says, was a *kitchee cheeman*, a paddle was an *apway* and a portage a *cappatagan*.

Elsewhere in the literature at the turn of the century, the canoe as personal vehicle makes sporadic appearances. There are several stories of canoe funerals, the casket in the lead canoe and the mourners in line behind. And then there was the Canadien in 1807 who couldn't wait any longer and paddled solo from Lake Winnipeg to Trois-Rivières—five and a half thousand miles—to marry, then took his Anne-Marie back along the same route for the honeymoon.

The canoe had the great advantage of not being at the mercy of the wind, as the sailing ship was. As long as the river had rapids and the Europeans fancied themselves fashionable in beaver, the canoe had a job—unless something came along that needed neither wind nor paddle for propulsion.

Sailing, because it was the wind's servant, was always more of an art than a science on the St. Lawrence. The winds moving over the river rarely prevailed. They flowed between cliffs, were bisected by islands, massed over the mouth and funnelled through the twists and constrictions of the tail. They could hold aloft the fineness of a fog or shoulder the brute weight of a tempest, then release one or the other with a jester's timing.

Ships heading out of the river and across to Liverpool were described, in the newspaper adverts listing their shipping times, as sailing "towards" their destination. That gave the schedule leeway for nature to put its hand on the rudder. Time of departure from the dock was a probability, but the time of arrival was wishful thinking. A guaranteed landing on a specified day was a long-standing wish for passengers and shippers alike.

In 1807, a man called John Molson read in the Montréal papers that the American inventor Robert Fulton, who was also a jeweller and an artist, had travelled to Scotland, the birthplace of the modern steamer (where Patrick Miller, a banker by day and experimenter by night, had fashioned a boat that went five knots under steam, with the poet Robbie Burns in the crew), to see the steamships in action there. Fulton returned to the States with a steam engine from England and put it into a ship called the *Columbia*, which puffed under its own power down the Hudson from New York to Albany. Molson was intrigued by the idea of a self-propelled boat, and he had the money to bring it to the St. Lawrence.

Molson had emigrated to Canada from Lincolnshire, England, twenty-five years earlier, with a contract to enter the business of Thomas Loid, a Montréal brewer. Not long after, Loid got into financial trouble and Molson, now his partner, bought the brewery at auction and ran it his way. The rest is malt-flavoured history. (On the subject of beer and the St. Lawrence, which have always mixed well, the other major Canadian beer family, the Labatts, started fermenting on the river at Prescott in the 1830s. The boathouse John Labatt built for shipping and receiving is still there. His brother opened a bigger business in Montréal soon after.)

A year after reading of Fulton's success, Molson imported the necessary talent to make a steamship in Montréal—two engineers from Britain, both also called John. Using their design, he put his trust in the renowned St-Maurice forge in Trois-Rivières to fashion the engine from scratch, and the Canadian craftsmen came through. The first all-Canadian steamship was launched, just a basic hull, on August 19, 1809. The *Accommodation* was of a very simple design, a cigar-shaped deck with a thin smokestack rising out of an amidships engine, forcing two wheels to mill the water. After some cursory trials it was fitted out for its first paying run on November 1, 1809. It accomplished the hitherto uncertain journey downriver from Montréal to Québec in three days. "Neither winds nor tide can stop it," said one reporter in Montréal.

The elements didn't stop it, true, but they did slow it down, and Molson made a loss on his first season. He had a chat with Fulton, his American counterpart, and together they worked out a more economical size of boat. The *Swiftsure*, twice as long as the *Accommodation*, made the Montréal–Québec run in less than twenty-four hours in 1812. The river had begun to steam.

The long-simmering American mistrust of the British—who were in the midst of tackling Napoleon—broke out into war less than a month later. The suspicions that set cannon firing across the St. Lawrence were rooted in four geographical areas. At the Great Lakes end of the river, the Americans had a distorted view of how chummy the Native peoples remained with the British. True, the British used the Indians of the interior as fur gatherers, gave them guns for the job and traded with them even when the furs had come from American land. The British

also made promises of Native sovereignty they had no intention of keeping. But perception is reality, and the Americans
feared that the British could order up a Native uprising at any
time. By 1812, the Americans and Indians of the so-called
Ohio country had drawn each other's blood several times.

Also by this time there were many thousands of ex-Americans
living along the north shore of the upper St. Lawrence. Their
former compatriots, who had fought the British to gain independence, had hopes that many Loyalists, and even more of the
less staunch "late" Loyalists—who felt their strongest allegiance
to the free land in Canada the British had used to entice
them—could be persuaded to cross back over to the republican
side of the fence. When the muskets began firing, the Americans
had their fingers crossed that it might develop into a redcoats
versus turncoats conflict.

Republicanism was certainly in the air. The American Revolution had been followed by the French Revolution, and the
British feared that the general lower-class disgruntlement with
the élites might prove contagious, particularly among the
French Canadians. The French had gone so far as to send
agents to North America in the early 1790s to try and provoke
unrest among francophones on the St. Lawrence.

Alongside the risk of ideological infection, there was also
some old-fashioned greed at play. The rich burghers of Montréal,
an island of Britishness in a province of Frenchness, controlled a
truly vast amount of land, and the Americans wanted it.

On the high seas off North America, the British navy was
superior to that of the United States. Raids on American ships
by British opportunists out of Halifax were irksome, and the
Americans were anxious to have control of the waters off their
own eastern seaboard. They were also keen to get a bigger slice
of the West Indies spicy pie than they already had.

For these main reasons, and several lesser ones, the old country and the new one got into it. This time around, the St. Lawrence was a stand-in for the Atlantic Ocean. On paper the Americans had the land battles won and the naval battles lost. A head count on New Year's Day, 1812, would have recorded around seven and a half million Americans. Although the French Canadians had gone forth and multiplied at a lusty rate, and the population of Lower Canada trebled between 1783 and 1812, there were still only a third of a million of them. All together, and not counting the Indians who did not stand still to be enumerated, British North America had a population of only half a million.

6

RIVERS OF THE BLOOD

It was all, in the end, about property values, the St. Lawrence being the most valuable property of all.

The War of 1812 (the title is an understatement—it lasted three years) left a deeper mark on the St. Lawrence than the attempted rebellion of 1775. As soon as the Americans made their declaration of aggression in June, a squadron of British shipbuilders were transferred from Québec and other smaller shipyards to Lake Champlain, which became ship-building central for the duration of the war. (Ironically, two of the major shipbuilders of the conflict, John Goudie for the Canadians and Henry Eckford for the Americans, both learnt their trades in the Québec shipyard of John Black.) The conflict was fought as much on the water as on land,

and the St. Lawrence was stage for the frequent play of cannon fire.

Wars leave their mark on the landscape. Meadows are transformed into graveyards, ships into wrecks. And when day is
done, the battle sites are preserved, not as they appeared when
they were in heat, but as fields of death and endeavour, pinned
down with plaques of explanation and statistics. Two centuries
after the smoke settled on the St. Lawrence, the modern
enjoyer of history can move slowly down the river, travelling
from plaque to graveyard, from shipwreck to battlefield, piec-
ing together the story of the last war between Canada and its
imposing neighbour. (It must be said, however, that it is hard
to decipher the identity of the winner from reading the battlefield plaques on the American side.)

Kingston was the bull's eye of the British navy, and the
inner bull's eye was Point Frederick, where the Royal Military
College of Canada is now. The Kingston dockyard started up in
1792 and set to work as soon as war was declared, launching a
series of ships with names that read like the arrivals at a London ball: the *Prince Regent*, the *Princess Charlotte*, the *Duke of
Gloucester*, the *Earl of Moira* and the *Sir Sydney Smith*.

The *Royal George*, a muscular corvette, was likewise built
at Point Frederick. It was also attacked there on November
10, 1812, like a fox in its lair beset by a pack of hounds. The
hounds were several schooners—one was actually called the
Growler—plus a brig commanded by one Commodore
Chauncey. The *Royal George*, chased off Lake Ontario, holed
up in the bay alongside Point Frederick. Cannon shots were
given and received, to no great effect. At dusk the American
schooners backed off, each side having lost precisely one
man, making it a draw. A plaque commemorating the battle
appeared one hundred and forty years later.

Wars are black holes for money, using up supplies at an accelerated rate. There are stomachs and ships' holds to be filled, and during the War of 1812 the St. Lawrence was laced, in the ice-free months, with convoys of bateaux moving the necessaries about. These convoys were usually protected by gunships, compact naval guard dogs with a single cannon up front. They were nautically ambidextrous: they could be sailed or rowed.

For many years after the war, at a place called Brown's Bay near Mallorytown in the Thousand Islands, a wreck sat on the bottom, not very far down. It was a playground for kids in swimsuits, and hunters used it as a hide from which to kill ducks. When the river was low, more of the wreck would appear in the air, as though the old boat were trying to rise again.

The wreck caught the curiosity of scientists at Canada's National Parks in 1966, and since then educated guesses wondered if it might be the HMS *Radcliffe*, built in Kingston in 1817. Officially, the ship is anonymous. Certainly it's the same model as the gunboats of 1812, and the only well-preserved example of one. Divers found articles from as late as 1861 around the Brown's Bay wreck, so it apparently enjoyed a long life. Parks Canada raised it in 1968, preserved it, and popped it into a shed for public viewing at the park at Mallorytown. Its skeletal remains have the feel of a forty-foot-long dinosaur, the wooden bones of something that once led an active life.

Whether the Brown's Bay gunship saw battle or not, there was undoubtedly a naval skirmish near where she was found, within days of the War of 1812 starting. Some smaller, unarmed American cargo schooners made a run for it up the St. Lawrence to get into Lake Ontario, but they were intercepted by keen Canadian civilians in bateaux, and two of them, the *Sophia* and the *Island Packet*, were captured. The rest retreated the way they had come to harbour on the

American side. The British promptly stationed two of the freshly built warships from Kingston, the *Earl of Moira* and the *Duke of Gloucester*, on the opposite shore. The Americans, it being their move, brought up the *Julia*, and after some preliminary barking the ships exchanged shots in midstream for most of an afternoon, a duke and earl versus a republican woman. The *Julia* gave better than she got and the British ships backed off, and next morning the American vessels finally made it into the lake.

Along the stretch of the upper river stippled with Americans on the south shore and Canadians on the north, there were (and still are) pairs of towns that faced each other, like pairs of lace holes in a shoe. Prescott (Canadian) and Ogdensburg (American) are two such towns; in fact they are closer to each other than to their neighbouring hamlets in the same country. In 1812, flags of war atop the opposing forts waved to each other in the same breeze. During the two winters encompassed in the affray, when the river became a field of ice, forces from these towns could not resist walking on the St. Lawrence to have a go at each other.

The first raid across the ice was provoked in early February 1813, when two hundred Americans, under the zealous command of Captain Benjamin Forsyth, sleighed from Ogdensburg upriver to Morristown. (Confusingly, there is a Morristown and a Morrisburg on the St. Lawrence within an hour's boating of each other. The town is American; the burg is Canadian.) After a night spent warming up, Forsyth marched his troop over to Brockville at daybreak and surrounded it. It was a rare sight: two hundred men in penguin-like formation walking across the river.

Forsyth had come to set free some Americans being held prisoner in Brockville (which was then known as Elizabethtown, since General Brock, who had saved the western frontier of Canada from American takeover and died in battle only five months earlier, was yet to be immortalized as a town). The American prisoners were freed, the British barracks torched and the town's guns carted back to Ogdensburg. The townspeople of Ogdensburg, who only months before considered the people on the Canadian side their neighbours, now sat and waited for the inevitable retaliation, meanwhile muttering about Forsyth under their breath. The British rebuttal came two weeks later, when six hundred men walked across the ice in file, then split into two flanks and besieged the town.

The counter-raid on Ogdensburg was also successful, although the captain leading the right flank took a bullet in each arm. The unpopular Captain Forsyth retreated, and was reassigned; he was wounded in battle a few months later and died in a house that has since become a funeral home. The British hung around Ogdensburg for a day, burned the barracks in their turn, plus two schooners that were iced in, then went back over to the Canadian side. (The story of this raid is explained in several numbered plaques around Ogdensburg. The trail makes for an imaginative stroll.)

The next day, the wife of the sheriff of Ogdensburg, a Mrs. Jenkins, walked over to Prescott in a one-woman ambush to retrieve her mirror, the only one in town. The precious object had been carried off in the general looting. Using only the sharp edge of her tongue, she fought well, and returned unharmed but empty-handed; a soldier claimed to have dropped the mirror through the ice. Her crossing marked the end to the cold war in that stretch of the St. Lawrence; after that the fighting was confined to warmer weather.

The war dragged on through 1813, the British losing more slowly than the Americans. Then, in the first week of

November, a major American flotilla carrying seven thousand men, commanded by General Wilkinson, ran past both Kingston and Fort Wellington (at Prescott) in the dark, and made camp on the Canadian side near John Crysler's waterfront farm near Morrisburg.

As soon as the flotilla had passed Kingston, a considerably smaller British force, with a Lieutenant Colonel Morrison in charge, set off in pursuit. They picked up some extra men at Fort Wellington, got within range of Wilkinson and took over John Crysler's farm, setting up HQ in the farmhouse while Crysler himself pondered the size of the chunk of bad luck about to fall on him. Meanwhile, the American force had been reduced: a brigade had split off to deal with some militia at the Long Sault rapids downstream. Nevertheless, it was still four times the size of the British contingent. Wilkinson, who was busy being seasick on board ship, handed over command to General Boyd.

When the fight came, ploughing up the farm fields with boots and elbows, the Americans could not shift the leaner but cooler-headed British force. As the sun set, American morale also sank, and Boyd ordered his men off the field. General Wilkinson, his queasiness gone and his pragmatism re-established, reassembled his demoralized force and marched them one day nearer Montréal, his ultimate target. Then he learnt that the other wing of the attack on Montréal had been broken a week earlier at Châteauguay, in Quebec. Wilkinson, glad of the opportunity to do so, called it quits.

A few months later, at the end of 1813, Kingston's shipyard turned out a sailing leviathan. The St. Lawrence, built by shipwrights from Québec on secondment to Upper Canada, sported one hundred and four guns and a crew of six hundred, a greater population than many St. Lawrence villages at the time. It was meant to be a bully and it succeeded, giving the British control of the water until peace made it redundant.

Peace on the St. Lawrence after Châteauguay and the *St. Lawrence* actually took a year to unfold. Many more died on both sides, on fields as distant as New Orleans, until, on Christmas Eve 1814, the two countries signed a treaty, and after a couple of sessions around the table in 1817 and 1818, etched out the border that still bisects North America. The cannonballs settled in the river's mud, and in time the plaques, like pages of a scattered book, stood in the calm fields.

History's finest quality may be its sense of irony. The British, with the help of Native people, conquered French-controlled Québec and Montréal over a period of seven years, but within twenty years lost their New England colony south of the St. Lawrence. Once they had gained their independence and become a republic, the United States then launched and lost a war against the exact same territory the British had won a generation earlier. With a great deal of help from the recently conquered French Canadians, the British held off the predatory Americans. It was all, in the end, about property values, the St. Lawrence being the most valuable property of all. When the cannon smoke settled in 1814, the Americans ended up with less than a tenth of the total riverbank.

7

Slow Rivers

And so, by 1850, it was plain, slow sailing from Kingston all the way to Montréal.

With the battle for the outline of Canada decided, the ship-yards along the river reverted to peacetime schedules, and freshly turned pine masts rose like exclamation points into the smokeless air. Some styles of ship went out of fashion—the last St. Lawrence snow, a two-masted square-rigger, was made in 1829—but most of the river's production was still fully rigged ships that weighed in at around a thousand tons. The shipyards of the St. Lawrence continued to turn out vessels destined for Britain, and for Liverpool in particular, built largely by French-men. (The use of oak, the *sine qua non* for British ships, declined as the great stands were cleared, to be replaced by the aptly named rock elm for the keel, dependable tamarack for the fut-tocks, plentiful but strong red pine for the planking, and the unwarping yellow pine for the decks.) Many exported ships were soon back in the St. Lawrence, carrying a human cargo.

As peace stretched on in the St. Lawrence valley in the sec-ond quarter of the nineteenth century, the restless poor of Europe began to decant into sailing ships and sail across the Atlantic Ocean and up the St. Lawrence—and the crossing still took as long as it had when Cartier made it. Some of the immigrants were people who had stared at their worn, empty farmers' hands and decided that anything was better than this. Some were fleeing persecution, while others were anxious to find somewhere fresh to practise their own brand of it. Soldiers who had been so long from home in the Napoleonic Wars decided that starting anew somewhere else made as much sense as going back to the old life. For a thousand different reasons they all went west and sailed up the river, turning left into the States, right into Canada or carrying on ahead to the frontier, where they set up homesteads in the forest, the trees diminish-ing in concentric circles around the settlers' chimneys until the clearings linked up and formed towns.

The Irish in particular were quick off the mark. Reverend William Bell and his family, for instance, left Ireland in April 1817 on the sailing ship *Rothiemurchus*, making for Upper Canada, there to farm, preach and eventually give the family name to a place called Bell's Corners. Bell wrote in his diary, on May 29:

> Still beating up against a head wind, but making little or no progress. Both shores uninhabited, hilly, and covered with wood. About noon, though still 280 miles from Quebec, we were met

by a pilot boat manned by a father and son. From
their cask, we had the first American water we
ever tasted, and they gave us a little maple sugar,
the first we had ever seen.

A little later in his journal, after the pilot has safely guided
them to Québec, Bell describes his preparations for the next
stage of his journey and shows us that, only five years after
John Molson's steamship *Swiftsure* carried its first paying passengers, travel by this means had become a fixture on the river.
New arrivals stepped off the sailing ship at Québec and onto
the steamship that would take them inland.

> The steam boat *Malsham* was that in which we
> were to take passage for Montreal. We were
> detained two days while it was undergoing repair.
> We had to hire Canadian carts to take our prop-
> erty from the ship to the steam boat. The drivers
> were very reckless, and did much damage in load-
> ing and unloading. As we had a good deal of bag-
> gage the captain of the *Malsham* said he would
> have to charge for it, as our passage ticket said
> nothing about baggage. So I had to go back to
> Col. Myer's office and get it altered.

Note that all the basic elements of modern travel are there in
Bell's testy report: a delay in taking off, a scary taxi ride, luggage
abuse, an excess baggage charge and some bureaucratic penance.
   Finally the Bells got underway.

> On the evening of June seventh, we sailed from
> Quebec in the *Malsham*, which is the largest and

the handsomest vessel of the kind I have yet seen. We had about fifty cabin passengers and a hundred and fifty others. The boat was large, splendidly fitted up, and the table abundantly supplied, and we had a pleasant passage to Montreal. There we found new friends. The Commissary, Mr. Clarke, paid us the greatest attention, in providing carriages to convey us up to Lachine, and batteaux to carry us up the river. On the sixteenth of June, after a voyage of eight days from Montreal, we landed at Prescott.

All was well that ended well, especially when one was travelling cabin class and not on a deck crowded with a hundred and fifty representatives of the common herd.

To put this into perspective, Reverend Bell's week-long journey by land and river between Montréal and Prescott now takes just over an hour in a loaded station wagon. Another immigrant, an Englishman named E. A. Talbot, made the same journey as Bell a year later in a small boat, and it took him thirteen days to get from Lachine to Prescott. Several times, Talbot says angrily in his account of that nightmarish trek, he had to sleep rough onshore, and on one occasion jump out of the boat in water up to his armpits and push. Unlike Bell, Talbot seems to have paid the economy fare.

The rapids between Montréal and Prescott were the reason for the extraordinary time spent travelling between these communities. There were six distinct eruptions of white water—Mille Roches, Moulinette, Long Sault, Farran's Point, Du Plat and Galops—and they were impassable except to the log rafts of the almighty timber trade. Dealing with the rapids was, literally, a drag, as big boats heading up or down the river had to come to a halt and unload into smaller boats, which were then poled and pulled by oxen on shore.

However, the curse the rapids represented for shipping was a blessing for the towns alongside them. Arranging for goods to be manhandled through the rapids and people to be taken on to Montréal or Prescott by land developed into a business known as forwarding. Prescott had the good fortune to be at the end, or the beginning (depending which way you were advancing), of the troublesome stretch of rapids. It consequently became the place where you took a load off or put it back on. For merchants, having their goods forwarded was an expensive part of their business—two pounds ten shillings per ton of stuff transported from Montréal to Prescott, compared with a pound per ton from London, England, to Montréal, Canada—and no doubt they sat in Prescott's bars, the Dog & Duck or the Black Bull, indulging in the Canadian national sport of wishing government would do something. Build some decent canals, perhaps, or hurry up and invent railways.

The forwarding trade made a boom town out of Prescott. Previously, it had just been the place where the ferry from Ogdensburg, New York, stopped. (The first Ogdensburg–Prescott ferry, a sailboat called *River Girl*, started making the short run in the late 1770s.) The first man in Prescott to call himself a forwarder was William Gilkison. Gilkison was a Scottish sailor who had tired of the sea, run a schooner for a while on Lake Erie and then come on land near Brockville to open a rope walk (a building for braiding long strands of hemp into rope) with a partner. Gilkison, perhaps at the end of *his* rope, saw an opportunity to develop a niche market and went into the forwarding business on his own. He built the first house in Prescott in 1811, and the necessary forwarding sturctures: an office, a warehouse, a dock and some wharves. When he offered cheaper rates than the

Kingston transporters, he was away, on track to a fortune.

The scent of money being made carried on the wind, and others soon arrived in Prescott. Within a decade there could be as many as a thousand travellers milling around town, waiting for a coach or a ship out, the poorer ones staying in tents or barns, the others in one of the twenty-four very active hotels.

While the forwarding trade flourished, the canal engineers were hard at work downriver doing something about those rapids that were easier to tame. Canal building was a growth industry in early nineteenth-century Canada for two reasons, and both had to do with speeding up the riverine transport system.

When the military and the colonial planners in London sat down with the admirals and generals and held their post-mortems after the War of 1812, they agreed that if the Americans got it into their republican heads to return to Canada, men and materials needed to move more quickly and successfully than they had during the conflict. A canal here, a canal there, and the problem would be solved—and that is why Ottawa got its famous canal. The Rideau Canal was the third side of a triangle that had the Ottawa and St. Lawrence rivers on the other two sides, and allowed Canadian forces to elude the Americans in any possible future war.

The second reason had to do with the pressure the rising population was putting on the river's cargo capabilities. The river had become a rope ladder for thousands of Europeans climbing up to the Great Lakes, and it was getting to be a busy place, ships and boats scurrying up and down, pushed by wind, pulled by rope or getting along under their own steam. As in the old fishing story where a man hooks a monster, watches the

rod bend double and says to himself, "I'm going to need a bigger boat," the St. Lawrence system needed an upgrade.

There was already a larger cargo boat to hand in the northern United States: the Durham. The Durham was twice as long
and half as wide again as the standard Canadian bateau, with a
short, raked mast down front and an elegantly bent oar as a
rudder. It was the same both ends, like the woof 'n' poof dog in
Dr. Dolittle. In the canal system as it stood, however, the
Durham was an elephant trying to get through the cottage
front door, and so in the early 1820s the canals already built
between lakes St-Francis and St-Louis were deepened and doubled in width to allow Durham boats in and out without a
scratch.

At the same time, the acrobatic rapids at Lachine that had
blocked Cartier, bedevilled Champlain and caused the
explorer Louis Joliet to lose the journal of his epic trip down
the Mississippi were finally bypassed, more than a century after
de Casson had tried it. The first edition of the Lachine Canal
was cut across the bottom tip of Montreal Island's nose, like a
bone thrust through it. It was eight miles long, took three years
(1821 to 1824) to complete, and was capable of taking a
Durham boat and a bateau side by side.

The government attempted some cost recovery through
tolls on the improved canals, and the accounting records of the
period give a sturdy portrait of traffic flow up and down the
river. Barrel making was a good business to be in in the early
1800s, because potash and peas, flour, salt and rum were
shipped in them, around twenty thousand tons a year upstream
and three times that many coming down, as trade and manu-
facturing around the Great Lakes began to grow. In 1832, for
example, eight hundred Durham boats went through the
canals, and almost twice as many bateaux. In the working life

of the river, this was a time of management's demand for increased productivity. And the workers kept on arriving.

The immigrants to North America did not bring many belongings with them, just a trunk or a suitcase each and some savings, because they were not rich. The prosperous, by definition, do not need to start new lives; the ones they already have are fine. The majority of immigrants came from the less wealthy parts of Europe, and there are contagious diseases associated with regions of poverty, diseases such as cholera, typhus and bubonic plague, which rhythmically descend into epidemic. And whenever an epidemic swept through Europe and congregated in the ports that exported poor people to North America, it was bound to hopscotch its way across the ocean. The emigrating viruses and bacteria were organisms that, like their hosts, were simply looking to stay alive, and forty days spent at sea in close, unsanitary proximity provided favourable conditions for them to flourish.

One of these epidemics, the cholera outbreak of 1832, carried into Europe by Indian soldiers, was so biblical in proportion, with deaths in the hundreds of thousands, that the Canadian government determined to stop it at the gates. The solution was to funnel the immigrants through a quarantine system that would detect and filter out the sick while allowing the healthy to percolate through. Ideally, the quarantine facilities, like prisons, needed to be on an island, a sort of natural isolation tank with a good harbour. A search committee was struck and, thirty miles downstream from the port of Québec, in an archipelago in the slipstream of the Île d'Orléans, they found just the place they were seeking: Grosse-Île. The first station on Grosse-Île consisted of quarters for the staff, two sheds, a hospital for the unfortunate and a bakery. They also placed three cannons—which are still there—pointing out into the passage between Grosse-Île and the south shore of the St. Lawrence to alert ships to the need to stop and be medically inspected.

The Americans have made much of Ellis Island, the turnstile through which their huddled masses entered. Grosse-Île is often called the Canadian Ellis Island, but that is a misnomer. Ellis Island was basically a reception hall, and the reception centres on the St. Lawrence were in Québec. Grosse-Île was a quarantine centre. It is certainly a sad and beautiful place, the piece of Canada that so many Canadians set their first footprint on, their dreams intact. It is also the last Canadian place that some of them saw.

"The dreadful cholera was depopulating Quebec and Montreal when our ship cast anchor off Grosse Isle, on the thirtieth of August, 1832, and we were boarded a few minutes after by the health-officers." These are the opening words of Susanna Moodie's account of her settling in Canada, the classic *Roughing It in the Bush*, published in 1852 to great success. The cholera was in the process of killing almost six thousand people in Lower Canada, and the next epidemic two years later would see off another two and a half thousand. When she laid eyes on Grosse-Île from the deck of the sailing ship *Anne*, Moodie was a twenty-nine-year-old, middle-class woman who had been married for a year and had left behind a modest writing career in England. The quarantine station was already in its first year of operation, bursting with humanity.

Moodie, through the filter of her genteel but robust sensibilities, described the look of things.

The rocky isle in front, with its neat farm-houses at the eastern point, and its high bluff at the western extremity, crowned with the telegraph—the middle space occupied by tents and sheds for the cholera patients, and its wooded shores dotted over with motley groups—added greatly to the picturesque effect of the land scene. Then the broad, glittering river, covered with boats darting to and fro, conveying passengers from twenty-five vessels, of various size and tonnage, which rode at anchor, with their flags flying from their mast-head, gave an air of life and interest to the whole.

Moodie got the chance (as a sightseer—she was not ill) to go ashore at the small bay that was the landing point and cast her literary eye over a less exquisite scene.

Never shall I forget the extraordinary spectacle that met our sight the moment we passed the low range of bushes which formed a screen in front of the river. A crowd of many hundred Irish immigrants had been landed during the present and former day; and all this motley crew—men, women, and children, who were not confined by sickness to the sheds (which greatly resembled cattle-pens)—were employed in washing clothes, or spreading them out on the rocks and bushes to dry . . . The people who covered the island appeared perfectly destitute of shame, or even of a sense of common decency. Many were almost naked, still more but partially clothed. We turned

in disgust from the revolting scene, but were
unable to leave the spot until the captain had
satisfied a noisy group of his own people, who
were demanding a supply of stores.

Moodie goes on to describe her progress to Québec, where
most of the seventy-two passengers on the *Anne* disembarked.
She takes up the story again when the *Anne* and two other vessels are towed, like a trio of English setters on leashes, by the
steamer *British America* to Montréal. In the darkness (a pro-
found darkness much different from the well-lit one the river
enjoys now) a lone piper struck up a tune on one of the sailing
ships, and invisible musicians on the other two answered the
call. When this small fleet reached Montréal, Moodie's nose
was, once again, the first part of her to react when she stepped
onto land.

The town itself was, at that period, dirty and ill-
paved; and the opening of all the sewers, in order
to purify the place and stop the ravages of the
pestilence, rendered the public thoroughfares
almost impassable, and loaded the air with intol-
erable effluvia, more likely to produce than stay
the course of the plague.

The Moodies, needless to say, left Montréal fairly quickly and
travelled overland to Prescott. There they "embarked on board
a fine new steamboat, the *William IV*, crowded with Irish immigrants, proceeding to Cobourg and Toronto," and spent some
time trying to console a Scottish couple in mid-emigration
whose six-year-old son had died that day and for whom the
journey to a new life had lost its meaning.

At Brockville, a bundle of ladies came aboard, some welcome extra tongues, and then the day turned stormy. Curtains of rain fell and hid the Thousand Islands. The steamer reached Kingston at midnight, the deck passengers soaked to the bone, and all slept fitfully in their rooms or in the open air till dawn, with the storm banging the steamer's sides. Outside the Moodies' quarters a drunken, yodelling Irishman was collapsed on the mat. This annoying stereotype "harangued his countrymen on the state of the Emerald Isle, in a style which was loud if not eloquent." Despite being kicked and threatened by a Dutch stewardess, the man was a firework that wouldn't go out, and he "kept up such a racket that we all wished him at the bottom of the Ontario."

The next day dawned wet and woolly, and the trip to Cobourg took longer than expected. The Moodies made it by midnight, and in a day or so worked their way into the bush to begin, well, roughing it. Like most of the British immigrants in the years after the War of 1812, they had bypassed Lower Canada and gone into Upper Canada, which was busy making itself into a Little England under the direction of Governor Simcoe and his wife, Elizabeth. The river had been like a seesaw until around 1800, with most of the weight of humanity on the lower side. Now the upper side was gaining weight.

Moodie's literary chronicle of ascending the St. Lawrence is one of many that drift up from those years of steam travel. Indeed, if everyone who wrote of the adventure were assembled on one mid-nineteenth-century steamer, it would make for quite a passenger list, including Walt Whitman, Mark Twain and a host of others not as well known but just as eloquent. All of them report on a river that resembled a vast stretched-out building project, with workers constantly being shipped in from elsewhere while the materials of progress scurried from site to site in small, busy barges and in boats that puffed smoke and churned their side-paddles, like grist mills broken loose from the riverbank.

As well as the stench of sewers, the air the Moodies breathed in carried the first scent of rebellion. Civil unrest, which broke out in 1837, was about much the same things in both of Canada's provinces. The rebels, who were republican in nature, were looking for a reduction in British arrogance and patronage in government, and an end to the perennial evil of land specula-tors. These aims were not dissimilar to the ones that had sparked the American Revolution two generations earlier.

A year after the twin rebellions of 1837 had come and gone, with twelve men hanged and dozens of French-speaking rebels deported to Australia, a curious little incident took place on the St. Lawrence near Prescott. The ragged story began on a cold Sunday morning, November 11. The regular ferry from Sackets Harbor on the American side of Lake Ontario was making its way downriver. At each stop an unusual number of young men with an Irish turn of phrase got on, and by the time the ferry pulled in at Ogdensburg, it disgorged a battalion of them. They were joined on shore by two hundred other members of a group called the Patriots, a paramilitary offshoot of the Hunters' Lodge organization, one of those boys' clubs with Irish history stuck to the bottom of their shoes that proliferated in North America at the time, and still do to some extent. The Patriots' plan was both simple and huge; they would sail across the nar-row strip of river to Prescott, take Fort Wellington, and use it as a base from which to generate an uprising among the defeated rebels of a year earlier, whose blood pressure was hopefully still high, and thus take Canada. The country would no longer touch its cap to the imperial Queen—Victoria's reign was a year old—and instead would become a monarchless democracy.

In various small boats and schooners, the force left the American shore the next day. The famous pirate William Johnston had joined them—any excuse to rattle the British and Johnston (a Canadian who had deserted to the Americans when the war started) was there—and he even dressed up as an admiral for the occasion. His uniform, however, was smarter than his navigation; his gunship ran aground. Another self-promoted officer, one "General" John Birge, was equally raring to go, and then, complaining of a tummy ache, had himself dropped off.

The rest of the force made it across, but they noticed a British naval vessel sailing nearby. Instead of chancing an attack on Fort Wellington, which would involve tackling a warship, they drifted downstream a mile or so to a defunct windmill. The McQueen family, whose failed enterprise the building was, offered no resistance, and the windmill became base camp for the invasion of Canada by the Hunters' Lodge. Meanwhile, the schooner that had brought most of the Patriots across the St. Lawrence abandoned them and went back to nearby America.

The local militia, apparently not in the mood for a revolution, soon pinned the Patriots down and sent to Fort Wellington for backup. The fort in turn alerted Fort Henry at Kingston, which dispatched a gunboat. The first cannonball the gunboat fired bounced off the sixty-foot stone structure without denting it at all, so the British went to Plan B. They laid siege to the windmill, and when a couple of thousand reinforcements arrived four days later, they stormed it.

At this point the great adventure, as adventures with guns usually do, ended up in a heap of dead young men. The Patriots, fighting for their lives, exacted a heavy toll on the British, killing over two hundred and fifty foot soldiers and mutilating several of them, while losing only twenty of their own. But they were all captured, shackled in pairs and shipped down to Kingston to face a military trial. Eleven of them were hanged, and a load of them sent off to Australia, whence they did not return. Two of the rebels on trial had their token defences written out by a young local lawyer named John A. Macdonald, who, unlike them, was on his way to better things.

The revolution that never really was had ended. The windmill in time became a historic site. Drive a little east of Prescott on the way to Johnstown and take a dogleg on the right and there is the windmill, where it blocks the view of the bungalow across the street. The windmill's sails are gone, and it now suffers only the light assault of people in comfortable shoes. There are flower beds where there once was blood. Ogdensburg is as close as ever, so close that the day I visited the windmill I saw someone going into Ogdensburg's Frederic Remington museum for a look at its fine, calm paintings of the St. Lawrence. The river was ruffled slightly by the breeze, but I called out a hello to America anyway and raised my arm to it. The waves, neutral as ever, waved back.

In 1842, Charles Dickens did a tour of the eastern United States. At the tour's end, in May, he effected a brief sortie into Canada, and recorded it in his *American Notes*. The novelist was only vaguely aware that the country was still settling down after the Rebellions of 1837. After seeing, of course, Niagara Falls (he thought their noise exaggerated) and Toronto, he took a steamer, loaded with one thousand eight hundred barrels of flour, to Kingston. By coincidence, Dickens got there when it was the seat of government; Upper and Lower Canada had become one in the Act of Union two years before, and were renamed Canada East and Canada West. Kingston was the compromise capital of the new democratic dominion until 1844, when the seat of government began bouncing around, finally settling on Ottawa a decade later.

Leaving Kingston for Montréal at half past nine, Dickens made the usual cooing noises about the Thousand Islands, and then turned sullen at the prospect of taking a stagecoach past the worst of the rapids and getting on and off steamers in between coach rides. At one point, going up on deck after both breakfast and a violent storm, he beheld the ponderous sight of a passing log raft. It was the biggest he had seen. "A most gigantic raft," he wrote, "with some thirty or forty wooden houses upon it, and at least as many flag masts, so that it looked like a nautical street." He boarded a stagecoach for a trot through a series of French villages, which he enjoyed, not-ing that the common people all wore a sash of a bright colour, usually red, even though they had no shoes. Then it was another steamboat, then off again at Lachine, and the last nine miles by stagecoach into Montréal.

Dickens's descriptions of the streets and views of Montréal, which had a population then of around fifty thousand, and Québec, thirty-five thousand, are cursory. His social conscience emerges when he travels back from Québec to Montréal on a steamer crowded with immigrants.

> At night they spread their beds between decks (those who had beds, at least) and slept so close and thick about our cabin door, that the passage to and fro was quite blocked up. They were

nearly all English; from Gloucestershire the greater part; and had gone through a long winter passage out; but it was wonderful to see how clean the children had been kept, and how untiring in their love and self-denial all the poor parents were.

The sight of this sends him into some vintage Dickens, wherein he wonders how the rich, so quick to label the poor as depraved and deserving of their state, would fare as parents if they were stripped of their advantage and put on this deck, bedless, with children in need of relentless attention. He doubts they would cope, and his "love and honour of my kind" is renewed.

⚓

The Colonial Office, shaken but not stirred by the rebellions and firmly back in control, as Dickens had seen at Kingston, were anxious to resume canal projects on the St. Lawrence. Pre-rebellion, the Assembly of Lower Canada had dragged its feet on spending money that would help shipping reach Upper Canada. The British, frustrated, had gone so far as to impose on the two Canadas a joint commission for canals to look into what should be done. The commission had recommended—no surprise—more and better canals.

A river like the St. Lawrence cannot safely be left in European hands.

—Thomas D'Arcy McGee, while editor of the Boston Pilot, 1845

The canals so far constructed were the joint-custody children of the military and the legislature of Canada, but in their own minds Canada West and East were still separate countries. For a while there had even been a customs house at the unofficial border at Coteau-du-Lac. Despite the Act of Union they continued to behave in a sort of left brain–right brain manner, with the British and their loyalists trying to keep a stiff Upper Canada that reflected the way things ran back in Great Britain and the hotter French blood in Lower Canada breaking out at regular intervals, usually resulting in a building getting burnt down. All of the bailiwicks wanted bigger and better canals of their own on their respective stretches of the St. Lawrence, and they were in a constant tug-of-war with the British purse strings.

Upper Canada in particular was anxious to get a canal system in place, because everything accomplished so far on the river was downstream, in Lower Canada. Tired of waiting for Her Imperial Majesty's money to drift their way and the French Canadians to get over it, the burgeoning city of Brockville had asked the Upper Canada assembly way back in 1834 to build a canal bypassing the rapids at Long Sault (near Cornwall). The assembly had provided the seed money and work had started, but the rebellions had snookered the project. Now, post-rebellion, a loan of a million and a half pounds to the new, single government of the Canadas got the shovels flying again. The loan came better late than never: the St. Lawrence, despite predictions to the contrary by the canal system's advocates, was not doing a roaring trade.

As far back as 1825, the Americans had carved out and opened the Erie Canal, and it *was* doing very well. The Erie made possible a southerly detour of all the rapids on the St. Lawrence, and so the ingredients for bread—wheat and flour—could go direct to New York without passing Montréal. And New York was closer to Britain than Montréal by a factor of a couple of days of seafaring.

Phase two of the St. Lawrence canal system had two simple notions in mind: firstly, the wider and deeper the canal, the bigger the boat that could thread through it; secondly, the fewer the locks, the quicker the getting through. Top of the list of motives for a beefed-up canal system was making the St. Lawrence the route of choice for western grain heading east. Canada was hard at work turning wheat into wealth, and the grain barons and the shipping barons were determined to get it onto the world's tables, baked, sliced and buttered, by whichever route was cheapest and quickest. Eager to work, the engineers got out their rulers and went at the river with money and determination.

By the time the mud settled at the end of the 1840s, all the rapids along the river had been circumvented. The Lachine Canal was deeper and had tidied up its lock count from seven to five. The first two lock basins were now deep enough, at sixteen feet, to take transatlantic sailing ships. The trio of veteran canals in the northern channel between Lac St-Francis and Lac St-Louis were usurped by a single, eleven-mile-long canal on the southern side, the Beauharnois, which sported nine locks. The firm building the Beauharnois stretch—named after Charles, Marquis de Beauharnois, who put in twenty years as governor of New France in the early 1700s—probably got it with the lowest tender, because the job was sloppy. One entrance jammed, the canal was too shallow and it was banana-shaped. The addition of two dams to raise the water level and a crack repair crew got it working.

Upriver, the pesky Cornwall Canal the burghers of Brockville had been after was finally finished. The rapids west of Cornwall were tamed with a group of canals collectively known as the Williamsburgs—at Farran's Point, Rapide Plat and Galops—with six locks between them. These last three were needed only by ships ascending the river against the current; coming down was a joyride. And so, by 1850, for the first time, it was plain slow sailing from Kingston all the way to Montréal, and vice versa.

With a viable canal system in place, the writing was on the wall for the forwarding trade. The last man to close up shop and make a career change in Prescott was Timothy Buckley, who stayed on in his stone house as a store owner. His sons carried on the business after him, and there was always a keg of beer available in their general store for customers to take a quaff or two (a notion worth reviving).

O boating on the rivers, / The voyage down the St. Lawrence, the superb scenery, the steamers, / The ships sailing, the Thousand Islands, the occasional timber-raft and the raftsmen with long-reaching sweep-oars, / The little huts on the rafts, and the stream of smoke when they cook supper at evening.

—Walt Whitman, "A Song of Joys,"
Leaves of Grass, 1855

One of Prescott's buildings that had been used for forwarding later became Canada's first Lifesaver Candy Factory, and when that went sour, it became a pickle factory. The warehouse that had been the centre of William Gilkison's operations had a series of other lives, first as an American consulate, then a lawyer's office, after that a laundromat and finally, fittingly, as a museum to the forwarding trade.

While Prescott declined, the other end of the now-deceased forwarding trade—Montréal—prospered. Canal locks, in the course of holding back water and releasing it, provide hydro power. That power could be sold to mill owners and factories, indeed to any cog of the Industrial Revolution eager for a force that can do the work of many men. Alongside the canals of the St. Lawrence, industries sprang up like dragon's teeth; ninety-nine leases for water use were granted at canals between 1847 and 1862, to sawmills, paper mills, tanneries and the like. The first two basins of the Lachine Canal, poetically known as Basin No. 1 and Basin No. 2, were rapidly boxed in by an industrial park, the biggest in Canada. Fortunes were there to be made, and men like Ira Gould made them. An analysis of Gould's empire conducted in 1856 revealed a cutting-edge scythe factory, three nail and barbed-wire plants, two metal works, a couple of sawmills and a brace of flour mills. Lined up beside these were factories pumping out sugar, rubber, cotton, doors, barrels and wool, and there were jobs for a thousand people.

8

LAMENT FOR A RIVER

La Chute Montmorency displayed power, beauty and flowing abundance, the virtues the newcomers were seeking in Canada.

The extra workforce needed to keep these wheels of industry turning came mainly from two sources: the poor of Ireland, who for five years had been in mass emigration from a recurring famine caused by a potato fungus and bad English governance, and the sons and daughters of the large French Canadian families. An average of thirty-five thousand immigrants, two-thirds of them Irish, entered the St. Lawrence in the years 1832 to 1846. (The population of Ireland was so drained by emigration in the mid-eighteenth century that it has yet to return to the numbers it boasted in 1845.)

The exodus from the prolonged Irish famine (an unnecessary

one—there were stacks of Irish produce being exported to England from the same docks that were shipping the starving to Canada) became a business opportunity for anyone with a boat they thought could make it, stuffed with vulnerable humanity, across the Atlantic. Most of the immigrants were desperate people who had chosen Canada as the lesser of two inevitabilities. An early death on Irish soil seemed certain; death in Canada was certain too, but it might be postponed. As history continues to show, however, there are bacteria and viruses that thrive on desperate people. The immigrants, despite themselves, were an easy target for disease.

Inevitably, typhus, carried in ticks and fleas, as well as in infected food and water, found the undernourished in the spring of 1847. It matured within them as they gathered at ports like Liverpool. It flourished in the sailing ships that brought the poor to Canada. In tens, then in hundreds, then thousands, they felt the first chills, followed by the fever, the telltale dark red spots on the thin skin, the swollen intestines. Typhus killed the immigrants by the hundreds even before they saw the new land, their bodies sent to the bottom of the ocean wrapped in cheap shrouds, like unhatched moths in their cocoons. If they survived the crossing, they sailed up the St. Lawrence on the death ships and hove to at the cannon's signal off the wharf at Grosse-Île. The doctor came on board, and if he found disease, the sick and the well were rowed over to the island and quarantined until they died, recovered or remained clean of it.

Grosse-Île is shaped like an eel facing upstream with its mouth open. It's a five-minute walk from the wharf to a small, undulating field midway across the lower jaw. Here and there in the field, small white crosses are the bleached, sad stalks of the epidemic of 1847. Some of the crosses, with the passing of time, have started to lean. The field is a mass grave, rendered tranquil by the years.

Underneath half the field are cheap wooden coffins, piled three high. It is called the Irish Cemetery because most of the coffins hold Irish bones. Six thousand lie below those waves of earth, all but a thousand of them buried in just six months in 1847.

The immigration authorities in Québec, despite letters to the city newspapers warning of increased immigration and corresponding sickness, were caught underprepared. Two years earlier the city had been hit by two fires that left twenty thousand people, *half the population*, homeless, and rebuilding had preoccupied much of the city's energies. Grosse-Île in the spring of 1847 had facilities for two hundred sick people and eight hundred in quarantine. The first ship bearing the infected, the *Syria*, arrived from Liverpool on May 14, and by the end of the month Grosse-Île was dealing with twelve thousand people, in sheds, tents or still on ships at anchor. One thousand three hundred of them were sick. In those two weeks a hundred children had become orphans, and one day in that dreadful May, thirty-two ships were anchored off the island like yachts in a marina, all of them bearing sickness. On May 21, five ships pulled in carrying seventeen hundred people, a third of them ill.

By the end of the month, the death rate was climbing past eighty souls a day. A priest, Father McGauran, spent five hours on a ship continuously administering the last rites to a hundred people. To relieve the pressure, selected immigrants who had not shown signs of disease for a week were sent upriver to Québec and Montréal, although the doctors releasing them knew that many of them would fall sick there and die. (They were right: three thousand expired in the wards of Point St-Charles hospital in Montréal by New Year's Day, 1848.)

After a month, the death rate, as a percentage of arrivals, began to fall even as the number of detainees on the island increased. Word had got back to Liverpool and health inspections there had been tightened up. But in mid-June, over a hundred and fifty people a week were still succumbing, and the island was a cross between a mortuary, a construction site, a tent city, a swamped hospital, a graveyard and an overcrowded port. The disease had also jumped over to the mainland directly north of Grosse-Île. The Québec *Gazette* reported that St-Joachim was now suffering an outbreak of typhus.

The most important thing now was to build, build, build and get everyone under a decent roof. Money and men were asked for and received. The end of July and all of August was spent moving people into newly constructed sheds and hospitals as soon as a roof was on. Like plucked weeds, the number of tents dwindled away. The worst seven-day stretch, death's heyday, came in the second week of August. (The only building that survives from this period is the lazaretto, down at the eastern end of the island, the last of a dozen sheds erected in August and September to get the as yet unsick out of tents and away from contagion. When I visited the island, this shed was being restored. The sound of hammers and sawing, and the bright beige wood, were an eerie echo from a century and a half earlier, when the labour had a more desperate purpose.)

Finally, in early September, the ships—and every sail breaking over the horizon must have seemed like a death bell—began to arrive less frequently. By the beginning of October, weekly deaths had dipped below a hundred for the first time since June 1, and the biggest problem was what to do about winter, when the island would freeze up. Anyone still there would need to be heated and fed. Those of the medical and caretaking staff who had not fallen to disease or exhaustion decided to evacuate the island of the remaining four hundred sorry quarantines.

The last person to die on Grosse-Île in 1847 was Mr. Lindsay, a member of the service staff, who passed away in the third week of October. By October 23 only ten people were left on the island: four caretakers; the medical superintendent, George Douglas, who had certainly passed the most trying season of his career; a notary who was there to inventory the belongings of the dead; a washerwoman, two assistants, and a patient who had been on the staff, a Mr. Hum.

On the first day of November the *Lord Ashburton*, the last of the four hundred ships that anchored at Grosse-Île that year, turned up. It was in wretched condition, and eight people died that night, still on board. All the *Lord Ashburton*'s passengers were transferred directly to a steamer, the *Alliance*, and taken to Québec. On November 3, Superintendant Douglas locked the door of his office and was ferried back to Québec. It was over.

In all, just under a hundred thousand emigrants left Ireland, England, Scotland and Germany that year, one in seven of them Irish. Fully half of those Irish steerage passengers fleeing the Grim Reaper of famine would contract typhus, the disease known to them as ship's fever, and one in five would die of it by Christmas. (Eight thousand Germans came to Canada that same summer, and hardly any got sick.) Close to nine thousand immigrants spent time in the hospitals on Grosse-Île. All together, over three thousand people expired there in the summer of 1847; another two thousand died on ships anchored just offshore, for a grisly total of five thousand, four hundred and twenty-four. Among the dead were four doctors (including John Benson, an Irishman who arrived at Grosse-Île in mid-May, offered to stay, and died there), plus twenty-two of the nurses, orderlies and cooks who fought to prevent the deaths of others. The field near the hotels was now full of wooden coffins.

A hundred and fifty years later, in a book of Canadian poetry by Carmelita McGrath, I find these lines: "Walk inland; beneath the trees that shelter this still place lie more bones;

walk shoreward; in stone cairns lie other, earlier dreams."

The orphans of Grosse-Île were taken in by families along the north shore of the St. Lawrence. The couples who had married there went off to start new homes and families. The babies who had been born and baptized there, such as James Maher, son of Eliza Waters from County Kilkenny, whose father had died on the crossing, went on to start their lives in a new country.

The island did not see another year that came close to being as bad as 1847, although cholera did break out again in Europe in 1854. Eyewitness accounts taken from journals of passengers on transatlantic sailing ships after 1847 show the island in a different mood. William Fulford sailed from England on April 5, 1848, as a steerage passenger on the *Civility*, which had brought timber to the old country and was returning to Canada to reload. Fulford organized religious services on the deck every evening at seven, and after holding forty of them he saw the St. Lawrence for the first time. A few days later he wrote:

> Sunday twenty-first, May. Continued fine. A fair wind. At half past seven this morning we arrived at Quebec Quaranteen Ground which is thirty miles from Quebec. We cast anchor, which is on the north side of the river. There is an English settlement and hospital under our Government, and doctors for the reception of sick passengers; but through the mercy of God it was fortunate for us: we were the most decent and healthy passengers the doctor had ever seen or examined. So we were detained only two hours.

Fulford must have known of the events of the previous year, and he can't be blamed for his obvious joy at not having to set foot on Grosse-Île.

Seven years later, another emigrant, William Gliddon, sailed from England on Monday, April 2, 1855, on the *Ocean Queen*. Six weeks later he was able to write in his journal, as they entered the St. Lawrence: "Tuesday, 15th. Weather fine and headwinds. Land on both sides. This evening we are becalmed and have had a splendid sight of the Aurora Borealis." The ship arrived at Grosse-Île on May 19. He pointed a telescope at the island even as his ship received a clean bill of health. Through the lens Gliddon saw people scattered along the shore washing clothes, and he thought this a pretty sight. The next day the *Ocean Queen* was allowed to weigh anchor, and Gliddon wrote this as the wind bore him upstream:

> We weighed anchor about 4 a.m. and proceeded. The Island of Orleans which bounds the North Coast is a pretty island, and one mile below Quebec are the falls of Mont Morencai, about 60 feet high and 20 wide. I think the scene up the Gulf and River St. Lawrence repays all the expense and trouble of so long a voyage.

Gliddon was a little off on the height of the Montmorency Falls—they are actually, at two hundred and forty-two feet, taller than Niagara—but they were a symbol noted in many a voyager's journal as he neared journey's end after stopping at Grosse-Île. La Chute Montmorency displayed power, beauty and flowing abundance, the virtues the newcomers were seeking in Canada.

9

OLD MAN RIVER

The trouble with the St. Lawrence, and it remains a problem,
is the fact that for a handful of months it ices up.

The river Gliddon ascended in 1855 was now churning with
steamer companies, from the big sturgeon who had got in at
the start—the dynasties-in-the-making like the Molsons and
the Torrances—to the young pikes who were lurking in the
reeds. The latter category included a river pilot, Jacques-Félix
Sincennes, who also wore the hats of farmer and merchant and
lived in Sorel at the mouth of the Rivière Richelieu, which
comes down from Lake Champlain to meet the St. Lawrence.

Sincennes's particular roster of jobs prompted him to go
into the produce shipping business. In 1845, he built a small
paddlewheel steamer and hooked a barge behind it; a man of

simple poetry, he dubbed the steamer the *Richelieu* and the barge the *Sincennes*. Twice a week he towed his rudimentary barge down the Richelieu and pulled in at a series of stops, where farmers from the river valley would drive their carts straight onto the barge. Reaching Montréal harbour, the horses were awoken and the carts driven off and up to the dockside Bonsecours market, where the farmers dropped the reins, hopped down and started selling from the back of the cart.

Sincennes made money, bought out the competition on the Richelieu as it rose up to challenge him, and became the chief executive of the Compagnie du Richelieu. When the railway arrived in the valley and started to cut into his business, he moved on to the big river, to Montréal, in 1853. As soon as he was installed in his new headquarters, Sincennes commissioned two well-crafted ships, one for each of the two languages in the streets around him, the *Victoria* and the *Napoleon*, and set them to work making, as each of their human counterparts had done, an empire.

Meanwhile, John Molson's lead with the *Accommodation* in the early 1800s had been quickly challenged by men like David Torrance. Torrance was a true son of the river. His father was a liquor shipper in Montréal and later an agent in the forwarding business in Kingston. Old man Torrance made barrels of money in Montréal from the War of 1812, and eldest son David held on to it as part of an extensive family of merchants importing tea from China. The Torrances took the logical step and got into shipping, with a towboat company in the 1820s. David, a man who believed that size matters, sought out and bought the most powerful steamer on the St. Lawrence, the *Hercules*, and later added to his collection of superlatives the two-hundred-and-forty-foot *Canada*, in its day the biggest and fastest steamer in British North America.

The Molsons and Torrances jousted with business plans, and in mid-century ended up going head to head for the Montréal–Québec traffic, the plum run on the river. Transatlantic sailing ships were arriving daily in Québec, and the contest for getting their passengers and cargoes upriver sparked a price war, like gas stations on opposite corners. In 1850, a dollar would get you a stateroom from Québec to Montréal, a throwaway price even then. If you were down to your last fifteen cents, you could go steerage and still have a couple of cents' change. The churning rivalry above water was matched by the churning of the paddlewheels below, and the banks of the St. Lawrence began to crumble as they were repeatedly slapped by the wake of powered ships.

There is a fine line between competition and rivalry, and the stretch of water between Québec and Montréal became something of a racetrack for steamer companies. The prize was the extra business that fell to whoever consistently got the incoming immigrants to Montréal first. Sporting crowds would turn out on Montréal harbour for the matinée arrival. Passengers would line the rails to cheer the first ship into Victoria pier, while side bets down on the dock were being settled.

Winning the daily Québec–Montréal dragster race started to get out of hand when stokers were asked by ships' captains to squeeze some extra speed out of the engines. They began supercharging the boilers with highly combustible materials such as resin and grease, or even, in one instance, pork carcasses that were on their way to market, thus adding pigpower to the horsepower. Sprinkling powdered colophony (the residue from turpentine manufacture) on the coals in the boilers also pushed up the pressure, sometimes over the red line, while the chief engineer stared hard at the dial and crossed his fingers. Like children playing with something sharp, this was an accident waiting to happen.

At four o'clock on June 26, 1857, the steamships *Napoleon*, wearing the Compagnie du Richelieu colours, and the *Montréal*, the latter from the Torrance stable, pulled rapidly out of Québec harbour together, racing for Montréal with full passenger lists. The plumes from both smokestacks billowed hard, and by Cap-Rouge, about ten miles into the run, the *Napoleon* was a figurehead in front. Then the deck of the *Montréal*, with three hundred people on board, caught fire amidships, right over the glowing boilers. Things quickly got serious, and the captain ordered his ship run aground. It did—on a sandbar a thousand feet from shore, in swift-running water a fathom deep and cold as a dead man's stare. The flames soon conquered the ship, forcing the passengers into a tight knot on the bow. Two lifeboats were lowered, only for one to capsize and the other to sink. Two hundred and fifty-three people drowned in minutes.

The next day the *Napoleon* tiptoed into Montréal harbour, her decks littered with the quick and the dead. The race was over.

The fallout from this terrible accident was considerable. No one felt like racing any more, and a round of mergers and closings ensued, leaving the Compagnie du Richelieu on top as the biggest shipper on the St. Lawrence, with the Torrance Line as part of it. For fifteen years thereafter, Sincennes's company enjoyed a maritime dominance clear down to the Gulf, and new ships were being added continually. First came a *Montréal* to replace the one lost, then the *Québec*, in tribute to the sailing ship left unfinished on the dock when Wolfe overran that city.

Meanwhile the Department of Public Works, which was handling coast guard duties on the river, was purchasing steamships of its own in the late 1850s to patrol its lighthouses and buoys and to tow sailing ships out of trouble whenever they got into it. One of the Department's ships, the *Queen Victoria*, was put on special duty in August 1864 when, as the Quebec *Gazette* reported, "The Hon: messrs J. A. Macdonald, Cartier, Brown, Galt, Campbell, McGee, McDougal and Langevin left on Monday evening by the Provincial Steamer *Queen Victoria* for Charlottetown." The honourable gentlemen were on their way to the Charlottetown Conference, where the notion of a Maritime union of Nova Scotia, New Brunswick and P.E.I. was dropped in favour of the grander one of a united British North America that would include the province of Canada, Upper and Lower.

In the space of a few short decades, steam had conquered the St. Lawrence. It was sending up smoke signals all along the river; clocks could now be used to pace a journey instead of calendars; and the phrase "day trip" had entered the language of river travel. Applied science had not taken a break, though. Even as the routes along the St. Lawrence were snapped up by steamer companies, marine engineers had been hard at work on the problem of increasing the number of times a ship could cross the Atlantic during the warmer months. The motive for the quest was simple: the more trips per season, the more money the shipping lines could make. A thousand tons of wood moving at ten knots with only moving air as fuel was an impressive sight, but harnessing changes in barometric pressure put you at the mercy of the wind gods. Hydraulic pressure was faster and more controllable. It was time to take the wind out of the sails.

Another motivation for making ships that could get back and forth across the Atlantic as quickly as possible was the desire for a quicker mail service. Mail was a hugely important concept in the quieter years before the telegraph and the phone. The British ran their colonies on it, and it was the only lifeline back to the motherland for all those thousands of immigrants. News of a birth, death or marriage in Brockville or Rivière-du-loup might not reach the relatives back in County Cork or Cherbourg for a month, and it would be another month before you knew that they knew.

The trouble with the St. Lawrence—and it remains a problem—is the fact that for a handful of months it ices up. Nowadays a set of power chisels—icebreakers—managed by the Canadian coast guard maintain a watery valley down the middle of the river to keep Québec and Montréal reachable, but in the nineteenth century the two ports were out of bounds from Christmas to Easter. (Ice, being a child of nature, can display irrational outbursts of behaviour. In the great freeze of 1976, the ice pack actually touched bottom between the Île d'Orléans and the mainland, a depth of thirty-five feet. That thickness of ice could support a skyscraper. By contrast, 1998 was so mild a year that the river abstained from closing at all, and the coast guard had to find other things to do, while seal pups birthed on the ice's edge in the Gulf of St. Lawrence drowned when it melted away beneath them.)

The nearest year-round ice-free harbour to the St. Lawrence's urban centres was Portland, Maine, and so a railway line was constructed, beginning there, to bring transatlantic mail and materials to inland Canada in winter. Portland being an American town meant that British mail was arriving in American sailing ships and that they, not a Canadian line, got the lucrative fee the British government paid to mail carriers. Mail carried in British ships in winter had to pay harbour fees to Portland and then travel on an American railway line into Canada. This would simply not do, and these distasteful facts, combined with the urge to reduce mailing time and speed up the country's business, prodded the St. Lawrence shipping lines to come up with a fast, all-Canadian transatlantic service.

A dozen years before Sincennes started his little firm on the Rivière Richelieu, the Canadians had proven that a steamship could cross the Atlantic. In 1833, the *Royal William*, a Québec steamer, was sold to an English firm. Delivery involved getting the ship across the Atlantic, and the steamship's owners decided to let the ship deliver itself. The *Royal William* accomplished the feat in nineteen days, using every scrap of coal in her hold and twice shutting off the engines to scrape them clean of the sea salt that had lined the boilers, like plaque in a kettle. As the *Royal William* came into sight of the south English shore, the era of the great liners was born.

The British Cunard Line, run by Samuel Cunard, an expatriate Canadian, was actually the first to put a steamer, the *Unicorn*, into Montréal laden with mail from England, in 1839, but for political reasons they dropped the service in 1845. After that, the mail came by rail via the United States for a few years, and then the job of getting it directly down the St. Lawrence on a ship was again put out for tender by Her Young Victorian Majesty in 1853. The British were still anxious to get a Canada–Britain mail service that bypassed the Americans, and so they sweetened the pot and offered a healthy monetary contract.

The banks of the St. Lawrence thoroughly cultivated and covered with houses and villages very like our own. All traces of the wilderness have disappeared; it has been replaced by cultivated fields, bell towers, a population as numerous as in our own countryside.

—Alexis de Tocqueville, *Democracy in America*, 1850

The conditions of the contract were that a ship must leave for England every two weeks and that the crossing must take no more than thirteen days. (Returning ships, going against prevailing currents, were given a day's grace.) For a while a Liverpool firm of shipbuilders who could talk the talk but not steam the steam carried the mail, but the best they could average was twenty days, in underpowered ships. It was Hugh Allan, second son of the famous Scottish sailing-ship magnate Sandy, patriarch of the sailing ships of the Allan Line, who navigated his way through the financial sandbars and made the St. Lawrence a viable turnstile for transatlantic liners.

Hugh Allan was only thirteen when he left a job in his father's counting house in Ayrshire and sailed to Montréal in 1814 on the Allan Line's star brig, the *Favorite*. Hugh studiously climbed the company mast and by 1839, at the age of twenty-eight, was in charge of the Canadian end of the firm, which was then still the thin end. Even so, after New York and New Orleans, Québec was the third-busiest port in North America. In 1854, after blowing some frustrated steam for a season, Allan, backed by investors with deep pockets like the man who owned Dow beer and the governor of the Hudson's Bay Company, applied to take the mail contract away from the Liverpool firm. They intended to operate under the name Montreal Ocean Steamship Company. They won the contract a week before Christmas. The river was of course frozen by then, but when it opened up in April, Hugh intended to have steamships worthy of the job carrying news of Canada to Britain, and vice versa.

To honour the conditions of the contract, Hugh needed the right tool, and in 1854 he had it fashioned in the form of the *Canadian*, an elegant ship that was tailor-made for the St. Lawrence and the adjoining ocean. In the anthropology of shipping, the *Canadian* was the missing link between sailing ships and the great ocean liners. The hull was iron, a quilt of sheet-metal squares joined by rivets that were tossed red-hot from the forge to the riveter and banged into place even as they cooled. Propulsion was accomplished by means of a sixteen-foot-diameter screw at the back, turned by an engine with cylinders as wide as a man's outstretched arms, rather than the outmoded side paddles, which froze up too easily. Big for her era, the *Canadian* was a hundred yards long, triple-masted, with baby masts that could provide some wind power interspersed by two red funnels. A reporter taken for a press junket on the *Canadian* had to reach into his bag for the adjective "refulgent" to describe the fittings. On deck there were two substantial ice houses and a cow house; the passengers could hear that night's dinner calling out as they strolled the deck.

The *Canadian* was the first of the St. Lawrence's divas, a celebrity whose comings and goings were loyally followed like a television soap opera. Three years into service, she left Liverpool in mid-May 1857 headed for Québec. On board were one hundred and seventeen first-class passengers and over twice that many immigrants in steerage, the former kept in genteel apartheid from the latter. Households all along the St. Lawrence awaited the mail and packages in her hold.

North America was in fog when the ship entered the river ten days later, and the *Canadian's* Captain Ballantine went on round-the-clock watch. As though a giant fan were suddenly switched on, visibility was perfect when they drew level with Matane, the first major port on the river's south shore. They glided to a halt off Île St-Barnabé at Rimouski to receive the pilot, Jean-Léon Roy of Saint-Michel-de-Bellechasse, who would shepherd them into Québec. The pilot was a middle-aged man of copious experience. Captain Ballantine, after following regulations and assuring himself that Roy was sober, handed over his ship to Roy as they slowed down by the Bic highlands to receive and unload some mail.

The last day of May provided the passengers with a glorious sunset and a detailed view of the tiny mail boat being loaded and rowed back to shore. Darkness followed the sun's display and the *Canadian*, taking advantage of a high tide, gathered speed. Just after midnight, as they overtook the lighthouse ship *Brillant* guarding the entrance to the Traverse St-Roch, Captain Ballantine stood down and handed over to the first mate, Dutton. Then he headed for his bed. They were in a stretch of the river prone to islands and isolated rocks, but for Pilot Roy this was as easy as tying his shoelaces; the moon was a flood lamp, making everything perfectly clear. Roy decided to navigate by eye, abetted by the rotating light of the Pilier-de-Pierre lighthouse standing on a postage-stamp-sized island in the middle of the south channel.

Then—and there is no word for this in English, but there should be—Officer Dutton got that first, blood-freezing inkling that something was terribly wrong. Landmarks that should have been there were not. The feeling grew so strong that Dutton broke a sea rule and asked the pilot if all was well. Roy seemed to come awake at the question, and right then La Roche-à-Veillon rose out of the water dead ahead, like a bull's horn, and impaled them. The ship shook as though to loose herself, rolled onto one side, then back over to the other. The roll knocked Dutton unconscious.

The same feeling of things gone swiftly wrong hit Captain Ballantine in his cabin as the ship shook, and brought him to the bridge at a run. He ordered an immediate stop to the engines. Ballantine realized his ship was hooked as though in the jaw of an animal that will not let go; when the tide turned and dropped, the *Canadian* would either sink her rear end into the water or roll over onto the rock. The Captain attempted a series of releasing manoeuvres, but luck had deserted him. It was time to abandon the luxury of the *Canadian* and attend to the safety of its passengers. With the help of several nearby ships—the ironically named *Eden* from England, sailing directly behind them, and the aptly named *Providence* , which hustled out from the southern shore and collected the remaining mail and the first-class entourage—everyone got off safely with just a few cuts and bruises.

With the passengers safe, attention turned to the *Canadian*. The innovation of steam power had produced pugnacious little ships that could push and pull—tugs—and the *Queen Victoria*, the newest and strongest of them on the St. Lawrence, chugged out of Québec and put its shoulder to the sinking *Canadian* to try to free it. No luck. Using lateral thinking, a team of miners tried to blast away the rock upon which the ship was fastened, but a storm shook the ship and filleted it on the stubborn rock before they could try. The *Canadian* sank in its own depth of water, the bow poking up. She was declared lost.

For his part, Pilot Roy faced a disciplinary board in mid-July. His claim that the lighthouse at Pilier-de-Pierre had malfunctioned was refuted by Ballantine and Dutton, and the full weight of the *Canadian*'s demise fell on Roy, ending his piloting days. The unwitting implement of destruction, La Roche-à-Veillon, survived all subsequent attempts to blast it level, and as a mark of respect to its obtrusive power, a lighthouse was put on it in 1878.

The sinking of the *Canadian* only three years after her proud launch presaged a plague of disasters of Old Testament proportions for the Allan Line. Over the next ten years the company lost nine luxury ships, all but one of them in Canadian waters, including: the *Indian*, with twenty-nine lives lost; the *Hungarian* a season later, with no survivors and over two hundred dead; in 1861, the *Canadian II* in ice; and the *Anglo Saxon*, lost to that great thief, fog, with over two hundred and forty souls taken. Each of those metal hulls touched bottom with the same final certainty as their wooden predecessors. The St. Lawrence, using a variety of weapons, had quickly learnt to overwhelm this new breed of engine-driven ships and add a cross-section of them to its collection of wrecks.

Nevertheless, the ships continued to be built and launched. The ocean trade made Hugh Allan rich, a transportation millionaire, in the same way that trains were making fortunes for their owners alongside the river. In fact, Allan had money in trains too, as part of the "vertical integration" of his empire. He was also a founder of the Merchant's Bank in Montreal; that bank lent money to his shipbuilding company; the coal, brought to the docks on Allan's trains to burn in his ships, was from mines he owned; and the ships that ran on that coal were insured by a company that Allan directed.

Having his fingers in that many pies gave Allan a stranglehold on the Atlantic trade for a quarter-century, until his death in 1882 in his house in the port of Montréal, and the company continued to prosper even after his demise. Allan's money allowed him to innovate and speed up his crossing times, and on the St. Lawrence the guy with the fastest ships won. The Allan Line built the first all-steel liner, the *Buenos Ayrean*. The *Parisian* had the first rustproof keel. The *Victorian* and the *Virginian* were the first ocean liners propelled by steam turbines. And slowly the ships swelled in size, passing the fifteen-thousand-ton mark, then the twenty. The ocean had become two weeks smaller and would go on shrinking to less than half that by the end of the century. The restless public, ever anxious to be somewhere else, were increasingly prepared to take the risk.

If there had been a gauge on the bridge of transatlantic steamers that registered the Canadian population—a populometer, perhaps—the needle would have shown a surge after 1867. Confederation of several adjoining smaller territories into one vast Canada had streamlined immigration, and the new government set about getting the country settled. Ships were bigger, stronger, faster, and more reliable at getting landed immigrants safely to the St. Lawrence, doorstep of the country. The Canadian population rose past the five-million mark by 1875.

Hand in hand with this bulging, stratified immigration (Britons came in three varieties: first, second and third class) came, fortunately, a leap forward in the prevention of the spread of disease. The Frenchman Louis Pasteur introduced vaccination in 1881, and went on to discover that heat destroys bacteria and that a clean pair of hands is a vital part of a doctor's equipment.

These two developments—class-structured transatlantic steamship travel and the use of disinfection to limit bacterial invasion—had an effect on the ambience and architecture of Grosse-Île. Three "hotels" appeared on the island, one for each class, with fittings and services to match. Residents of the first-class hotel, awaiting release from quarantine, could enjoy a fine view of the river from the veranda over the roof of the washhouse, with its constant flags of river-washed sheets waving in the wind, while in the dormitories of the third-class hotel the poor slept separated only by low partitions.

The man who saw all this building and improved medicine through was a doctor, Frédérick Montizambert. More than a mere doctor, he was a bacteriologist, then a branch of medicine only just becoming influential. Montizambert was ferried to the island to begin his work as Chief Medical Superintendent in 1869, and he stayed for thirty years.

Dr. Montizambert's waking concern was that the confirmed sick and the healthy make absolutely no contact, and his benign apartheid practices, coupled with his attention to inspection and disinfection of both ships and facilities, made it much harder for death to haunt the island. As the science of fighting germs expanded, Montizambert incorporated innovations such as fumigation chambers resembling steam-train boilers into the island's most evocative building, the solid, two-storey wooden embarkation and disinfection hall, which was built in 1892. It is still there, intelligently restored and preserved to allow the imagination to picture its former daily life, a vast piece of medical equipment designed to try and make sure that diseases like smallpox, scarlet fever, tuberculosis, polio and diptheria did not gatecrash Canada.

When immigrants disembarked at Grosse-Île, their luggage was tagged and put in wire cages of the sort that might be used to trap raccoons, which were then conveyed on small flatbed railway cars a hundred yards into the disinfection hall. Once inside, the belongings headed for the fumigation chambers, while their owners filed upstairs to the second floor, into a waiting room filled with pews that had the air of a Quaker meeting hall. As their names were called from the passenger list, each humbled disinfectee went into a cubicle, changed into a smock, then stood for the practised, swivelling eye of a doctor in search of familiar symptoms.

The next stage of the assembly line was the showers, which ran in gangways, as though at a public swimming bath, except that here there were several rows and enough showers for over a hundred people. Tepid water tinged with lye shot out of three C-shaped nozzles, at head, waist and knee height. Downstairs, dressed again in clothes that now reeked of formaldehyde and with luggage retrieved, the immaculate, germ-free immigrants were handed a grey postcard with the word DISINFECTED written diagonally across it. Now, and only now, they were assigned hotels according to their station in life. If they were not required for quarantine, they reboarded the fumigated ship and moved on to the immigration hall at Québec.

It would be intriguing, on a future census, to determine how many Canadians have ancestors who suffered through the disinfection hall and emerged, cleansed of their old lives, clutching that small card.

10

END OF ALL RIVERS

*Most of those who hired themselves out to shotgun
the rapids were from Kahnawake.*

At the other end of the river, in the Thousand Islands, as
Hotel Canada continued to fill, the relentless rate of settlement was supplanting an older way of life. Several thousand
years of nomadic canoeing, of following the migrating eels as
they departed the St. Lawrence, was undergoing a slow death.
Acre by acre, as the value of real estate increased, the territory
of the Native peoples was shrinking. Native settlements on the
islands of the St. Lawrence were falling silent as the song of the
birchbark faded.

On the large and fertile island of Grenadier, near Brockville,
the Iroquois had long had cornfields and permanent longhouses,

from which they launched armadas of war canoes to deal first with the Huron, then the French. Jesuits wrote of the village of Tonionta on Grenadier, but by the time of the American Revolution it was a ghost village. The Iroquois had moved south, replaced at the head of the St. Lawrence by the Mississauga.

In their turn the Mississauga, neophytes at the real estate game, sold off bits of territory in naive deals. The British bought up land wholesale to hand out in free parcels, like party favours, to incoming Loyalists. In 1783, waterfront land around Kingston was purchased—*nabbed* might be a better word—for, as the governor at the time put it, "an inconsiderable sum," and quickly turned over to the faithful, including Molly Brand, a maternal Mohawk elder. On the American side, a rich fur trader named Macomb and a partner bought almost all the islands lying in New York State in 1792 for less than $200,000. At the beginning of the 1800s, the first two Loyalist families moved onto Grenadier; their names were Root and Fish. Eight hundred and eighty-one St. Lawrence islands were bought from the Mississauga in one fell swoop on the nineteenth of June, 1856, in "surrender for sale for the benefit of the tribe," as the paper pertaining to the deal put it. The signatures at the bottom of the bill of sale were John Sunday, John Simpson, Jacob Sunday, John Pigeon, Joseph Skunk, Thomas Frasure and James Indian, all Mississaugas, most of them no longer living on the river.

As their territory shrank, job prospects for young Indians in the fur trade were likewise diminishing. For two hundred years the Indians had been there in the great canoes on the Great Trail. They had signed on with the mighty North West Company, founded in 1776 by immigrant Scots and headquartered in Montréal. The Nor' West, as it was called, employed the canoeing skills of the men who mapped Canada and outlined an empire—men such as Alexander Mackenzie and Simon

Fraser, both of whom found water routes through the Rockies, and David Thompson. These explorers had picked up their skills from Native guides, and could rebuild a canoe in a day or make a serviceable, smaller one out of a rock-ravaged wreck.

For a time, helped by these surveyors/land mercenaries, the top-rate Indians who went with them and the interior Indians who trapped for them, the Nor' West held its own against the rival Hudson's Bay Company. However, with an 1821 act of parliament the Nor' West was folded into the Hudson's Bay banner. In that joining a bell tolled for the working canoe. The new Hudson's Bay governors favoured the York boat—a plank-sided craft that one rowed or sailed, not paddled—over the canoe. The canoe yards at Trois-Rivières and the voyageurs—Native or French Canadian (or both)—were effectively downsized, and the canoe as a symbol, which had featured in the Nor' West coat of arms, did not carry over into the Hudson's Bay crest.

There was one remaining place, a niche market, where Native voyageurs could find work. For the powerful men in charge of the St. Lawrence, the lords of the river, having Indians ferry them about in deluxe birchbark canoes was a status symbol, the chauffeured stretch limo service of its day. The gaudiest display of Native chauffeurs was mounted by the Scotsman George Simpson, a man with indestructible ants in his pants and an equally restless sexual itch. Simpson sailed in from London in 1820 and became governor of the Hudson's Bay Company six years later. He made his headquarters on the St. Lawrence at Lachine and lived on Montréal's Île Dorval, where he died in 1860, still in charge. It was Simpson who ordered the switch in rowing stock from the canoe to the York boat, yet he kept a personal fleet of express canoes. One of Simpson's water-cadillacs tailed out at forty-two feet, thought to be the biggest ever built. Manning these beauties was an élite force of Iroquois. When Simpson came into town, there were bagpipes playing, cannons firing and a matching set of Indians trimming their paddles as the canoe glided alongside the wharf. It was all showbiz, in an era when importance and wealth were measured in ostentation.

The swan song of the great canoes came the same year as Simpson's death, long after most of them had been broken up. Several were hauled out of mothballs one more time when the Prince of Wales, not yet twenty, on his honeymoon and already a man-in-permanent-waiting for his turn to become king, made a royal visit to Lachine in August 1860. The Prince arrived and left on the *Great Eastern*, Isambard Brunel's great wonder, the largest vessel afloat. "Her five thin funnels belching clouds of black smoke, her paddles and propeller churning up the water, and her great white sails bellied out by the wind," is how a contemporary spectator described her going past Baie St-Paul.

After doing the usual royal thing and opening a bridge—the spectacular and world-famous Victoria, a covered railway bridge with breathing holes in the roof where smoke would pop out as the train passed through—the Prince was installed on a barge and treated to a display of synchronized canoeing. The team consisted of, as the *Gazette* reported it, "one hundred Iroquois . . . costumed *en sauvage*, gay with feathers, scarlet cloth and paint." Later that day the Prince did some paddling of his own and, when he left, was presented with a genuine voyageur canoe. It went back to the Prince's rumpus room in the palace, and he would occasionally take it out for a spin. One of the other birchbark canoes from that day, which became known as the Quebec canoe, ended up, naturally, in the United States, in the boathouse of the Buffalo Canoe Club. It perished there in a fire on Christmas Eve, 1990.

In one area of expertise the Indians remained acknowledged

masters: getting boats through the Lachine Rapids. This was a talent that had remained exclusive to the Native peoples for two hundred and fifty years after Champlain wrote about it. For a time it was actually a condition of insurance that the pilot of a boat going through the dangerous waters be an Indian. Most of those who hired themselves out to shotgun the rapids were from Kahnawake, a Mohawk reserve on the south shore next to the town of La Prairie. The Mohawks' status as pilots through the Lachine and the Long Sault Rapids west of Montréal became legendary, and they continued in that role into the twentieth century, in a father-son chain, taking ships through and then catching a train with the nickname "the Moccasin" back home.

The most famous Native navigator was Big John. His last name was in fact Rice, and he learnt as a child how to avoid the cross-currents that could kidnap a boat and ditch it on an unseen boulder, how to sidestep the eddies that were like leghold traps, and how to avoid unseen entities that could gut a hull. When a canoe or steamship stood poised to go through the Lachine obstacle course, Big John would appear and, with the help of the four men it took to manipulate the rudder, take both ship and squealing passengers down the path of least resistance.

Big John's talent passed into white hands in 1858 when a young man named Édouard Ouellette spent the winter with him. Ouellette had left the family farm, where there were eight brothers ahead of him in line, and headed to Montréal to find work. When Big John, now an old man, offered Édouard a job as one of the four rudder-wrestlers, Édouard took it. Big John, sensing a successor, showed him the way.

In 1860, the Compagnie de Richelieu added an iron-hulled steamer, the *Algerian*, to their roster, designed to go along the rapids without being gored by rocks. The company, at Big

John's request, let Édouard take the *Algerian* on her maiden voyage down the relatively tepid nine miles of the Long Sault Rapids, intending to pick up Big John at the head of the Lachine. When the ship got there, however, Big John could not be found. With their hands over their eyes, the officials let Édouard nose in to the whitewater and pick up speed. In a matter of minutes they were at the other end, intact. Édouard Ouellette became a full-fledged pilot and Big John retired.

For the few Native canoeists who hung on to their trade and fishing routes in the Thousand Islands, the territory they called Garden Place of the Great Spirit gradually clogged up with ships and boats that got bigger and noisier, and canoes were increasingly forced to work the margins. Native craftsmen continued to travel among the islands selling beadwork and handmade baskets, manoeuvring their homemade, wood-strip canoes among the mahogany launches until one day, when no one was looking, they were gone.

11

Moon River

*Skiffs moved about the maze of islands like water bugs,
scarcely breaking the surface.*

It would be easy nowadays to spend a summer's day burning
gas, trailing through the Thousand Islands in something loud
and made of fibreglass, and never see a St. Lawrence skiff. A
century ago this would have been inconceivable. Then, skiffs
moved about the maze of islands like water bugs, scarcely
breaking the surface. Some pilots, with a single sail up, might
be seen guiding their oak-keeled crafts along an unseen gust.
Other skiffs might be carrying couples, he moustached, be-
hatted, in a worsted suit, rowing along with great ease and
speed, using seven-and-a-half-foot oars, she seated at the
front on a wicker-bottomed seat, dressed as though for a

church supper, staring idly at the local real estate.

The origins of the St. Lawrence skiff lie embedded in its name. "Skiff"—some locals still say "skift"—is a corruption of a word that pops up in several European languages, including French (*esquif*) and German (*schiff*) and it usually means "a light rowboat." Most likely the Europeans ferried the word across the Atlantic. When the second-generation French, English and German immigrants moved inland and settled in the upper St. Lawrence, they kept the name but adapted the boats of their fathers to suit the kaleidoscope of currents, sudden storms and capricious winds of the Thousand Islands.

By 1840, the basic St. Lawrence skiff design was settled. The small, light craft of elegant proportions gave a long, firm glide for every pull on the oars. It carried farm produce between mainland and island, and when paying passengers arrived from inland New York State, looking for a guide to the premier fishing holes, there was an ideal boat already available. A tourism advertisement placed in the Kingston *British Whig* newspaper in July 1848 announces just such a service: "Skiffs for Hire. Fishing parties and other persons wishing for good safe skiffs can be supplied at all hours."

Most of the established St. Lawrence skiff builders, men like Louis Lachapelle of Brockville, active in the 1860s, had names that were French in origin, as though it were particularly strong in Gallic genes. (And indeed, France has more miles of river than any other European country.) The skiffwrights built boatyards on both sides of the river, with a slender majority on the American shore between Lake Ontario and Alexandria Bay, starting at Cape Vincent, where Leon Peo conducted his business.

Leon Peo, like his rival skiffmakers, published a yearly catalogue. In one edition there is corroboration of the origins of the skiff, plus evidence of how highly craftsmen esteemed their product. Peo's catalogue states:

> This unique embodiment of the boat builder's genius is neither a discovery nor an invention to which any one man, or company of men, can lay claim, but it is in fact an evolution of the genius of construction during all the years since its prototype, the batteau of the French "Voyageur" was first launched upon the waters of the St. Lawrence River.

Ending with a flourish, Peo had his superlative-spewing copywriter declare:

> Of the best procurable material, fashioned by the best mechanical skill into a beauty of model, and a finish unsurpassed, the upper St. Lawrence River Skiff, as constructed by Leon Peo & Co., of St. Vincent, N.Y., is simply an Oarsman's Ideal.

The reference in Leon's flyer to a "company of men" laying claim to having invented the skiff was in fact a cocked snoot at his main rival, Xavier Colon of Clayton, another riverside town, halfway between Cape Vincent and Alexandria Bay. Colon is sometimes hailed as the progenitor of the St. Lawrence skiff, and he did nothing to dissuade people from this view, but it isn't really so.

The St. Lawrence skiff as made by Colon, Lachappelle, Peo and others became the symbol of an era in the Thousand Islands, one that began at the end of the American Civil War. It was an era marked by "big"—big money, big hotels, big houses, big fish and big stories. It's one of those eras referred to as Golden, a label more sentimental than factual. But it was an era that shone with the gleam of fish scales and silver dollars.

The lure that enticed big money to the top of New York State was fish, the chance for wealthy men to tell arms-outstretched fishing tales back in the club rooms of the big city. Angling is the most-practised sport in the world, not least because, like golf, it takes place in first-class, unpopulated scenery, and it is also sometimes defined as a sport that gives men something to think about while they are talking. The St. Lawrence Native peoples had the fish supplies to themselves for a considerable while, then the dirt farmers who tilled the islands took their share in relative privacy, but the word eventually got out. It told of princely bass, large and smallmouth, pan perch that were a reason to get up in the morning, abundant ten-pound northern pike that could be taken winter or summer, and portly walleye pike (who later suffered when the Seaway took great chunks of their habitat). Most of all, tales were told of the mighty muskie, the middleweight boxer of the fish world, the hooking and landing of which is an athletic act in itself.

They are a puzzle to the oldest sailor on the lake, and we don't pretend to know even their names. For that matter, most of them have no more names than a child that dies before it is christened.

—description of the Thousand Islands in the 1740s from James Fenimore Cooper, *Pathfinder*, 1840

It was these monster fish that became the golden fleece for sportsmen. The upper class generally did not like to return from a nature outing without a large, dead animal, and all ready and waiting when they got to the St. Lawrence was a guide with a perfect boat to row them around all day. Most likely the guide was a farmer making some money on the side, who could steer them to the secret spot, over by Forty Acre Shoal, where Moby the muskie was hiding. Some of the summer people grew to know the fish and the river well enough to dispense with guides. The records show that in 1876, Augusta Mann, a redoubtable angler who rowed herself about, hauled one hundred and seventy muskie into her sailing skiff.

Anglers need a bar in which to tell stories, and Crossman's Hotel in Alexandria Bay fitted the bill. Its smoky air supported a nightly quota of lies, and the hotel grew as the record muskie grew with it. Crossman's was already well known by the time George Pullman, the millionaire who put his name to a first-class style of railway carriage, bought an island just off Alexandria in the middle of the Civil War. When Pullman invited Ulysses S. Grant, then president, up to his "cottage" for some fishing in a St. Lawrence skiff in 1872, it put the islands, and their muskie, on the map.

Soon, big summer hotels sprouted up to cater to the medium-rich, with wraparound porches on each floor and towers in the middle, at the ends and in between. In front were landscaped lawns for promenading; behind, water for boating.

Squiring these weekend warriors and holidaymakers around the Thousand Islands became a full-time job. With their signature luxuriant moustaches and hats like small hills parked on their experienced heads, the fishing guides became regional legends; stories about them swirled with the cigar smoke back in Albany and New York. As always when one class hires the expertise of another, the guides took amusement at the expense of their clients. When asked by nervous, fog-enclosed passengers how far it was to the nearest land, the inscrutable guide would give the distance straight down to the riverbed. The picnic luncheons provided by the guides' wives were also matters of fame. George Lalonde's wife, Sophie, provided her own delicious pink dressing for her husband's customers to enjoy on their salads. When Mae Irwin, a famous actress and gourmand of the time, took a trip with George in the early 1900s, she got the recipe from Sophie, named it and passed it on to the chef of a New York hotel. From there, the Thousand Islands dressing spread far and wide.

When the railway tracks reached Clayton and the neighbouring holiday towns in the late nineteenth century, the cycle of summer invasion and winter evacuation that still goes on in the Thousand Islands began, although the railway is now gone. In the Pullman carriages at the front of the train were the millionaires. They hired two kinds of guide, one to hunt for fish, the other for real estate. The islands became pieces of showy jewellery as the millionaires tried to out-castle each other. Once installed, the lords of the islands would take their rest or indulge in the fashionable turn-of-the-century pastime of playing catch with medicine balls.

The Hope diamond of the islands was Boldt Castle on Heart Island, built by Prussian immigrant George Boldt. Boldt reached America in 1864, beginning as a dishwasher and ending up owning the Waldorf-Astoria, the legendary hotel where Thousand Islands dressing was first put on the menu. In 1902, Boldt ordered a castle built on the island as an edificial love token to his wife, Louise. He had the island remodelled in the shape of a heart—a rich man's version of a Niagara Falls honeymoon bed. When Louise died overnight of a heart attack in 1904, the castle still in mid-construction, Boldt abandoned the building there and then. He never set foot in it again, although he did come back to the islands, of which he owned several. Boldt's castoff castle sat unused until 1918, when the man who had made millions out of Life Savers candies bought it.

While the skiffs scurried about the islands, the natural virtues of canoeing allowed it to adjust to the end of the fur trade and take on a recreational role. The packs of furs on the canoe floor were replaced with packed lunches. The mid-1800s are full of stories of wealthy Europeans, men like the Earl of Dunraven, an Anglo-Irish politician, who sampled canoeing in Canada in the late nineteenth century and declared it "the poetry of progression," being guided hither and thither on Canadian rivers, all the while hauling wildlife from the water or knocking it out of the sky.

As the islands filled with a chorus of strikes and shots, the canoe itself was shedding its skin and taking on new forms. The birchbark canoe was a traditional craft, on the whole better made by people raised to it. The newcomers did not abandon the concept—they knew a perfect thing when they saw it—but applied their temperate-zone, technological ingenuity to getting around birch. Canvas, tin, the wonder metal aluminum, strips of cedar, even layers of manila paper were all pressed into service. The silhouette of canoe and canoeist was redrawn as the double-bladed paddle, various decks and sails, even for a brief moment a steam canoe, appeared on the waters.

The New York Canoe Club was born in a room full of gents on a Saturday night in 1871, and six years later four of its members paddled from Lake Champlain down to the St. Lawrence, two of them in Canadian-style, strip-cedar canoes, the other pair in double-masted canoes with a deck. Two of the four, Messrs. Habberton and Norton, wrote up the trip in a book, *Canoeing in Kanuckia* (a smart-aleck reference to

Canada). The New York club duly spawned, in 1880, the American Canoe Association, and fairly soon they were holding regattas, wives and girlfriends lolling in gazebos while the men competed on the water. By 1884 the association had hundreds of members, and they were looking for new, spiffy places to hold their rallies.

One section of the St. Lawrence offered up all the beauty any canoeist, rich or poor, competitive or capricious, could need: the Thousand Islands. The border between the two canoeing nations was etched on the water, the setting magnificent. The American Canoe Association's 1884 and 1885 meets were held on Grindstone Island, at a place they sensibly dubbed Canoe Point. At the 1889 canoefest, held on Stave Island on the Canadian side, war canoes were raced for the first time, the Canadians winning. This was indeed "re-creation," as the canoes were exaggerated versions of the old fur-transport canoes made at Trois-Rivières. The war races, the wildest of the classifications, became the highlight of the meets, with novices sweating hard alongside veterans.

War canoe clubs broke out all along the river in the 1890s; there was one in Montreal and three in Brockville. At an informal meeting between two of those clubs in 1900, the Canadian Canoe Association took shape. Reflecting the difference in mentality between the two nations, the Canadians eschewed the American penchant for a variety of styles and concerned themselves with chaste racing in standard, open canoes. It took both associations until after the Second World War to allow women to race.

In 1903, with membership up past fifteen hundred, the American Canoe Association, looking for a permanent venue, bought an island on the Canadian side near Gananoque and renamed it Sugar Island. They have held their meetings there ever since. The campsites on the island have hosted generations of bonfires, accompanied by the smoky, loose harmonies of the songs that open-air flames seem to induce.

12

BIG RIVER

The whole business actually took three decades, and in the process the river gained both a new canal and a new style of boat.

When the *White Wings*, a privately built barquentine, slipped down the launchway in 1893, the age of wooden shipbuilding at Québec came to an end. The peak year, the records reveal, was 1853, when seventy ships left the "ways," as the shipyards were known. The city's trade in wood and sail had lasted two and a quarter centuries, and from the hands of her artisans sixteen hundred ships, the vast majority of them square-riggers, had gone out into the world. Men with certain skills retired or looked for work elsewhere, and the smell of wood being worked into long, fine curves dropped to a faint tang.

The era of the sailing ships was closing, although the existing stock sailed on, still useful, senior employees in a business that had refitted itself; wood had become metal, sail had become paddlewheel, then propeller. Along the St. Lawrence, one by one, the other shipyards saw a similar launch of the last wooden hull, such as the one at Garden Island at the river's western end, just off Wolfe Island, where the Calvin family held sway. The great timber rafts, the largest man-made structures of the nineteenth century, drifted on, and the smaller wooden boats, like the shallow *chaloupes* of the Île aux Coudres that wrestled the rafts and fished the waters, contin-ued to be made. Masts still broke over the horizon as home-ward-bound ships came into view, and women watched as the sails grew larger and the moment of recognition, and of relief, came into their faces.

In 1877 our first post office was opened here. From four winter mails we have reached ten now, and from a monthly summer service have grown to a ten-day one. The little yawl, double-ender, or fishing boat, which ran between Rimouski and the North Shore in the old days, has given place to two modern steamers.

—Napoléon Comeau, *Life and Sport on the Lower St. Lawrence and Gulf*, 1908

As the *White Wings* sailed away from Québec, the master at the port, forty-six-year-old Joseph-Elzéar Bernier, understood her significance better than any man there; she was the full stop after an age of construction in which his family had been intimately involved. There is many a family along the St. Lawrence that put several generations on the high seas, and the Berniers were as generous as any.

The Bernier family produced an honour list of captains, shipmasters, shipbuilders and pilots for whom the St. Lawrence was the threshold of their working lives, beginning with the first Bernier who sailed into Québec, in 1663. Flip through the history of any family that put its men on the St. Lawrence and there is an early grave somewhere, a shortened arm or leg, an eye lost or a finger, and the Berniers paid for the right to work the river with their share of flesh.

Jean-Baptiste Bernier, grandfather of dock master Joseph-Elzéar, was shipwrecked on Anticosti Island in 1828–29, in a snowstorm that took down several other ships in the same area. Jean-Baptiste and his crew of eight lived off one half-wild horse they killed, as well as some game and fish. They were there the entire winter, until a sealing schooner finally picked them up in May and dropped them at Gaspé. After a month's trek along the south shore, they made it back home. Jean-Baptiste traded captaining a ship for manning a lighthouse after that, but he went back to sea in 1833, ferrying immigrants from Grosse-Île to Québec. Then, his sea blood aroused again, he was back on the oceans. He retired, at the age of eighty-two, two years before his death.

Jean-Baptiste saw all his sons follow him up the gangway. The eldest became a pilot for the Allan Line, a position he held for fifty-one years. The next, Eucher, likewise a pilot, drowned in the wreck of the schooner *Sutherland*. Two of the younger boys, Joseph and John, also served as pilots. Joseph, after forty years avoiding the hazards of the river, was drowned in a canoe accident in unruly ice off Cap Tourmente, now a sanctuary for ducks and long-legged waders. Yet another son, Thomas, lost an arm. But the story of shipwreck that truly makes the blood run cold concerned one of Jean-Baptiste's nephews, Bernard, a captain. An early winter storm, hungry for ships, pushed Bernard's vessel onto a wall of ice on the treacherous north shore. The ship jammed fast into the ice like a pick, and as each monster wave crashed over it, another man was swept away. Bernard, when he knew the ship could not break free but only break up,

lashed himself to a mast, a knife in one hand. As he was repeatedly submerged and then unveiled into the freezing air, his ship
disintegrated around him.

The moment came when he had to take to the water. Cutting himself free, Bernard sprinted for the pilothouse, itself on
the verge of breaking off. He clung to the roof as the small
square of wood rushed against the ice wall between him and
the shore. The wall was high—so high that he could not jump
from the pilothouse onto the ice beyond and the next stage of
safety. Death began to enfold him. Then a giant wave roared in
and banged the pilothouse hard against the barrier. He was cat-
apulted into the air, like a stone flung over a castle wall, and
onto the ice, breaking both his legs. He crawled forward in
slow motion, then passed out.

When he awoke, he was in a fisherman's hut, on a table. He
was alive, but even his rescuers could tell that his frostbitten,
mangled legs needed amputating below the knee. This they
did, and several days later they managed to get Bernard to a
doctor, who saw that he would have to go to Québec. Once
there, the botched first amputation was extended above his
knees. Bernard worked out the rest of his life as a St. Lawrence
telegraph operator, and died in his seventies.

Although it tried several times in the seventy years he spent
on it, the sea also failed to claim Joseph-Elzéar Bernier. He was
born on New Year's Day, 1852, at L'Islet-sur-Mer, on the south
shore just east of Québec, where most of the Berniers settled.
Late in life he was persuaded to write and publish his rolling
memoirs, and he proved to be a fine, articulate writer. The stories he penned of his family's maritime doings in *Master
Mariner and Arctic Explorer: A Narrative of Sixty Years at Sea
from the Logs and Yarns of Captain J. E. Bernier* read like a boy's
own adventure novel.

Joseph-Elzéar Bernier went to sea at the age of two years and two months, sailed to the West Indies at age three, and helped his father build a hundred-ton ship when he was nine. At the age of seventeen he became a ship's master. In his long career as a captain he rescued many another ship that had run aground; deliberately ran one of his own commands onto a shoal to save his crew; prolonged the life of a number of geriatric ships with his skill; laid out more than his fair share of drunken cooks (a chore that figures in many a captain's log); and had a long association with Québec, where he built several ships of his own, supervised a shipyard and eventually became the dock master. Occasionally, Bernier forsook the sea and tried to make a go of it on a calmer surface. He started up an ice company in Montréal, growing the stuff in a converted dry dock and selling it in handy chunks, and even ran the Québec jail for three years in the late 1890s, but he was happier looking up a mast than the side of a building, and back he went over water, as his forebears had done. The Berniers form a backbone to the river in its time under sail, just as royal dynasties do on land, a bloodline down the centre of a region's history.

As one era slowly dissolved into history, another was steaming in. The age of the canallers commenced as the century turned. The long-running project to renovate the canal system was nearing completion, and the river was poised to take off like a runner in the blocks.

Despite the large dollops of money and sweat poured into the canals in the mid-nineteenth century, they had not been the roaring success their builders had hoped for. The Canadian government, which had shouldered much of the financing for the canal expansion, had been chasing its own tail. To make more money in tolls from the canals, they had to move more goods; for the shippers to move more goods, they had to make bigger, heavier ships, which sat lower in the water; that in turn meant making bigger canals, which meant spending more money—and the financial Ferris wheel made another turn. An 1870 commission looked deep into the problem and recommended canals that were twelve feet deep, which is a fine depth for a grave but not quite enough for the new era of marine architecture that had already produced ships in the Great Lakes that drew more than that. The shippers and canalside industrialists had to nudge the bureaucrats to add two more feet, which, to their great frustration, took five years of steady pressure. Eventually they got it, and fourteen feet became the standard.

Making the canals deeper was easier said than done, because they were already in use and couldn't simply take a break while they were reconfigured. In most cases a deeper, parallel set of locks was built alongside the old one, and then the old one was brought up to speed when traffic shifted into the newer lane. The whole business actually took three decades, and in the process the river gained both a new canal and a new style of boat.

The new kid on the block was the Soulanges, on the north shore between Grande Île and Montréal. An old argument about whether the canal should be on the south or north shore had resurfaced, and this time common sense triumphed over patronage. The Soulanges was a state-of-the-art canal, made more of concrete than of stone, and by now history had ushered in the trick of generating electricity from moving water. The Canadian government started building an alternating-current power plant at Niagara Falls, one of the first in the world, in 1891, and it was on-line by the mid-1890s. The Niagara experiment was the model for the plant on the Soulanges as the twentieth century began, a grand building that looked like a French château. The canal locks were duly lit with electric lights, which meant that they could raise and lower ships twenty-four hours a day, doubling their workload with the flick of a switch. The turbines could also invest winches with enough donkey power to haul two-thousand-ton steam barges through the lock, a far cry from the days when passengers hopped into waist-deep rapids to shoulder a towing rope and drag a York boat foot by foot towards Prescott.

By 1901, the beginning of the century that Prime Minister Sir Wilfrid Laurier had promised would be Canada's, all the canals between Prescott and Montréal were of a size to handle the new ships designed for the new canal system, the canallers. These boats were like pedigree dogs bred to a special purpose, all hull and hold with a minimum of superstructure. Homes along the river each had a spyglass on the windowsill, ready to read off the Olympian- or Indian-sounding names on the gliding sterns of the ships: *Juno, Acadian, Doric, Kipawa, Ponoka, Stadacona, Magog,* and others with names that told of Canada's European links, like *Chapleau, Waterloo, Burlington* and *Oxford.*

Never had so much freight been handled on the river by so few seamen. The canallers did a quick-slow, quick-quick-slow dance up and down the river, negotiating its new slalom of locks with only inches to spare. The system was now one vast, coordinated conveyor belt of train and tanker. Night and day, trains arrived at the Soulanges Canal from Depot Harbour on Lake Huron, obese with grain that had sailed across the Great Lakes. The grain was stuffed into a plain, enormous elevator with the size and air of a Mayan temple, then downloaded into canallers destined for Montréal. There it was transferred into oceanic tankers, the so-called salties, and carried out into the latitudes. The St. Lawrence was a hard-working, twentieth-century river now, carrying the weight of the world on its back.

13

RIVER OF DREAMS

*As the boat's prow neared the tumbling hayricks of water,
passengers would gather outdoors and anticipate the rush.*

In the first decade of the twentieth century, Canada, with a
population of around six million, was at the end of a very busy
waterslide. The slide began in Europe's ports and ended in the
St. Lawrence, and it spilled more than a million new pairs of
hands onto the landscape between 1900 and 1914, a delta of
working humanity fanning out ever westward. It was the greatest influx Canada has ever witnessed. In light of this surge of
immigration, the newspapers could not help but make an omen
of the nine-ton whale that swam into Montréal harbour in
November 1901. The whale became a spectacle and several
people used it for rifle practice. The tormented creature was

eventually landed, stuffed (which took a sweating taxidermist an entire month) and put on exhibit.

Montréal harbour was now continually dredged to keep it hospitable for ocean liners, and there was even talk of keeping it open all year round, thus bringing money into the port every week. The city's *La Presse* newspaper, using a hired combination steamer/sailboat, organized a showcase mission upriver in March to demonstrate that winter access was possible. Things were going fine until the ship was almost past Île d'Orléans, when it struck ice and bent the propeller. The sails were hoisted and the ship came in the old-fashioned way. The case had been half proven.

A ship under sail was becoming a rare sight on the river. Schooners were demasted and used as barges, suffering the ignominy of being towed about as though invalid. And as the sailing ships grew obsolete, the motor car was arriving. A real estate agent had taken Montréal's first horseless carriage, a Crestmobile from Boston, around the town just before the turn of the century, and the grand Victoria Bridge was widened to accommodate four-wheeled traffic a year later.

The honk of that car's horn on the streets of Montréal was counterpointed by the arrival of two ocean freighters that were also signs of the way the century was heading. The *Fremona* and the *Jacona* came into port in the 1901 season bearing fresh fruit from the Mediterranean, a feat made possible by a new invention called refrigeration. Now, food from anywhere could go anyplace, and the ports along the St. Lawrence experienced a growth spurt as a whole new line of produce began to reach city markets.

Canada's booming population signalled a shakeup in the business of moving people around the country's eastern seas and rivers. Big frogs from nearby ponds moved in to try their luck, and the big fish commenced eating up the little ones.

Canadian Pacific, already established in the west coast immigration business, leapfrogged across to the eastern waters. In the summer of 1906, CP brought on line a duo of fourteen-thousand-ton liners and set them running between Liverpool and the St. Lawrence. They bore a title that would become a fixture on the river: they were *Empresses*. In honour of the countries currently supplying Canada with the most immigrants, the sister ships were called *Empress of Britain* and *Empress of Ireland*. As a bit of marketing fangdoodle, the company announced that only ships offering the very best first-class suites would be worthy of the name *Empress*.

The CP ships took to the St. Lawrence just as the ocean liner business was moving up a gear. The Germans had built the first superliner, the *Kaiser Wilhelm der Grosse*, and slipped her into the water in 1897. There was a floating pool at the beginning of the 1900s of rich people being courted by the liner companies. Their way of life deliberately mimicked royalty, and so the ships they travelled on became palaces. The *Empresses* were Canada's entry in these "starboard wars," and they were destined to be a resounding success. Eventually.

On Thursday, May 28, 1914, just before four-thirty in the afternoon, the five-hundred-and-fifty-foot *Empress of Ireland* sailed out of Québec with a Captain Kendall on the bridge. Kendall had earned some cachet the previous year, on a different ship, as the man who discovered the escaping English murderer Dr. Crippen, travelling in disguise with a young woman he had abducted and forced to pose as his wife. Kendall had apprehended Crippen and had him taken off at Québec. Among the Captain's passengers this time was a large delegation from the Canadian Salvation Army, en route to a conference in Britain. There was a smattering of British high society in the lists as well, including Lord and Lady Astor. As the ship edged away from the harbour, the *Empress*'s tabby cat, of its own accord, ran down the gangway and remained on the dockside, mewing farewell.

Among the crew was a young doctor making just his second voyage on the liner. Dr. James Grant was originally from Wellington, Vancouver Island. He had headed east to take up medicine and graduated from McGill in 1913. While interning at Montreal General, his already unsteady health worsened. Sea air was recommended, and Grant went to work for Canadian Pacific as a ship's surgeon. The good health of one thousand and fifty-seven passengers and four hundred and twenty crew was in his charge.

By two in the morning the *Empress* had dropped the St. Lawrence River pilot at Pointe au Père and was four miles from shore, heading for the Gulf. Grant was fast asleep in his quarters on the right-hand side of Upper Deck, among the second-class cabins. At nine minutes past two he awoke on the floor of his cabin, tossed there by some force he didn't understand. There were no lights, and he could hear screams. When he located the door and opened it, he found he was looking *up* the passageway. It was slowly rising, like a drawbridge.

On hands and knees, fingernails clawing at the carpet, Grant ascended the passageway and got his head into an open porthole, through which he could see stars. A passenger standing on the level side of the ship reached in and de-corked him. Grant found himself standing on the ship's flank with hundreds of other passengers and crew, none of them panicking, all just numbly trying to fathom what had happened. Almost immediately, the ship slipped away beneath them, and Grant was forced to stumble into the deep, near-freezing water. The *Empress* went down in one hundred and fifty feet of water fourteen minutes after she was hit amidships. She sank in less time than it takes a quarter to run out in a Montréal parking meter.

As Grant treaded water, the fog that had enveloped the ship dispersed. Ahead, Grant saw the nearby lights of another vessel. Behind him, the rigging and funnels of the mortally wounded *Ireland* were crashing onto people already in the water or in lifeboats. Grant began to swim towards the lights and was soon picked up by a lifeboat crowded with shocked and shivering people. The boat returned to its mother ship and unloaded the rescued.

Grant, who was still in his nightclothes, now borrowed an outsized pair of trousers, used a piece of string for a belt, and got to the business of healing. The boat Grant was on was the seventeen-thousand-ton Norwegian collier *Storstad*, the very ship that, in the dense fog, had cut like a cold chisel into the side of the *Empress of Ireland* between her two funnels, directly below Grant's cabin. Had Grant punched a hole in the floor of his cabin when the accident occurred, he would have been looking at the deck of the coal ship. The *Storstad* had been going the opposite direction to the *Empress*, with six thousand tons of Sydney coal belonging to the Dominion Coal Company.

Throughout the night, until all the survivors were transferred to shore, Grant battled shock and broken limbs. He organized relays of artificial respirators, and when necessary laid out the dead with dignity.

With the dawn came the horrible outline of dozens of bodies stacked on the wharf at Rimouski. Two-thirds of the passengers on board the *Empress* died with her, including a hundred and thirty-four of the one hundred and thirty-eight children, and all but forty-one of the over three hundred women. The final death toll was one thousand and twelve. Grant was written up in the newspapers as a hero, and a few weeks later he was given a silver medal and a duplicate medical diploma to replace the one from McGill that had gone down with the ship.

A stoker called Taylor also survived the sinking of the *Empress of Ireland*. Two years previously, Taylor had escaped death on the *Titanic*. (A year after the *Ireland* disaster, Taylor shipped out on the *Lusitania*, which was torpedoed off the Irish coast. After that, Taylor retired, with six lives still intact.) As for Dr. Grant, he returned to Vancouver Island after his solitary disaster and continued to work for CPR—on land—as chief medical officer until 1938. He raised a family of four and died of an ulcer at the age of fifty-nine. At the time of his death he was living on Cold Harbour Road.

The subsequent inquiry into the tragedy discovered, as inquiries are meant to, that there were two sides to the story. The *Empress*'s rudder, it emerged, had recently been repaired. Also, thirty miles upriver on the same night, there had been a near-accident between the *Empress* and another Norwegian freighter. Furthermore, Kendall had made some sort of manoeuvre as he entered the fog, and signalled it with his horn to the *Storstad*, whose lights and hence orientation he swore he was aware of. The captain of the *Storstad*, Thomas Andersen, admitted he had not been on the bridge when she struck the *Empress*. After the *Storstad* had cut into the bigger ship, her captain had tried to keep his ship within the *Empress*, knowing that withdrawal would open the wound and allow the sea to rush in, but she had slipped out as the big ship sailed on. In the end, the board of inquiry, which was entirely British, had to set the word of the Norwegian captain of the *Storstad* against that of Captain Kendall. Official blame was accorded to the Norwegian corner. Whatever the facts, which died with the captains, the sinking of the *Empress of Ireland* was, and still is, the worst maritime tragedy to occur in

Canadian waters. The river had claimed the tithe it regularly extracts for being used as a highway.

A year after Canadian Pacific's greatest disaster, the company was back in the news for a different reason. It announced that, six years previously, in 1909, it had acquired the Allan Line and, for undisclosed reasons, kept it a secret. With this bold move CP became a player in eastern Canada, just as the other Atlantic rim countries—Germany, France, Britain and the United States—had all entered the competition for the superliner trade.

As often happens in big business, in the wake of Canadian Pacific's moving and shaking there were similar amoeba-like movements from others. The Compagnie du Richelieu in particular, still headquartered in Montréal and still run by French Canadians, became a target. A game of musical boardrooms ensued, involving the likes of the Montréal monarch of mergers, Louis-Joseph Forget, a utilities millionaire. The company changed hands and picked up the English name of Richelieu and Ontario. In 1911, the Niagara Navigation Company was folded into the R & O. In its turn, a year later, the R & O was swallowed up by a Canadian go-getter named Grant Morden, a man with little knowledge of shipping but possessed of a superior ambition. Using British money from the deep pockets of Lord Furness, Morden was able to oust the Forgets. (Morden was himself later nudged out, and died bankrupt and blind.) The new company was dubbed the Canada Steamship Lines, and so the fleet that had started with a barge and a tug steamer on the Richelieu had now grown into a mixed herd of cargo and passenger ships.

Floated end to end in parade, the passenger steamships working the St. Lawrence would have made a pleasing sight; they had an elegance of workmanship and materials that is still possible but no longer viable. In the early twentieth century, steamships became less like trains on water and more like floating hotels. As the population around the Great Lakes and along the St. Lawrence developed a sizable middle class, a cohort of passengers appeared for whom simply being out on the water, on a ship whose fittings reflected their opinion of themselves, was the whole point. They were tourists, taking a break from their lives. They strolled the decks and chatted idly in the lounges, or took to the dance floors, perhaps to the tune of *Sunset on the St. Lawrence*, an innocuous waltz by Maxine Heller published in 1907. Looking at a photograph of the SS *Kingston*, a paddle-wheeler built in 1901, weaving its way through the Thousand Islands, with its mahogany arches, decorated panelling, potted plants, Parisian light fixtures, filigree ironwork, carved pews out-side the cabin doors and burnished wooden floor, it is hard not to sigh with regret for being born out of her time, and the time of her sister ships, the *Toronto* and the *Montréal*.

The CSL divided the St. Lawrence into three sections, a bit like organizing a swimming pool into lanes, with different pas-senger ships catering to each section. Steamers left daily from Toronto, making for Prescott. On any Friday afternoon in the summer, office workers by the hundreds fleeing stuffy rooms lined up at the departure dock at Toronto to buy a return ticket to Prescott, to get out on the cool water with a breeze on their brows, in suspended animation from their daily lives. During this aquatic rush hour the ticket sellers on the dock were so overwhelmed that they made no attempt to count the money they took over the counter; they simply backhanded it onto the floor behind them, and the heap of bills and change was collated and counted once the steamer had left the pier.

At Prescott, those continuing downriver transferred to one

of the "Royal Family"—the *Rapids Queen*, the *Rapids King* or the *Rapids Prince*, all built between 1892 and 1910. The *Queen* was the senior ship, the *Prince* the youngest. The *Queen* and the *Prince* sat high in the water, drawing only six feet, and were flat-bottomed. With that kind of profile, they almost snow-boarded through the angry rapids between Prescott and Mon-tréal. The *King*, however, sat six inches lower in the water than its sister ships (a construction oversight), which was enough to make it run aground with frustrating regularity. (Six inches can indeed make all the difference.) Eventually, the pilots refused to take it through and the *King* was sent to work in exile on the Great Lakes, where it rolled so much that even the crew would lose their lunch. Finally, it was scrapped.

The roller-coaster ride through the Lachine Rapids provided by the *Queen* and *Prince* was an early tourist attraction on the river. As the boat's prow neared the tumbling hay ricks of water, the more solidly stomached passengers would gather outdoors and anticipate the rush. When it came, it was attended by squealing and a churning undertow of fear of the river's power.

The myth that only Native pilots could get a vessel through the Lachine dragged on long after it was no longer true. Pas-sengers expected to see a headdress on the bridge, and Cana-dian Steamship Lines was anxious not to disappoint anyone. They hired a Mohawk named John Nine (he was missing a fin-ger) from the Kahnawake reserve to stand on the bridge and do what many a waiter has learned to do: look busy without actu-ally doing anything. Passengers in mid-shriek as they went bouncing down the rapids could look back and see feathers and a stern countenance on the bridge, and know they were going to make it. At the Montréal pier Mr. Nine would, for one dol-lar, have his picture taken standing next to you.

The third section of the river started at Montréal, went past

Québec into wilder and even more beautiful scenery, all cliffs and bays, and down to the postcard-perfect town of Tadoussac. There the steamers made a left turn into the Saguenay, a river of unspoilable beauty reputed to be the deepest in the world. From the ship's rail, passengers were likely to see part of one of the nine species of whale that inhabit the salty stretch of the St. Lawrence.

As the steamers, old and new, plied the river, they were spotted and their names marked down in notebooks by earnest boys who hung like seagulls around the docks, catching a friendly wave from passengers. The boys collected the post-cards of the various steamship lines, with hand-painted photographs done as a series of portraits. Postcard albums allowed them to encase a whole set. When a ship retired or sank, its card was duly moved to the back of the album.

Antique emporiums along the river have boxes of these postcards, usually on a table at the back. The earliest one I have is dated 1889, and depicts Québec harbour looking down from the Citadel; there are sailing ships and steamers side by side at the quays, oxen and horses housed in the same stall. By far the commonest card shows a steamer happily shooting the rapids, the upper deck crowded with thrill-seekers. The prettiest ones show a steamer wending its way through the Thousand Islands, usually at sunset, as though they were still photographs from an early motion picture romance.

Lewis Evans was just such a card-collecting boy. He was born in 1907, the year a paddle steamer called the *Cayuga* was built, one of five famous ships that had names beginning with C and ending with A that worked the river. Evans lived his whole life on the St. Lawrence, dying in Brockville at the age of ninety-three, a pebble's throw from the riverbank. He wrote about the St. Lawrence, sailed on it, taught generations of other boys about it, collected its tarnished stories and retold them till they shone, and summered for seventy years straight in Tadoussac. Human beings are seventy percent water; in Lewis Evans, most of that was St. Lawrence.

One of Evans's first reminiscenses in a loving memoir called *Tides of Tadoussac* is of being five and taking a horse-drawn cab—his father, a chaplain, insisted that the horse have a white star (the name of a shipping line) on its forehead— down to Montréal's Victoria Pier. It was June 1912, and the Evans clan were heading for Tadoussac again. Waiting for him at dockside was "the familiar beloved sight of the wedding-cake superstructure and twin funnels" of the *Quebec* or the *Montréal*. Also in Montréal harbour that season was the largest dry dock in the world; it had been towed across the Atlantic and installed there, a headline event that drew a throng of sightseers.

The feast of boarding one of those steaming confections remained with Evans, and in his seventies, when he wrote *Tides of Tadoussac*, he could recall it fluently: "The gangway, the lobby, the row of stiff chairs, each with its polished brass spittoon, the brass-edged stairway with its ornately carved banisters, the carpets with an R & O design, the gingerbread woodwork, the narrow cabins, the upper bunk where you could see out the window." When darkness fell, Lewis pushed his nose into the glass and searched for "buoys dancing past like little red and black soldiers with their hands on their hips; the stop at Sorel where always men seemed engaged in dropping iron pipes on other iron pipes; the swishing nothingness of Lake St. Peter; and most of all, passing the upward-bound steamer, which swooped past in a blaze of light and flurry of foam."

Reaching Québec by early morning, the Evans family transferred to a boat headed for the Saguenay River, perhaps the

Scottish-built *Saguenay* itself, the first of the St. Lawrence ships to do away with paddlewheels and install twin screws. Or it might have been any one of several paddle steamers, including "the *Murray Bay*, previously named the *Carolina* and later the *Cape Diamond*, or the *St. Irénée*, once the *Canada* and afterwards the *Cape St. Francis*, for the policy was to change names after any accident, trifling or otherwise, or even, it seemed, after a new paint job."

The male fascination with engines got a full workout on the old paddle steamers. The designers catered to that segment of the population who found confirmation when they stared at massive pistonry in action.

> Inside, amidships, there was an enclosure with windows bordered with coloured panes, where you could watch the shiny steel pistons from the walking-beam plunging up and down into the vitals of the ship to turn the drive shaft of the paddle-wheels. And as you toured the deck you found your way blocked by the curved paddle-boxes; there was a glorious thumping and sloshing from within, and at full speed the water squirted at you from leaks between the boards.

And so on towards darkness.

> Freight deck jammed to the overhead beams, already an hour or two behind schedule, the first boat of the season would slide past the lush green hump of the Island of Orleans, and head for the looming blue capes of the North Shore. Then out on the widening estuary to meet the darkness

flowing up from the Gulf, and the long sweep
round the Prince Shoal Lightship into the mouth
of the Saguenay. The welcoming lights of
Tadoussac and its wharf in the little cove called
Anse à l'Eau, disembarkation, the frenzied dog,
the smiling caretaker who had come to meet you,
the fourteen pieces of luggage and the seventeen
checks, the buckboard ride through the sleeping
village, the cottage with that smell of all summer
cottages just reopened, the creaking stairs, the
cold damp sheets, and the dreams of the steamer's
paddles plunk-plunking up the deep Saguenay, if
it was foggy her whistle sounding as they could
time the echo from the cliffs, headed for Anse
St. Jean, Chicoutimi, and her turn-around for
Quebec. And all summer lying ahead.

Also lying ahead was a world war. Two summers later Europe
went to battle, and almost at a stroke immigration into Canada
dropped away, the hubbub in the embarkation hall at Grosse-
Île falling to a whisper. The flow of humanity was now in the
other direction, as six percent of the Canadian population
went overseas to fight with the Canadian Expeditionary Force.
The Canadian navy gave eight thousand of its sailors the task
of guarding shipping in the Atlantic, which was being harassed
by a new breed of weapon, the submarine.

The war, as wars always are, was a benefactor to shipyards.
The British government, which lost a million tons of shipping
in 1915, placed orders in its dominion of Canada for ships to
ferry supplies and men to the European killing fields. On the
edge of the narrow-streeted, no-frills town of Lauzon, the
Davie Shipbuilding and Repair yard, already a century and a

half old, went into increased production. "Davieship" was the prime place on the St. Lawrence to construct warships. There were no messy, narrow canals between the launch ramp and the open sea that led straight to Europe. Ships could grab a tide to ease them downriver, and winter's icy blockade was not a problem. Work could continue around the calendar.

Besides the new shipping, much of the St. Lawrence's standing fleet of cargo and passenger ships was commandeered for overseas service. They were additional vertebrae in the huge supply convoys that sailed out of Canada over the four years of conflict. After unloading their grain and guns in the London docks, several ships were seconded into the French navy or shuttled between English ports and the continent. The greatest convoy, nicknamed the Great Armada, left for Plymouth in September 1916, the ship at the rear unable to see the lead ship as the curve of the earth obscured it.

There were ships that did not return to the St. Lawrence, sent instead to obscure graves off the English coast, including two of the Empress line, the *Fort William* and the *Midland*. On September 16, 1918, with British shipping losses now at nine million tons, and sixty thousand, mostly young, Canadian men buried in water or mud, the CSL cargo ship the *Acadian* was sunk by a U-boat, and all but one of the crew drowned.

Two months later, the war ended.

14

The River is Wide

*The daily onboard routine of
a riverbound life was a tonic in itself.*

The returning veteran ships of World War I passed under a
new bridge on the St. Lawrence, at Québec. A year earlier, on
September 20, 1917, the centre span of the Québec railway
suspension bridge was nudged into position by tugboat and
slowly hoisted into place. The headline in the Québec newspaper that day read: "Quebec Bridge span bolted in place and
engineering dream of many years is at last a reality." The bridge
was a wonder of its time, then the longest suspension bridge in
the world, another giant staple across the St. Lawrence linking
north and south. A month later the bridge was ready to open,
and on a cold and cloudy October 17, the first locomotive

pulled two flatcars and one chair car across the span. The chair car was for dignitaries and the flat ones, draped with Union Jacks, for selected workmen and their wives.

Certain technologies make a habit of leaping forward in wartime. As well as bridge building, the airplane was a far more refined thing by war's end than it had been in 1914, the year the Wright Brothers were finally given a patent on motorized flight. More speed meant the possibility for a faster Canada–Europe mail service, a goal as cherished by communicators then as a faster modem is now. Until planes could be developed that would fly the ocean non-stop, the idea was to unite a liner and an airplane in a relay race to provide a transatlantic express service, the ship handling the ocean, the plane the inland portion. By way of a dummy run, on the third of September 1927, the *Empress of France* steamed out of Southampton and made it to the Rimouski pilot station in record time, and the mail was rowed ashore. An airplane was standing by; the mail was thrown inside and the plane set off down the runway. As it lifted off, it clipped a tree and had to land in a hurry.

Ten days later, they tried again. This time the *Empress of Scotland* raced across the ocean, but she made Rimouski after sundown, too late for the plane to fly. To make it third time lucky, it was decided to switch direction, and on the twenty-first of that busy month of September a plane flew from Montréal to Pointe-au-Père, the mail was rowed across to the *Empress of Australia*, and the recipients were reading their letters in London on the twenty-ninth.

Right at the end of the season they got the east–west run sorted out. The *Montnairn* left England on the third of November, zipped to Rimouski by the eleventh, the mail boarded the plane at four-thirty in the afternoon, and it was in Montréal just after nine that night. By midnight it was in the right mailboxes with "This mail was carried by Postal airplane to Montreal" stamped upon it. The mad dash had shaved twenty-four hours off the regular service.

The following year, 1928, an express mail service was offered (for a little extra cost) to Montréal, Ottawa and Toronto. As an advertising stunt, a package of silk was ordered via telegraph from a London supplier by the Canadian firm of A. Sheldrick and Son, merchant tailors of Chatham. The order was placed on the afternoon of Friday, June 15. By exactly 12:53 p.m. the following Saturday, eight days later, the package was in the tailor's window, with a crowd of Chathamians staring at it as though it was a two-headed sheep. By September 1930, using seaplanes that could fly to the edge of the continent and land right by the liners while they were still at sea, the London *Times* announced a special five-day delivery service between Canada and Britain. That is faster by a factor of one-half than it is seventy years later.

With the arrival of art deco, a style of restrained elegance that was as much North American as European, the liners became gilded lilies. The liners sailing into New York were gilt-edged flytraps for the rich trade, and Canadian Pacific saw the need to commission a palace of its own for the St. Lawrence. The hull of the *Empress of Britain II* was launched in Scotland in 1930, an event carried on an empire-wide radio link-up that was, at the time, the most extensive in broadcast history.

On June 1, 1931, the *Empress* docked in Québec for the first time, at a purpose-built wharf, five days and half an hour after leaving Southampton. The Western world was in a financial depression, and this sleek, floating grand hotel of awe-inspiring expenditure was a bravura antidote to the hard times. The city was drawn to her arrival as though she were royalty itself. Coming into port at ten at night, the *Empress*, a sixth of a mile long, slid down a liquid red carpet of reflected setting sun, spotlights playing on her funnels. Well over a hundred thousand Quebeckers gathered at the city's edge to wave her in, and two members of America's celluloid royalty, Mary Pickford and Douglas Fairbanks, waved back from the rails. The next day, eight hundred of Québec's élite dined on board at the captain's pleasure, and she was jammed for days with tours. The *Empress* then began her regular runs, and because she could make twenty-four knots with her twin screws, she took the Blue Riband for fastest Atlantic crossing several times.

$$\downarrow$$

The period between the wars was the heyday of the St. Lawrence passenger steamers, with the CSL ships under the command of William Coverdale. Coverdale could claim to be a son of the river, at least by birth. He was born in Kingston in 1871, as he was fond of remarking, "under the shadow of the asylum and the penitentiary." That was sentimentality on his part; in fact he made his money in the United States as a consulting engineer and a rescuer of ailing companies, and lived there even while he headed CSL, keeping a summer estate and a yacht at Kingston. A large, penny-pinching, brusque man with a military voice and a

As regards the St. Lawrence . . . familiarity with it breeds no contempt. On the contrary, the more it is known the more it is admired. Without exaggeration, it may be called the chief and prince of all the rivers of the world.

—Charles Mackay, editor of the *Illustrated London News*, 1858 relentless stare while interrogating employees, Coverdale was head of CSL for over twenty years.

From the moment he moved to the head of the boardroom table in 1922, Coverdale made plain his romantic attachment to the passenger side of the business, to what CSL dubbed "The Great White Fleet." The fleet's whiteness was its trademark. Every winter the ships were docked in ice and painted a gleaming ivory from bottom to top. The well-wrapped painters stood on the ice and began at the waterline, working up to the tunnels before spring thaw.

In his enthusiasm for the steamers of his fleet, Coverdale went so far as to commission several writers—and himself—to produce guidebooks on the Arcadian joys of taking the *Richelieu*, the *St. Lawrence* or the *Saguenay* on a long weekend jaunt. CSL published the books (today we would call them infomercials) themselves and made them available for purchase on board. In a book penned by Coverdale, he was able, straight-faced, to write prose such as this: "Unique is the fact that all the wonders of this last stand of romance lie close beside a mighty river that has been the grand highway of Canadian civilization for four centuries." Coverdale expected the same standard of his hired pens, who no doubt needed a swig of inspiration before composing to such a level.

These books are now available in second-hand stores in towns along the river. I have the seventeenth edition of *The Saguenay Trip*, bought for the price at which it first sold to steamer passengers—one dollar. It is abundantly illustrated with colour prints showing white steamships comfortably dwarfed by majestic scenery, plus pen-and-ink sketches of little homesteads with smoking chimneys, Group of Seven counterfeits, photographs both hand-tinted and black-and-white, and at the very back, a fold-out map giving copious explanation of the route the original reader was moving down.

The text, which includes two sub-Wordsworth poems, one in French, shows how far copywriting—the art of making an invoice resemble literature—has come in sixty years. It is a translation from the French, and anglo readers are warned in the introduction that they may detect "a slight fragrance of French in the groupings of Saxon words." It starts with a quote from an earlier journalist, of 1859, on assignment from *Harper's* magazine:

> The moisture from the storm that had prevailed on the St. Lawrence for almost a week had penetrated everywhere, and we found the berths in the state rooms dangerously damp. The obliging steward brought us dry mattresses and flannel blankets, with which I soon made up three comfortable beds at the dark end of the saloon. To make assurance doubly sure in guarding against agues, each one of my immediate company swallowed a hot gin sling before retiring. The precaution was effectual.

From there on, the book's intention is to cast a spell of forced mythology. After some highly selective history, it ends with "true" tales of legendary figures of the river. The pièce de résistance concerns Pierre Soulard, a part-time ferryman and drinker who had a fondness for the liver-pickling beverage *bagosse*. Soulard's ferry route was between Île d'Orléans and Beauport on the north shore. One day, as a student on spring break, Pierre attempted to cross against the tide while drunk. He overturned the boat, killing several people. Later that same binge, two years later, Soulard tried the same route again, during ice breakup, and was decapitated on the sharp edge of a small iceberg when he was jettisoned from the boat. The head, it is said, still bobs along in the St. Lawrence; to see it is to know you will die before winter comes.

The booklets also made fanfare of the hotels that passengers could stay in en route. CSL had inherited two major hotels from the Richelieu and Ontario Company: the Manoir Richelieu at Murray Bay and the Tadoussac. Coverdale—a man who, with age, allowed his reverence for the river to get the better of him as a businessman—had architectural dreams for both of them. He got his wish with the Manoir Richelieu when it burnt down to the vaults in 1928, just after the end of the season. In eight freezing months, using five hundred off-season workers from the Davie shipyards, who toiled behind a sort of vast wooden condom designed to keep out the weather, Coverdale got the new manoir. It was done out in impersonation of a seventeenth-century French château, and opened in time for the traditional start of the season, June 15. The golf course was directly behind, the fifteenth and eighteenth tees so elevated that players had to use a funicular railway to reach them. All great hotels market themselves on the celebrities who visit them, and the Richelieu offered the merely well-to-do and obscure the chance to inhabit the same dining room as the king of Siam or ex-president of the United States William Howard Taft, both of whom were on the celebrity A-list of their time.

Downstream and just a touch downmarket, the three-storey, red-and-white Tadoussac hotel was plainer but homelier. In the hotel grounds Coverdale popped some history, re-creating the trading post originally built there by Pierre Chauvins and incorporating some of the original stones. He also spruced up St. Anne's chapel, which contains the very bell that rang out the first Christian call to prayer over the St. Lawrence, in 1647.

Neither of these hotels ever made money; that wasn't their point. They were somewhere for the steamers to arrive, somewhere for the rich and the upper middle class to reinforce their status in suitable surroundings, a place where they could escape the grind of making money while remaining wrapped up in it. As background, patrons enjoyed the relatively unsullied wilderness of the north shore, and for foreground they had the wide, salty flow of the St. Lawrence.

For many who used the steamers, it was simply the getting there that appealed: the ritual of the mile march—six laps of the upper deck—every morning; high tea taken to the strain of a gently swelling orchestra; and bagpipers announcing that it was five o'clock and time to dress for dinner. The daily, on-board routine of a riverbound life was a tonic in itself. There was a gang from the Quebec Institute of Accountants who travelled every year to its general meeting in Québec by steamer from Montréal. Gradually, the farther downriver they got, the less the business of debits and credits, of accounts receivable and payable, figured in their conversation, and a life of facts gave way to the simpler facts of life.

15

TOO MANY RIVERS

*Money was in a good mood
in the twenties, and the engineers had a plan.*

In 1932, a panel of six super-engineers, three each from Canada and the States, made its final report on the future of St. Lawrence shipping to the International Joint Commission.

The idea the engineers espoused of a rapids-free, deep-water channel that could provide plain sailing for the big grain ships travelling from the Great Lakes to the Gulf was actually first mooted in 1895. The topography of the St. Lawrence's riverbed dictated that such a channel would have to zigzag between the United States and Canada, which meant the two countries would have to get around a desk and forge a deal. On the way to the deal, they created sub-commissions that begat studies. The studies begat surveys, which begat possibilities, which begat meetings, and so it went for four decades as the two countries inched towards legislation at the speed of politics.

From 1895 to 1932, a revolving door of presidents and prime ministers signed the various papers put before them that created treaties, commissions of navigation and terms of hydro power production. World War I had been a prolonged distraction, but money was in a good mood in the twenties and the engineers now had a plan.

The 1932 report by the coven of engineers recommended exploiting the river in two ways: first, through the rebuilding, dredging, damming and flooding of a navigation channel, which would be a uniform twenty-five feet deep and extend from Kingston to Montréal; and second, by siphoning off over two million horsepower of hydroelectric energy from the river in a series of power stations. The power was sorely needed. The first hydro plant on the St. Lawrence, a small, stone, one-storey building, started making electro-power in Iroquois in 1901. By 1930, the electric stove, invented in Ottawa, sat side by side in the kitchen with the fridge, and air conditioning was filtering into common use. Also, the factories that made the appliances, as well as the commuter cars that people were using to head downtown and buy those appliances, were multiplying at the rate of locusts, and they all required electricity.

The engineers' timing, however, was not the best. Either side of the border, the Depression had taken deep hold. A million and a half Canadians fell unemployed, and countries cut back on trading with each other. Shipping on the St. Lawrence was cut in half, and the idea of spending six hundred and fifty million dollars on a single project in the east of Canada did not seem politically astute. The river got a reprieve.

If there was little movement towards developing the river's potential for increased traffic and electricity production, in other areas there was progress. In August 1937, the quarantine station on Grosse-Île was closed. The science of immunology and the control of contagion had reduced the island's caseload to minor illnesses and what were called childhood or minor diseases, and such quarantine as was needed could be handled in Québec. Radio was now a standard item on passenger ships, and a ship's doctor who had spotted illness on board could call up assistance from the pilot station at Rimouski or alert a Québec hospital. The steamer companies had long been in favour of avoiding the island, a stop everyone had to make, and proceeding directly to Montréal without delay. They got their wish.

The hotels, the brick hospital and the embarkation hall were emptied, some buildings dismantled and equipment shipped to mainland hospitals. The last two doctors, Crétien and Laurin, were transferred to do good elsewhere; the interpreters, bakers, schoolteacher, ambulance driver, carpenter and telegraph operator found employment off the island; and the unique clan of people who could claim to have been born on the island began to dwindle.

For a brief time the village on Grosse-Île was a ghost town, with an uncommonly large complement of ghosts. Children no longer hunted rats among the graveyards. Almost immediately, however, the benighted island was pressed back into service. German expansionism was abroad in Europe again and war was inevitable. The Defence Research Board chose Grosse-Île, because of its history with germs, as the site of an experimental station to look into the use of anthrax, a cattle disease, as a biological weapon.

⚓

After Britain declared war on Germany, a week passed while the Canadian Parliament pretended to ponder the matter of joining in the contagious insanity already underway in Europe. Then, on September 9, 1939, the declaration was made. The speed of the Nazi advance, and the early defeats suffered by the Allies, scared the Canadian government, which had hoped for a low-key involvement, into more action than it had intended. Almost overnight, as though a great switch had been thrown somewhere, the country surged out of Depression and into production.

The shipping lanes during the Depression had been as quiet as a small town at midnight, but when war broke out, it was 1914 all over again, and the traffic got heavy. In fact, in 1939 shipping jumped to twice its 1936 level. Vessels that had been laid off were sent out to get their bows wet again, delivering ore and coal to the armament-producing steel mills, and men who had been laid off packed their lunch pails and headed for the factory gates. Only fourteen steamships bigger than a hundred and fifty feet were launched between 1930 and 1939; now, shipyards were cranking out merchant shipping vessels like doughnuts as well as ships to guard those vessels as they crossed the Atlantic. In Lauzon, the Davieship yard delivered the first made-in-Canada corvette, the *Wildflower* (a curious name for a killing machine), to the British navy early in 1940. The yard also filled orders for minesweepers, frigates and landing craft.

Lots of corvettes—small anti-submarine boats given the slightly derisory naval term "cockleshells"—were the order of the day. German U-boats had not ventured as far as the mouth of the St. Lawrence in World War I, but in this round they intended to nip the supply convoys in the bud. As well as making new corvettes, the shipyards converted several luxury yachts, some of them donated by wealthy owners, and these fairly inadequate machines stood on guard at the river's entrance. Two of them had no guns on their decks, having to settle for a wooden silhouette of a gun turret. A menagerie of such converted yachts, all named after Canadian wildlife—the *Raccoon, Grizzly, Beaver, Musky, Moose* and so on—protected the convoys as they sailed down the gangplank into the Gulf—and into the viewfinders of German periscopes.

The first of the guardian fleet to go down from enemy fire was the *Raccoon*. A prowling U-boat, a full seventy miles upriver, took the muscle yacht out with a torpedo on September 7, 1942, and thirty-eight men joined the ranks of the St. Lawrence's dead. In the subsequent one-sided battle of the St. Lawrence, torpedoes added another two hundred and eighty-six to that total: the crews of the *Otter, Charlottetown, Chedabucto, Shawinigan, Clayoquot* and *Esquimalt*. One torpedo even attempted to go ashore, missing the boat it was aimed at and exploding on impact with the beach at St-Yvon, a fishing village on the Gaspésie coast, making it the only Quebec village that can claim to have suffered a direct hit during the war.

War leaders do their best thinking well away from falling bombs, which is why Québec was chosen as the site of two planning conferences, in August 1943 and again thirteen months later. (Prime Minister Mackenzie King was not invited to either conference; Canada was considered to be a minor lifeboat lashed to the deck of the British Empire.) While the Allied leaders were sealed up in Québec at the 1943 conference, debating the course of the war, the British and American chiefs of staff spent a day and a night as the only passengers on the steamer *Tadoussac*. As all boat owners know, the water at night offers a haven of peace and quiet—the first two victims of war. The heavily guarded big brasses debated strategy back and forth, their secret dreams and schemes absorbed by the well-varnished wood panelling while the boat strolled in a deliberately random pattern about the mouth of the Saguenay.

The planning on board the *Tadoussac* paid off and the tide of war turned towards the Allies in 1943. The battle of the St. Lawrence, so far from Berlin, receded as the U-boats were called home. In October 1944, the last successful torpedo was fired in the river when the *Magog*, the lead frigate in a convoy that was setting out across the Atlantic, was sunk by a German submarine. The explosion took place in plain sight of the assistant lighthouse keeper at Pointe-des-Monts, Robert Kavanagh. Three men died, and the hulk of the frigate had to be towed away and scrapped. Some of the survivors were brought to the lighthouse and stayed several days before being shipped upriver, their war over.

Four years after the armistice was signed and the century's second great conflict was over, William Coverdale died in a New York hospital after twenty-seven years in the big chair at Canadian Steamship Lines. Coverdale's passion for the steamers of the St. Lawrence had never waned, but the concept of passenger steamers certainly had. The era of one man, one car and a new model every year was underway.

One by one, the Great White Fleet was laid up or sold. The *Montréal* had been taken by fire in 1926; the *Toronto* sustained fatal damage in heavy weather in 1936; the *Saguenay* went to Singapore in 1941 and later drowned in a typhoon; the beautiful *Kingston* sailed on after the war until 1949, then just died of old age. A newspaper headline in the Montréal *Gazette* in January 1950 that read "ABDICATION OF AN AGED PRINCE" announced the end of the *Rapids Prince* and the joyride through the Lachine Rapids. When the old steamer took its last trip through the churning water, the pilot was Captain Joseph Ouellette, Édouard Ouellette's grandson. That same year, the company tried to scrap the forty-three-year-old *Cayuga*. Her faithful passengers were so upset at the news that seven hundred of them bought her and she did four more seasons as an independent before they admitted defeat. Finally, only three ships, all working the Montréal–Tadoussac route, sailed on: the *Tadoussac*, the *Richelieu* and the *St. Lawrence*.

Almost before Coverdale was cold, his order for two new passenger steamers—a denial of the fact that luxury river travel had gone the way of the Newfoundland auk—was rescinded by the relieved CSL board of directors in Montréal. The intended steamers were subverted into freighters as the company, and the river, came about and headed for the dividends that would come from supertankers. When the directors left that meeting, got into their cars or onto airplanes and headed for the next important thing, the elegant era of passenger steamship travel on the St. Lawrence was effectively over.

As one concept expired after the war, another resurfaced: the revival of a continuous seaway from Great Lakes to Gulf. The two federal governments had signed a treaty in 1941 and even set a date, 1948, to have the Seaway up and running. It is an unbreakable rule in life that any project, be it a new backyard fence or building a bridge, takes twice as long and costs twice as much as forecast. If a government is involved, double that; if two or more governments have their hands on it, a factor of ten applies. The Seaway involved a Congress and a Parliament, and two second-level houses, the legislatures of Ontario and New York State. Applying the formula meant that the river might never see a Seaway at all.

Since the idea had been mooted, there had been powerful opposition to the Seaway from everyone who stood to lose money by it. The losers' list included privately owned eastern utilities, which would surrender business to government when the power plants were built, and the eastern railways, which would lose freight to the shipping lines if boats became big and cheap. The anti-Seaway gang had money, and they mounted a campaign that would have made the National Rifle Association proud. For half a century they had tripped and blocked the project, but with the advent of the 1950s and the dawning of modern, electrically powered affluence came their downfall.

In 1950, the population of Canada was half as much again as it had been fifteen years earlier, while the United States had grown by a third. The combined industrial production of the two nations was rising like a Rockie mountain; it had quadrupled in a decade and a half, and customers were lining up to plug into the Seaway's power as soon as it was available. Meanwhile, the United States needed iron ore to convert to steel to make, among other things, cars that would take the workers to the factories where they made steel. Canada had a treasure house of ore in the ground along the Quebec–Labrador border, which would be carried in ships—made of steel—to the metal-forging mills of the Great Lakes.

With the flow going against it, the anti-Seaway lobby was losing political favour, but it still had enough juice to make Congress drag its anchor. Then, four days before Christmas, 1951, the Canadians did an amazing thing: they called the Americans' bluff, a manoeuvre that has otherwise failed every time it's been tried. The Canadian Parliament went ahead and passed its own

Seaway Bill, allowing Canada to make unilateral power from its rapids. The American Senate, not used to being forced into a decision by its neighbours, rejected a resolution on the floor to go in with the Canadians in a power-sharing deal, but the exasperated state of New York and province of Ontario went ahead and made a deal on their own. This time the tail had wagged the dog, and the International Joint Commission authorized it. The Seaway was going to be built.

16

LOST IN THE FLOOD

The side streets became gravel hills, mountains of desolation looming in front of shambles that had been home addresses (above: Morrisburg, ON, before the Seaway was built).

By the middle of the twentieth century, cargo ships a thousand feet long were spending their working lives corralled in the vastness of the Great Lakes, unable to get out, like those pit ponies of old that were born underground and never saw the light of day. These giant ships simply could not reach the sea; fully loaded, they drew too much water and would have grounded in the locks or on the upper riverbed. To release them, and to allow the world's ships of equal size to enter the Great Lakes, the river itself would have to become bigger.

In 1953, with Dwight Eisenhower's golf clubs freshly unpacked in the White House, the St. Lawrence Seaway Development

Corporation was created and the signing ceremonies began. The newspapers carried pictures of distinguished and indistinguishable men in suits sharing a joke with laughing men in full Native dress—the Mohawks of St-Regis or Akwesasne, the reserve just south of Cornwall that extends into the United States that would be affected by the Seaway.

On the tenth of August 1954, a clutch of chairmen of power companies, a governor, a premier and a prime minister met at Cornwall and stood before a tacky billboard showing a giant goateed Uncle Sam and a mustachioed Mountie. The twin caricatures held a power station between them like a loaf of bread, while men in hats made speeches below them. Later the same day, the party decamped across the river to Massena, and there made the same speeches in reverse order. The fact that it was St. Lawrence's Day, and therefore four hundred and nineteen years to the day since Cartier had inadvertently named the river, had not been lost on the speechwriters. A golden shovel went into the ground and turned over a couple of pounds of earth, and then they were off. Gentlemen, start your engines.

The speech platforms were cleared away, and the heavy machinery and men in hard hats moved in. Their mission was to alter the very outline of the river on both sides of the international border. The river would lose the shape it had maintained for ten thousand years.

The concept of "big" is an appealing one for engineers. The opportunity to make something larger than life, which also solves a physical problem, and that endures after they are gone, engages them the same way a symphony engages a composer. Size matters. Big rivers attract big projects, and forcing a river to do as it's told is an act of muscular divinity. The St. Lawrence Seaway Development, or the Seaway, as it came to be known, was a labour worthy of Hercules, and the engineers were oiled up and the big machines ready to rock and roll.

When the word went out that a megaproject was underway on the St. Lawrence River, it attracted a wave of migrant workers. To a man, so it seemed, they'd heard there was ten-dollars-an-hour work to be made, moving cemeteries. It was true that a total of eighteen graveyards faced relocation, but the dead alone could not supply a living for that many men.

There was, however, plenty of other work for the surplus gravediggers. Twenty-two thousand men in hard hats, handling seventy-five million dollars' worth of machinery, went at the landscape, jacking up old bridges, erecting vast, temporary dams, gouging a channel down the river three storeys deep, blasting aside avalanches of rock, pouring a great lake of concrete, and rearranging earth and water. A coal-digging machine capable of wrenching twenty tons out of the earth in one bite, nicknamed The Gentleman, was brought two thousand miles from Kentucky by land and sea to speed up the work.

Mighty feats of engineering became commonplace as the St. Lawrence devolved into a vast sandbox between Iroquois and Montréal harbour. The venerable Victoria Bridge, in order to remain part of the Seaway, had to raise her skirts eighty feet while engineers inserted a lift bridge to allow ships to pass below. The Jacques Cartier bridge was jacked up fifty feet in one span, and the fourteen other spans were raised in increments to the new working height. Traffic on either bridge was never halted for more than a few hours at a time.

Also, according to the blueprints, seven entire villages faced partial or complete eradication. This was because of the required rise in the river to make it bigger, and hence drown the rapids. Aultsville, Dickinson's Landing, Farran's Point, Iroquois, Milles Roches and Moulinette would disappear off the map, with Morrisburg undergoing amputation. Five hundred and thirty-one existing homes were slated to be moved, and three hundred and forty-nine new ones built, as well as three dams, one each at Iroquois, Long Sault and Cornwall. The seven vanishing villages would be rolled up into just three, two with new names. There would be Ingleside (the new home of Dickinson's Landing, Wales, Farran's Point and Aultsville), Long Sault (Moulinette and Milles Roches) and a new town with an old name, Iroquois, where the local historian, Beryl Morrison, would be given the task of naming the new streets.

There was an air of Monopoly about the whole proceedings—people losing homes and gaining houses, new agglomerates being built, large sums of money changing hands. And the people holding the dice for everyone were Ontario Hydro, who sent teams of negotiators into the villages. These teams moved swiftly among the households, spelling out the forms of disruption available and naming the date by which they needed an answer. The residents slated to move were given the dice and told there were three possible rolls. One: they could have the house they already owned moved to higher ground, and the move would be paid for. Same house, different view. Two: the old house would be demolished and a new one built elsewhere, and they could have a hand in the new design. Different house, different view. Failing either of those, they could become Seaway displacees, take a cash settlement and go buy a house elsewhere. (Some people's homes could not be moved; the limit for the machines was two hundred tons.)

Depending on whom you talk to—on which side of the kitchen table they were seated during the negotiations—Hydro was either efficient or bullying. In the midst of dinner, that debate can still surface in forty-year-old houses in Ingleside and Iroquois. Some of the home-losers later found out that the National Research Council had used their houses to do burn tests, setting fire to them and clinically observing the logistics of the flames, and that got their dander up.

A house being moved is a roadside attraction, so the spectacle of entire villages being slid across the map became a tourist draw. I recall, as a child of eight, heading down to the St. Lawrence on a midsummer's day in 1958 to see the mighty goings-on. On the way back we were stopped by a man with a red flag to let a big flat truck with a small wooden church on it go by. There were plenty of other such wonders to be seen. Several of the islands that were due either to go under in the floodwater or to become part of the park system had summer cottages on them. These were removed simply by skidding them across the ice.

One act of relocation was truly monumental. For a century and a half, the stone obelisk marking the battle at John Crysler's farm had stood, appropriately, on the site of the blood-shed. The historic fields were destined to become riverbed and so the monument was moved. Soil from the battlefield was piled up in a mound, several trees were artfully planted, and the old monument got stuck on top of its fresh mounting in a calm park, marking the exact spot where the battle didn't happen. Even the amalgamation of the graveyards in the new Union Cemetery drew a crowd. On request, bodies could be moved along with their respective tombstones to new, eternal quarters. Those of the deceased whose relatives elected that they stay where they lay were sealed down with stone slabs.

In November 1957, the last house, the five hundred and twenty-fifth, was relocated. It was a mock Tudor, steep-roofed affair that had stood on Main Street in Morrisburg for a generation. The machine that moved the house, as it had moved all the others, was owned by an Iroquois company called Hartshorne. The phonetic irony in the two words making up that name was not lost on the displacees.

Many of the people who were moved between 1955 and 1957 later, when their dust had settled, put pen to paper to describe what had happened to them. Trauma often forces people to put on record their side of a story in which they had no real choice, and to be relocated is to undergo the down-to-the-roots trauma of being involuntarily repotted. In 1988, Leonard O'Dette, in his eighties and living in a seniors' home in the new village of Ingleside, self-published his scrapbook. *Relics and Requiems* was a salvationist project he undertook in the old folks' home, an ersatz Proustian mélange of newspaper clippings, lists, diagrams and pictures of vanished buildings with a smattering of marginalia by Leonard himself. It's a curious but enjoyable thing, a magpie's nest of random, shiny moments in the folk history of his doorstep. On one page of *Relics and Requiems* are two pictures of the farm Leonard grew up on near Farran's Point. One is shot from overhead before it was flooded, and the other, post-1958, shows a clear expanse of water.

Another displacee, Thelma Cameron, wrote a moving (in all senses) testimonial to the disruption of her place of living, in September 1958, a few months before the Seaway was opened:

> Iroquois, Ontario, with its population of eleven hundred, was the largest of the river towns to be completely cleared from the path of the St. Lawrence Seaway and Power Project. Citizens finally came to an agreement with the Hydro Commission of Ontario on June 14, 1955, and impatient bulldozers roared into operation. It took many months for the uprooting; a common sight was that of huge moving machines labouring along the highway bearing whole houses which, after being lifted from their usual environments,

left their grounds looking like empty picture frames. The demolished buildings rose in piles of lumber beside stacks of doors and windows. These wares of the salvage dealers were arranged carefully along the main street where people who were interested could buy them to carry away. Bathroom fixtures and furnaces looked strange indeed, when assembled on the side of the pavement. A bath tub remained four weeks in front of the Royal Bank of Canada. The side streets became gravel hills, mountains of desolation looming in front of shambles that had, a short time before, been home addresses for the residents of Iroquois. The sole activity during working hours was the din and clatter of trucks loading and dumping. After six o'clock each night the abandoned township was black and lifeless.

With the Monopoly game over, the day came for the great levee holding back the river near Cornwall to be dynamited with thirty-one tons of explosive. The day and night before, June 30, the old canals were stripped clean of power lines and lock gates, their working lives over. Bonfires along the canal banks lit the work after the power was turned off. At eight in the morning on July 1, 1958, the blasters on Sheek Island pushed the switch and two one-hundred-foot-wide wedges of dirt and boulders roared into the sky. The water broke through in a six-foot tidal wave and found its man-made contours in a new lake, Lake St. Lawrence, bracketed by the westerly Iroquois dam and the easterly Long Sault dam. A family of muskrats who had been caught in the flood fought against being symbolically sucked into the intake of the Massena power station, and lost. By nightfall the water was a dozen feet deep and had reached the new beaches and the seemingly stranded Long Sault Marina, which only the day before had been two miles from the nearest water.

The flooding of the Seaway deprived the Canadian landscape of dozens of islands, seven communities, two hundred and twenty-five farms, forty miles of railway and a section of the old highway. On the less populated American side the count was a hundred farms and five hundred cottages. Altogether, thirty-eight thousand acres of former land, shaved of everything more than a foot high, from buildings to bushes, slipped under water. When the water settled, the United States and Canada between Iroquois and Cornwall were farther apart. Ree Graham, born on a dairy and apple farm near Iroquois, recalls going down to the shoreline before the flooding to chat with her mother, standing on the opposite bank. Mother and daughter did not have to raise their voices to be heard. After the flooding, they had to shout.

The Seaway had two openings, one for business and one for the Queen. The former was on April 29, 1959, day one of the navigation season, and a processional flotilla sailed upriver, first threading the St. Lambert lock, with much wine being served on deck. The coast guard led the way with the *d'Iberville* and *Montcalm*, then they fell back and Captain Norman Donaldson took the canaller *Simcoe* all the way to the Great Lakes. The *Simcoe* was over two hundred and fifty feet long and just over forty feet wide, and since 1900 that had been as big a boat as it was possible to sail from Montréal to Chicago. As a muskie is to a pike, ships three times that length and almost twice as wide, their bellies stuffed with grain or iron ore, could now travel from lake to sea and back to lake again without scratching their sides.

Two months later, on June 26, the bow of the royal yacht *Britannia*, with the Queen of Canada and the President of the United States aboard, broke a ribbon stretched across the channel at Montréal and set out for the head of the lakes, stopping along the way to let off the Eisenhowers. Thousands went down to the new shoreline to wave at the royal yacht as she passed under the thick electric wires sluicing power down into New York State and beyond.

As the sixties started, the St. Lawrence now had grafted into it an artificial spine three hundred miles long, a channel kept to a depth of twenty-seven feet by a slow-moving navy of dredgers. The Seaway could support ships of thirty-five thousand tons and over, penetrating two thousand miles into North America, by which time they were six hundred feet above the distant mouth of the St. Lawrence. A new fleet of bulk carriers, a dozen emanating from the Davie shipyards alone over the next seven years, took advantage of the enhanced river—muscle ships like the *Saguenay* that weighed in around forty thousand tons loaded, ran on diesel and could be sailed almost single-handedly from the bridge.

17

WON'T YOU LET ME TAKE YOU ON A SEA CRUISE?

*A glorious musical closed, one that had enjoyed
an extended run for four hundred and fifty-two years.*

There is a generation of Quebeckers, now in their sixties, who remember with fondness a ship called the *Homeric*. It occupies the same place in their memories where others put their first car, first night away from home or first holiday romance. The *Homeric* also holds a place in the broader memory of the St. Lawrence, for she was among the last generation of scheduled passenger liners. When the ships came in after that, everyone was at the airport.

Built in Massachusetts in 1931, the *Homeric* started life as the *Mariposa*, running from San Francisco down to Australia. During the war she did a stint of troop transport, and then passed a few years collecting rust in dry dock. She was bought by a Quebec shipping line, given a thorough facelift, complete with air conditioning, and added to the Laurentian Line in time for the 1955 Montréal–Québec–Normandy season. The overhauled, souped-up engines made her fast enough to hold the record for that run, thirty-five minutes short of five days. Leave Quebec on Monday, collect the key for the new *pied-à-terre* from the concierge in Paris on Saturday morning.

The ambience aboard the *Homeric* as she glided through the Atlantic nights was mostly one of release. The collar of the church in Quebec was starting to loosen up in the late fifties, and university students from the cities and *petites villes* were the first generation to really grab the chance of an education abroad. The argonauts on the *Homeric*, a thousand of them in tourist class occupying berths that could be had for as little as three hundred dollars return, meals included, were escaping. They made a party of each crossing, and that party lasted nine seasons. Then the *Homeric*, leaking money for its owners, was reassigned to the warm waters of the South Seas.

In the fifth year of the *Homeric's* tour of duty, the river witnessed its last great maiden voyage. The marine affectation of using "maiden" to mean "first time out" comes from horse racing rather than a ship's virgin state of experiencing the ocean's embrace. A maiden filly is a horse that has yet to win a race. Maiden voyages were office parties for the river, and since Intendant Jean Talon had celebrated the first in Québec in the 1660s, there had been thousands. The grander ones saw Montréal harbour decked out like a village fête.

The *Empress of Canada* was launched in May 1960 with a very large bottle of Canadian white wine. She was the third ship to carry the title. The launch was a smooth affair (unlike the début of the *Montréal* in 1907 from the same pier, when that luxury liner caught fire while they were still putting up the bunting and the town turned out to watch her disappear). The newest, and destined to be the last, *Empress* got off intact, and a year later she went into regular service. It was as though a skyscraper had detached itself from the Montréal skyline, fallen over and floated out to sea. Her architecture was of her times, streamlined and clean, sleeker and heavier than her older sisters, the *Britain* and the *England*, with a bow that would have looked good on a clipper ship. (A personal note: I was due to sail on that maiden voyage as a ten-year-old emigrant to England. The need to leave earlier forced passage on the *Empress of Britain* instead. I've been haunted by the great liners ever since.)

Inside, the *Empress of Canada* had been given the full treatment, in a style that anyone who bought furniture in the fifties, or is buying it now as retro, would recognize. The five salons on the ship were thoroughly Canadianized. On the walls of the St. Lawrence Club on the upper deck, an artist by the name of Cronyn had done two contrasting murals. One depicted the seventy-six-foot brig *Jean* going upriver, the *Jean* being the first ship sent over to Canada by Alexander Allan in 1819 to make a regular oceanic run. The other mural showed the history of commercial development along the river, a comforting choice of subject for businessmen in their armchairs on a carpet of river blue, sitting beneath portraits of sailing ships by Gordon Ellis.

In the Canada Room, the first-class watering hole, the domed ceiling was painted to show the positions of the northern stars and the moon on the day the ship was launched. This was an old conceit, a tradition on luxury steamers. First-class people wandered in from the Canada Room to the Salle Frontenac, the first-class restaurant, named after the first governor of Quebec, while tourist class supped in the Carleton Restaurant, named after the British governor who prevented the

Americans taking Québec in a wicked snowstorm on New Year's Eve, 1775. The Carleton Restaurant's murals, produced by the patriotic brush of Edward Bawdon, illustrated the shift from French daily life in Quebec to English daily life in Ontario as one proceeded upriver.

As she pulled out of Montréal, the *Canada* would often give a friendly hoot to the three domestic steamships of the Great White Fleet still sailing. That exchange ended on November 10, 1965, with this terse message from the board of directors of Canada Steamship Lines: "We regret to announce discontinuance of the Company's passenger ships on the St. Lawrence River." They blamed the "inroads of automobile and air traffic." The *Richelieu*, *Tadoussac* and *St. Lawrence* were quickly hustled out of the country to a breaker's yard in Antwerp. There, the *Tadoussac* got a reprieve and became a floating hotel in Copenhagen.

The *Empress of Canada* was destined to work the St. Lawrence for only ten years; she was the right ship at the wrong time. Passenger liners existed in a numbers game, and the numbers sailing on her did not justify perpetuating the service. A full load was one thousand and forty-eight people, and the most she ever carried was twenty-two short of that. On November 18, 1971, the Montréal *Gazette* reported that at seven-thirty in the evening, with a last-post blast on the horn, the *Canada* was pushed away from Pier Eight by two St. Lawrence tugs, with a crowd of around twenty to wave her off. A band assembled from the crew played "Now Is the Hour," and three hundred people made the final crossing, her one hundred and twenty-first. It was the finale of sixty-nine years of Empress activity on the Atlantic. The *Empress of Canada* is still on the water, in the harbour at Piraeus, just outside Athens. She too has been converted into a floating hotel.

With the last Empress gone, the once legion fleet of trans-atlantic liners calling on the St. Lawrence was reduced to three: the Russian *Alexandr Pushkin*, the Polish *Stefan Batory* and the lofty *Queen Elizabeth II*, which made occasional visits to Québec. When the *Pushkin* retired in 1980 and the *QEII* was drafted into the Falklands War in 1982, the *Stefan Batory* was the lone wolf. By then the ship had been in service for forty-one years.

In 1950, the daughter of one of the directors of the Holland-America Line, who had married a Canadian officer during the war, wrote to her father, bemoaning the price of getting from Canada to Holland. The world was not the same postwar. Large numbers of working-class men and women had tasted seabound travel and seen Europe under the worst of circum-stances. In peacetime they wanted to go again, but cheaply.

In reply to his daughter, the Holland-America director introduced a set of ships called "the economy twins," which almost entirely dispensed with first-class cabinage and instead were flooded with basic, comfortable tourist class. The tourists also had the run of the ship, meaning they could go anywhere on it, without restriction. One of these ships, the *Maasdam*, first sailed out of Montréal in August 1952. The ships were floating salons or coffee houses, full of students, artists, profes-sors and other cultural cross-sections of the chattering classes.

In 1966, the *Maasdam* took over full-time duties in the St. Lawrence, never sailing less than three-quarters full, although Atlantic liner traffic was heading downhill at the time. The Poles, who were bucking the trend and expanding their pas-senger trade, bought the boat two years later and renamed it the *Stefan Batory* after a favoured king of theirs. Boats, inside

and out, are mirrors of their eras in much the same way buildings are, and the Poles added a teenage club, coffee saloon,
playroom, Mountaineer's Cottage and cinema, and first class
was all but eradicated. The new and improved *Batory* arrived in
Montréal at the end of April 1969, and it made nine voyages
that season, all of them close to full. There was no direct air
route from Poland then, although there were nine million
Poles living in North America, so demand was up to supply,
and the boat became a Little Poland. In its spare time the little
passenger freighter did side trips up the St. Lawrence and the
Saguenay, as in days of old.

Sadly, even patriotism and a loyal cohort of cash-strapped
but cultured Canadians could not keep the *Stefan Batory* in
business. Advancing Canadian environmental law and many
years of political unrest in Poland contrived to scupper the last
of the passenger steamships. In October 1987, after a season
that included no stops at Québec and only four Atlantic round
trips, the veteran ship, a tribe of one, made her final eastward
crossing. She did brief public service in various trouble spots as
a refugee hostel, then went to Turkey in 2000 for demolition
into her various parts, including the original Dutch panelling
of finest Zeeland elm.

When the *Stefan Batory* pulled away from Pier Eight at
Montréal in 1987, a glorious musical closed, one that had
enjoyed an extended run for four hundred and fifty-two years,
since Cartier had ferried ten Stadaconans to France in 1535.
The *Batory* was the last sustained note of the score as it faded
away to nothing. A package of sounds went with the little ship,
made extinct by time's passing: the deep-throated, bullish bel-
low of the liners' horns as they arrived and departed; the
shouted verse and response of hail or farewell delivered
through cupped hands from the quay and from the ship's rails;

the slap of luggage piled high on skids and wheeled away; the clatter of feet on the boarding ramps.

The big ships were still out there, but their luxury now served a different cause. The passenger had become the tourist, and the voyage had become the cruise. It took some time, while other, sunnier seas milked the booming cruise trade for all it was worth, for the notion of the lower St. Lawrence as a cruise-ship destination to catch on. Apart from Québec, the cities along the lower river showed the world a pockmarked face; industry and decline had left some bad optics, as marketeers call them. Determined to cash in, the St. Lawrence's boosters began the search for its retail virtues. Come fall, the maple trees along the river unwittingly put on a natural display of colour, a farewell fanfare of foliage before winter, and this product carries no refitting or maintenance costs. Montréal and Québec—still North America's only walled city—both had the foresight to put their oldest quarters and most attractive architecture close to the water. The lower St. Lawrence in the summer is a string of festivals airing most of the arts. The Saguenay is just a left turn away, and there were more exotic features too, such as guaranteed whales and Indians, and the lingering echoes of wars of conquest. Best of all, this being Canada, everything was safe.

Meanwhile, a secretariat was set up, headquartered in Québec and charged with the task of increasing the number of ships of all kinds that used the river. By applying the hyper-language of marketing to the river's virtues, the St. Lawrence began to sizzle in the minds of tour organizers. The St. Lawrence could not go anywhere now without being described as "mighty," and its blessings "comparable to what is to be found anywhere in the world." A rating system using stars was applied to the "attractions," and the St. Lawrence became a constellation.

Journalists stringing for foreign travel magazines were hooked, landed, fêted and returned to their homelands to produce glossy hymn sheets in praise of the river. Gradually, the lower St. Lawrence was remoulded into an enticing environment, part of what the marketeers labelled the New Atlantic Frontier. It became a "destination."

The pushing and shoving worked. The number of cruise ships parked at Québec and Vieux Montréal began to rise. The smokeless funnels of various shipping lines were added to the skylines of the river's twin major cities, and a new set of postcards was hatched with great wedgelike white ships posed like supermodels against the Québec waterfront, the ramparts and the Château Frontenac arranged in the background.

The great white ships that now work the St. Lawrence are entertainment pavilions with a whiff of art deco, floating Las Vegas hotels with casinos at their hearts and kitchens in their bellies that decorate raw food with the skill of fashion designers, producing menus that would make Henry VIII smile. The clients of these aquatic mansions are destination hunters wielding credit cards named after precious metals, who collect scenery and places on digital cameras. Unlike their predecessors, who came into the river's harbours with roots ready to plant, the cruise people are merely passing through, their lives already made elsewhere.

Just before the end of the twentieth century, a foreign-flag cruise vessel entered the St. Lawrence, went sailing past Montréal, negotiated the length of the Seaway and penetrated into the Great Lakes, finally docking at Chicago. This was a feat that had not happened for twenty-two years, and it took a special ship to execute it. The C. *Columbus* is capable of carrying four hundred and twenty passengers, and she was custom-built for the Seaway's lock and lift-bridge system. Retractable wings on the bridge fold in on hinges to make it narrower, and the sides are close to vertical. (Most cruise ships tend to bulge out as they rise, a design feature that excludes them from the Seaway's high-sided locks.) Thus, the entire river has now become cruisable.

There is no doubt that the invasion of the cruise ships and their tourists will alter the look and feel of the river in the twenty-first century, just as each wave of strangers has done before. The saying "perception is reality" is true enough, but reality also has a habit of adapting itself to fit perception. The terrible paradox of modern tourism is that, in taking you somewhere different, all the different places become the same. Beauty becomes entertainment, wildlife becomes a chorus line, history becomes quaint. All of this is inevitable, but for true travellers seeking something deeper than shopping and sightseeing, there are better ways to get to know the St. Lawrence.

A secondary fleet of smaller, middle-class touring ships have risen up and are offering shorter, cheaper and more informative visits. Quartered in simple, casino-less comfort, one forgoes ostentation and instead attends to the local historians and naturalists brought on board, who supply knowledge rather than information snacks. It is still tourism, prefixed by the nouveau tag "eco," but the river is treated with respect.

In 1997, a freighter company called Canmar, a shortening of Canadian Maritime, began taking passengers to Europe, one way or return, on two of their container ships, the *Fortune* and the *Courage*. Departure is from the Racine Container Terminal in Montréal (an authentic experience in itself), the accommodation is familiar to any university student, and the spicy meals reflect the gastronomy of the crew, which is mostly Indian. For this transatlantic journey you will need a calendar as well as a watch.

Once you have found your cabin, unpack a ration of books and then make for the upper deck. I recommend starting with Stephen Leacock's *Montreal: Seaport and City*, written in 1944 when he was seventy; then moving on to Hugh MacLennan's *Rivers of Canada: The St. Lawrence*; the University of Toronto's reprint of the 1874 *Tales of the St. Lawrence* by Gardner Chapin; a fictional account by Andrea Barrett of the terrible events of 1847 on Grosse-Île called *Ship Fever*; and *The Oxford Book of the Sea* edited by Jonathan Raban. Eight days, many pages and much swelling ocean later, you are in Felixstowe, England.

18

BY THE RIVERS OF BABYLON

The river flows on into the next generation
(above: Brockville, ON).

On the twenty-fourth of August, 1996, two dozen people went for a swim in the St. Lawrence, among them a doctor and a geographer. It was a warm, sunny day, so there was nothing especially courageous about their dip. It was where they swam that was impressive—in the busy, brown-water Louise Basin in the port of Québec. A decade earlier, any thoughts of bathing there would have been contrary to medical advice, but there had been a sea shift in the quality of the St. Lawrence during those ten years. Now the doctor, treading water in the midst of large ships, spoke cautiously of oases of relative purity reappearing along the river, making bathing possible once again.

The swim made the newspapers, as most swims do not, and it was reported as if a much-loved entertainer had made a comeback after overcoming a severe drug problem.

For the voyageurs of the seventeenth century, paddling their grand canoes along the St. Lawrence, the concept of self-contamination was inconceivable. In mid-paddle they often refreshed themselves using a "canoe cup," a ladle in the shape of a hollow breast, carved from wood or rendered in pewter, dipping it in the clear water, then pouring the contents down a warm throat in one clean motion. Back then, the relatively few Indians and voyageurs had nothing to fear from taking a mouthful of St. Lawrence. Lacking anything much in the way of technology, they had nothing much to pollute it with. And the ratio of potential polluters to the volume of river was almost negligible.

Gradually, dipping a canoe cup into the river became a risky business. Try it in the mid-1800s, away from a sewage-strewn harbour, and you might escape illness, but an 1850-vintage gulp of Lachine Canal water was a drink from a tainted cauldron. In time, outboard motors and discharging freighters swept down the highway, leaving an oily wake. Meanwhile, hornets' nests of urban dwellers pointed their derrières at the river and let fly on a daily basis, unwittingly adding E. coli to the mix. The factories and mills of the big five polluting centres—Montréal, Sorel, Cornwall, Trois-Rivières and Massena—laid down wood, clay and plastic sphincters that piped away industrial waste. The chemical industry, full of itself after World War II, offered its alchemy to business and agriculture, and potions of PCBs and pesticides made their way to the water table.

By 1985, every day of the year, the equivalent weight in copper of one well-fed man was being dumped into the river. In addition, the weight of five men of chromium, ten each of zinc and lead, and several hundred of iron splashed into the soup. Horror stories of toxic outrage reached the bar stool, and riverine legends were born of giant worms occupying acres of barren riverbed, one end anchored in the sludge, the other blindly waving in the dead water. Belugas were discovered washed up on shore, murdered by modernity, the corpses disposed of not as meaty carcasses but as lumps of toxic waste. It took only four hundred years, a blink of the river's eye, but by 1990 man could look into the shit-filled, oil-stained, gaseous, toxin-riddled, reconfigured, muddy, crapulous, humiliated St. Lawrence River—and see his own reflection.

The usual suspects for this environmental crime were not hard to name. They were us, in towns and on farms, working and resting on the banks of the St. Lawrence. Additional donors lived on the sibling rivers and the Great Lakes, where thirty thousand chemicals were in industrial use, feeding the main flow of the St. Lawrence. In Quebec, well over two thousand manufacturers were deliberately siphoning toxic by-products into the river. Add in the oops! factor—the three hundred and seven known spills of hazardous waste between 1978 and 1988—and the river was a chemical soup whose homicidal effect on living cells was impossible to figure.

Meanwhile, almost half of the six million thirsty people living on the edges of the St. Lawrence drew their drinking needs from the river, from a trough that stretched as far as Lauzon, the last town able to draw off non-saline water. A vicious cycle of input and output had been established: take dirty water out, clean it, dirty it again, put it back. Technological advance always comes with a built-in debit, and the St. Lawrence had paid with its purity, with—and there is no better word—its spirit, the primal poetry of nature. For every part per million of crap slid into the river over the centuries, an equal part of poetry had been forced out, and by 1990 it was time to offer up some compassionate economics as an act of contrition.

All environmental movements turn to nature for a face to put on the cause. Two hundred different species of fish swim in the St. Lawrence, and one hundred and twenty species of bird nest on its wetlands, so there was plenty to choose from. Without anyone officially deciding, it was the toxic belugas—the lost tribe of Arctic whales that rode the Labrador cold current into the St. Lawrence estuary—that became the river's mascot.

Belugas, the white whales, as Cartier called them, were a fine choice. Beluga skeletons eleven thousand years old have been found on the St. Lawrence riverbed, but after colonization their bones began falling to the bottom at a greater rate than could be replaced. They were hunted without mercy or fatigue. In 1870, five hundred belugas, the same number as the entire present population, were killed on a single tide, and until 1960 one could still collect a bounty on them. Now they are protected from direct slaughter, but indirectly they are still dying. It would be no surprise if they were extinct by now, but they continue to resist the chemical holocaust bestowed on them, and resistance is always a cause for hope.

Dan Brunton, a soldier-bee Ontario naturalist capable of driving off much larger enemies, once witnessed their persistence first-hand. In 1975, Brunton was two years out of college, attending a conference in Québec on communications in the nature business. Finding himself in a tidal zone for the first time since graduation, he played hooky and crossed the river to Rivière-du-Loup. Standing on the ferry dock, looking out to the mud flats where shallow water raced to the pull of the moon in white-capped waves, and Arctic eider duck flashed past, Brunton couldn't help but notice the garbage littering the water. As though to confirm his worst thoughts, he looked directly below and saw a fridge. Then the fridge moved, and a larger fridge appeared beside it. It was a mother beluga and her calf, the porcelain white of the calf's skin close enough to enamel to fool even a naturalist. Despite the centuries of abuse, these ancient mammals continued to breed. If the remaining belugas could take all that and survive, perhaps the St. Lawrence, symbolically, could do the same. Save the belugas and, in so doing, save the river.

The first step in redeeming the river was the decision, taken jointly in Quebec, Ontario and New York State, to dipstick the river and determine the level and nature of toxicity. By the end of the eighties, reports were coming out of the St. Lawrence Centre in Montréal trying to answer the simple question, how undrinkable is the water? At the back of the reports were some shy, stammering conclusions. They said that of the forty-five testing stations along the Quebec section of the river, all but one were "located in waters of deplorable bacteriological quality." That the river was, so to speak, officially full of shit was not news; groups like Friends of the St. Lawrence and TIARA, a property-owners' association in the Thousand Islands, had long raised their own levels of complaint. And the plants, fish, animals, insects and birds had registered their outrage with death and deformity—the crossed jaws of a pike like a pair of twisted scissors, or the third eye nestled in a frog's throat.

Governments are notorious for requesting information and then cold-shouldering it. The true business of governments is to govern greed and administer compassion, but the overlords of the St. Lawrence, by ignoring the problem for so long, had consistently done the opposite, filing the river under S for sewer, not R for renewable resource. Nevertheless, there was something about the scale of the St. Lawrence's fall from grace that prompted a reversal of inertia. The "something" was not shame, nor did the governments feel blame for what had happened. Perhaps it was the historical significance of the St. Lawrence, its role as the mother river. More likely, it was about property values and votes. Whatever the means, the end was a just one, and public money to pay for the majestic cleanup was forthcoming.

As the scummy tide of history was slowly turned back, the St. Lawrence began to float in acronyms. Dividing the labour, the river was partitioned into two budgetary sections—one might call them parishes—with the dividing line at Cornwall. West of the line, Ontario and New York State acted in unison; to the east, Quebec was on its own. The westerly pollution-busters identified hot spots and named them AOCs, Areas of Concern, while their easterly counterparts called them ZIPs, Zones d'Intervention Publique. An acronym attack was then launched on the river, which was to be SLAPed and RAPed. SLAP, a Québécois five-year plan that got underway in 1988, was the St. Lawrence Action Plan, while RAP, the Remedial Action Plan, was its western counterpart. The Holy Grail for the SLAP and RAP groups, the impossible dream, was to make the water drinkable again.

With environmentalists and scientists on one side of the table, business on the other, and government leaning both ways at once without falling over, talk became action. By the century's turn, SLAP had become Vision 2000, RAP was still going strong, and the ZIP and AOC committees were working their way down one of the world's greatest spring-cleaning lists. There had been preliminary acts of delayed hygiene all along the two-thousand-mile St. Lawrence shoreline. A small mountain of tainted soil was shifted by the Reynolds Metals Plant on the American side. Discharge waters were now filtered as they left Massena's industrial sites. A rayon factory in Ontario was told to take prophylactic precautions against its tendency to make spills, and in Quebec the top fifty polluting companies were named, and shortly thereafter began reducing their poisons. Farmers, who make chemical warfare on the bug, their greatest enemy, had reduced their use of a particularly nasty pesticide to the point where the St. Lawrence fish were almost Mirex-free.

There was also redemption for the holy trio of lakes, St-Francis, St-Louis and St-Pierre. The St. Lawrence takes its time flowing through these lakes, and like a poor rinse cycle this allows sludge to build up that is rich in heavy precious metals, like mercury. The middle lake, St-Louis, the one nearest Montréal, was underlined with the worst sediment, while the other two ran close behind. The fact that the St. Lawrence is downstream from the Great Lakes compounded the problem. Step one was to find a way for the many dredgers, which keep the lakes' deep-water channels deep and whisk up the sediments, to remove the sludge without overclouding the water. They did.

By the late 1990s, people were talking about the river in new tones, even poetic ones. The almost biblical cast of the following quote, from the opening remarks of two scientists who spend their daily lives worrying about the St. Lawrence, is testament to the way the river is shedding its old skin:

> Sadly, Ontario's water, like that within much of the rest of the earth, tells a story of a culture in which water has not been afforded true respect. Yet water's voice will not be silenced. Perhaps out of pure necessity, or perhaps from the strength of deeply buried human sensitivity, our culture is beginning to appreciate that life cannot be sustained without this most precious of elements.

The two men end on an upbeat note.

> Although the fallout from human-induced prob-
> lems will be manifested for many generations,
> signs of hope are beginning to appear.

Signs that now line up in the right direction.

Despite the triage and subsequent new health regime imposed on the river, the scientists and environmentalists working in Montréal's St. Lawrence Centre and Cornwall's St. Lawrence River Institute—benign institutions both, which have replaced the military forts that once guarded the river—know they must not lower their guard, especially when they hear statements like "one of the least polluted rivers in the world" and "cleanest it's been in fifty years" pour from politicians' lips. The river flows on into the next generation, and the cleaner their inheritance, the easier it will be to keep it that way.

There is also no point to making the river safe for humans if they can't get at it; clean it and they will come—but can they access it? Much of the river's edge is out of bounds to the average recreationalist. Léonce Naud, the geographer in that Québec bathing party of 1996, put this rhetorical question to reporters as he symbolically treaded water, demonstrating that he thought all is not yet well:

> In Quebec, there's been the river of historical
> accounts, the river of poets, the river of big
> money and . . . the river of fecal coliforms. Then
> appeared the river of whales, fish, birds, insects
> and plants of all kinds. As for me, a two-legged
> frog, held back behind the guardrails rising
> above the sea or confined to a pedestrian

crossway—what use for me is left of the St. Lawrence River?

More, one hopes—more beaches, more riverside parks.

In unison, the extended family of the world's great rivers became dysfunctional in the twentieth century, the sins of the fathers added to the sins of the sons and daughters. It will be up to this freshly unwrapped century to decide if the great rivers live or die. The St. Lawrence has been moved from the intensive care ward and is now listed as critical but improving. However, the day will never come again when a canoe cup can be dipped into the St. Lawrence for a refreshing quaff of clear, clean water.

Away in the St. Lawrence there would be a flash as an immense white fish jumped. Against the little gulfs and rock coasts at my feet were washing a few white logs of driftwood.

—Rupert Brooke, on the beach at Tadoussac, 1913

Two and a half thousand years ago, the Greek philosopher Heraclitus said that you cannot step into the same river twice. In the case of the late twentieth-century St. Lawrence, that was a good thing. And, as I saw one day with my own eyes at Tadoussac, as nine of them paraded past me a few feet away on their journey downriver, the belugas are still there.

Second Watch

RIDING THE WAVES

The
flat banks, stretching along the river.
Reeds and rushes. And sea grasses, long-stemmed eel-
grass, swaying in the wind. Like ripples along the water's edge.
The groom waves his whip against the July sky. Points out the islands.
Names each one, slowly, as if they were human beings . . . Île aux
Corneilles, Île Providence, Île aux Patins, Grosse-Île . . . The
long expanse of muddy banks. The smell of low tide fills the
air. The water blends with the sky. You can't see
over to the other side.

—Anne Hébert, *Kamouraska*, 1970

19

RUNNING DOWN THE RIVER ROAD

With boatyards and boathouses jammed into every inch of the waterfront like books on a shelf (above: Alexandria Bay, Thousand Islands).

The ferry to America from the southern side of Wolfe Island is a modest affair, leaving Point Alexandria and taking no more than five minutes, at the rate of a dollar a minute, to get four or five cars over to the States. Disembarkation is at Cape Vincent's simple wharf, where an unhurried customs official emerges from a hut and in a northern New York accent submits you, if you are Canadian, to a gentle interrogation. When he's done, he tells you what kind of day to have, says "Go ahead, then" and you do, into a foreign country.

A few years after the American War of Independence, and again shortly after the War of 1812, the United States and

Britain (Canada's headquarters) sat down and argued out where exactly one country ended and the other began. On land, the argument was easy enough to settle—the forty-ninth parallel continued to fit the bill—but the border's stretch on water through the Great Lakes and down the St. Lawrence took some careful drawing with a sharp pencil. Now, a zigzag line, like a solved join-the-dots puzzle, runs down the river between the neighbouring shores, starting about a mile off Cape Vincent, hard by Wolfe Island. An expert angler could cast from the wharf at Point Alexandria and catch an American fish. The international border then dodges through the islands for a hundred and twenty miles until it reaches St. Regis and the Akwesasne reserve, where Quebec takes over.

Cape Vincent is an unflustered town, its population holding steady apart from in the cemetery. The ample clapboard houses are set a respectful distance from each other, there being no need for them to crowd. The Cape has a lighthouse, at Tibbet's Point, one of the seven historic towers pinned to the landscape between here and Chippewa Bay. Built in 1827, the Tibbet's Point light shines its automated, unmanned beam first over Lake Ontario, then down the St. Lawrence as it makes its rotations. The lighthouse is the eastern end of the Seaway Trail, a series of stopovers and "things to do" that the Americans are boosting as a tourism route, shining up the old battlegrounds and heritage homes, putting in pocket-sized parks, promoting the chance to reel in fifty-pound carp or see river otters at play. The northern parts of most American states that border Canada tend to be lower-income zones, the residents driving older models of cars, and that is true here in New York too, except on those island sanctuaries that fly the Stars and Stripes on the flagpole, where the big money is. The Americans, to boost the dollar flow in Jefferson and St. Lawrence counties, are turning to the past and what remains of the river's natural beauty to provide some revenue for the future.

Standing on Tibbet's Point, looking back at Canada across the moat of calm water, I become suffused with that unanchored feeling I always get when travelling in the States, a sensation of being pressed like a weed onto a page of someone else's history book. It's a big fat book I've read snatches of, and keep seeing lying around Canadian living rooms, where it is much discussed. It's an exciting, exasperating read.

The Americans did not reach today by the same route as Canadians. Their history is entwined with ours, and both stories were nurtured in the same European pot, but the colonial sagas diverged after Columbus set them in motion. To be sure, the boats leaving the Cape Vincent marina travel in miles per hour, not kilometres, the meals in the main street eateries reach right to the edge of the plate and would choke a horse, the accent is bolder, the pervasive cheery politeness a little thinner, but those are superficial differences. The essential point is that the Americans got out from under the British a lot sooner than the Canadians, who have yet to complete the trick, and that may explain the Stateside tendency to individualism that is only just taking hold in Canada. The main difference, I've decided, is that Canadians worry about becoming Americans, but Americans never worry about becoming Canadians. So we make our sorties into the States with our eyes wide open.

Cape Vincent has its share of historical stories, and it retails them in its own unfussy way. It boasts, for instance, a connection with Napoleon Bonaparte, who never set foot in the place. The Cape is French in origin, named after a count Vincent LeRay, and after the Emperor was exiled some of his followers migrated to America. Count LeRay gave the immigrants a chunk of his land on which to start again. In their more nostalgic moments these old soldiers, four thousand miles from home, would plan a hit-and-run to pluck their exiled leader from St. Helena, but Napoleon died in 1821, and that was that. No small town ever misses a handy legend, however, so the story goes that one of the houses that used to stand in Cape Vincent, from all accounts an odd-looking cup-and-saucer arrangement, was being prepared for the retrieved Napoleon. In fact, the house was the residence of a French expatriate, with a room devoted to Napoleon in it. It burnt down in 1867.

Cape Vincent is fully American now, but it still throws a party on Bastille Day, the way other towns go a little crazy on St. Patrick's Day. The Cape stays in touch with the river via its pilot station at the transition point between lake and river, and the locals still hold an annual Blessing of the Fishing Fleet festival in mid-June (although it was cancelled in 1999 because the river was so low that sailors were walking out to their beached sailing vessels). The local fisheries station has a quaint aquarium in the basement, and one of the rebels (the local schoolteacher) hanged for taking part in the futile 1838 invasion of Canada at the windmill near Prescott was from here. It is a typical river town, not unlike its cousins on the opposite bank in design, although much better armed.

Down at the docks of Cape Vincent, I hope to come upon some wooden boats. This was once wooden boat country, and a century ago skiffs were as common here as RVs are now. But they are thin on the water in Cape Vincent, so I head east along the Seaway Trail with the flow of the river to Clayton, where I'll find more wooden boats than you could shake an oar at. On the Trail, through the treeline and the trailer parks, I catch glimpses of Carleton Island, where several Mississauga chiefs signed away most of the northern side of the St. Lawrence to the British in 1783 for the usual price of booze, blankets and a bit of money. The British promised to let the Americans have the island at a treaty meeting in Paris the same year, but because it had a nice fort on it, the local British commanders refused to give it up. Thirty years later the Americans, within days of war being declared, captured the fort and took it prisoner. By then it consisted of exactly one sergeant, three invalid troops and two women.

Clayton is the mahogany mecca for "woodheads," the collective noun for people like me who are borderline obsessives about wooden boats. Apart from their largely vanished craftsmanship, wooden boats are a symbol of a lapsed era in St. Lawrence history, one that, like all eras, is best viewed through a rose-coloured telescope. Certainly they are an ambivalent symbol, possessed of poetic lines but so expensive to own and maintain that they were for the privileged only, ensconced in their Thousand Islands mansions. To the wealthy go the spoils and, like America itself, the boats made envy and puritan unease rise together in the throats of the economically challenged. We now have a new set of fibreglass symbols, but the age of wood lives on in Clayton and every year, a few days prior to the first of August, the smell of wood oil, varnish and reawakened outboard engines begins to concentrate over Clayton and waft outwards in concentric circles from the Antique Boat Museum. The museum's annual regatta, a sort of boating Brigadoon, starts today, and I'm driving into the swirl of it.

The town of Clayton sticks like a thumb into the St. Lawrence, with French Creek Bay on the thumb's left-hand side. The bay was the start of an old booze-smuggling route down into New York State, and the setting for some artillery action in the War of 1812, when an American shoreline battery twice took on several British gunboats and sailing ships and drove them off. When peace returned after 1814, William

Angel rigged up his timber rafts in French Creek Bay and started a quality shipbuilding industry that lasted over a century. Clayton also had its own bad-tempered pirate who lived and died here. Bill Johnston bust out of Kingston jail in 1814 and took a fast ship across the border, and he was the same man who ran his armed barge aground during the attack on the windmill at Prescott in 1837. While he was on the loose, the British tried to catch him, but they never did, and with a pardon from his exhausted pursuers Johnston retired from pirating. The line of work he took up next is mentioned in a folk ballad by Alex Sinclair:

> Both governments soon put a price on my head
> 'twas then to these beautiful islands I fled
> with a ship that could dance like a bird on a breeze
> I robbed and I plundered so easy
>
> We burned and sank the pride of the St. Lawrence fleet
> but the citizens failed to fall down at our feet
> those Loyalist fools didn't want to be free
> not for William Lyon Mackenzie
>
> When I got pardoned out of the Albany jail
> nearby where I'd burned down the *Sir Robert Peel*
> they made a lighthouse keeper of me
> and I live out my life a bit more cautiously
> but sometimes I still dream of days of past glory
> with William Lyon Mackenzie

The most recent anti-establishment celebrity to inhabit Clayton was Abbie Hoffman, a famous radical outlaw from the sixties. He turned up in the town shortly after the end of that mythic decade, using the telltale surname Freed, and when the American Corps of Engineers got the idea in their heads of making the river navigable from Montréal to the Great Lakes in winter, Hoffman, smelling an old enemy, pulled the area's opposing social groups together into the Save the River coalition. The river savers routed the Engineers not once but twice, in 1978 and 1984, and the St. Lawrence remains shut at that end when the ice comes. Hoffman revealed who he really was in the course of the campaign, and for a while Clayton attracted journalists as well as tourists. Hoffman was found dead of a drug overdose in 1989.

The clamour of Clayton's shipbuilding days, once a steady hum of planes and hammers, has fallen to the occasional whisper in the back alleys of Frenchtown when repairs are made to an injured wooden runabout. When the railway stuck its nose into Clayton in the late nineteenth century, the town wrestled with itself as to whether to carry on making ships or milk the tourists. Tourism won, but a stubborn line of store owners and innkeepers on the tip of the thumb have resisted attempts to move them and open up the river view, so the downtown has a pleasant air of arrested development. A muskie-shaped weather vane graces the old opera house. The world-record muskie—an ounce short of seventy pounds—was caught just off Clayton, and it was here, in the oldest part of town, on the steps of Dick La Port's barbershop, that the fishing guides used to gather, load their pipes and discuss ways to hide smuggled booty in a skiff.

The Antique Boat Museum, a woodless modern main building of blue-grey siding and glass flanked by some new wooden outbuildings, takes up the nail of Clayton's thumb. This being the day before the official opening to the public, there are tents going up on the grass opposite the museum entrance, a small fair of boat paraphernalia. One stall is devoted entirely to model classic outboard motors. They are the size of a small finger and cost as much as the real thing. Another entrepreneur is selling a miracle varnish in a can: "One coat, one hour, one-derful!" An antique croquet set from Abercrombie and Fitch is going for seven hundred American dollars, a remnant of the days of leisurely summer games on the lawn of Thousand Islands House followed by single malt Scotch on the porch at sunset. On the road between the fair and the museum a barker is extolling the virtues of his "e-boat," a battery-driven, solid wood reproduction of a four-seater launch, with a canvas awning like you might see over a Dickensian market fruit stall. This runabout, a thing for commuting to and from picnics, is manufactured on the St. Lawrence, in Montréal. Being electric-driven, it moves at a gentle trot, and that too is promoted as virtuous.

The grounds of the fair, busy with exhibitors setting up, consists of a large hall stuffed with motorized beauties, several outlying barns, and long finger docks hosting private boats, their languorous reflections forming watercolours in the river. Several of the boats in the main hall are over a century old and still seaworthy. Gazing with envious eyes at these wood sculptures, I know them for what they are: talismans of luxury once owned by people who could afford that most precious of commodities, time to idle away. The king of the castle in the main hall is the *Pardon Me*, the era's last, teak-scented gasp, forty-eight feet from bow to stern, fashioned from the finest African and Philippine timbers at a total cost of a thousand dollars a foot—in 1948. The engine was a supercharged V12 Packard that sucked up aviation fuel at the rate of one hundred and fifty gallons an hour, outrageous then and immoral now.

I have long cherished a desire to ride in one of these thoroughbreds, and when the chance comes for a berth in the exhibitors' afternoon outing, I take it. As the drizzle that has marred the day clears and the prodigal sun begins to shine, the *Zipper*, a cabined runabout of uncommon luxury, pulls out into the river like a state carriage at the head of a line of exquisite wooden boats, racehorses trotting down to the field for exercise. I'm sitting next to the Benoits from Plattsburgh, and the talk is of wood and its blessings. In 1985, Jack Benoit took third-best in the show for his "thirty-three," meaning a boat built in that year. "The summer I met him, he mostly had his butt in the air, leaning into that damn boat," Susan Benoit says.

As we serenade the day, I notice the sheer volume of waving going on as landlubbers and passing boats acknowledge us. Waving is more than a common courtesy on the St. Lawrence; it is a statement about you and where you are on the river of life. Boaters, because they are alfresco, wave to each other all the time and so develop a signature that can be read from afar. "Is that the Boswells?" "Wave and see." "No, can't be. Left-handed, terribly straightforward." "A rental, then." The raised hand, fingers loose, palm out, is the base wave, with embellishments added to that, building a personality into the gesture the way golfers or tennis players customize their address of the ball or serve. A touch to the forehead on the upstroke, rotation of the wrist when the arm is upright (known as "doing a queen"), holding for an extra beat at the apex, and many more choreographed variations grace the river's daily exchanges.

After threading through islands large and small, the *Zipper* pulls into the Boldt yacht house. Boldt built the Tudor-esque, larger-than-life barn for his wooden boat collection on Wellesley Island, and the doors are cathedral-sized, capable of admitting a yacht with its mast erect. Boldt had a passion for water races, and in 1910 he commissioned a fleet of twenty twenty-eight-foot runabouts with killer engines from a builder in

Ogdensburg. He distributed them among his chums on Millionaires' Row and they raced them annually. Six of them survive. Two of them, called *This* and *That*, are on display in the boathouse, proof that the difference between men and boys is the price of their toys.

After lunch on the grounds of an island mansion built in 1892 by a Cuban millionaire with the unlikely name of Marx and largely preserved as it was then, we return to the museum, which is now buzzing with enthusiasts. After rubbing a few cedar-strip canoes and gasping at the reserve price of the boats due for auction at the end of the regatta, I pause in the main hall and look at a freestanding map portraying the exploits of Homer Dodge, true son of the river. In 1904, at the age of seventeen, Homer made an epic, five-hundred-mile voyage around the Thousand Islands in a rowing skiff. As the bookend to that youthful act, he circumnavigated the considerable girth of Grindstone Island in 1977 at the age of ninety, accompanied by his son. That turned out to be Homer's last journey, and he died five years later. There are men and women like Homer dispersed along the river who over the course of their lives map out the landscape before them, voluntarily locking the geography of one small sliver of the planet into their heads, the way the St. Lawrence Iroquois must once have done. What is a maze to others becomes intimate to them, and in the process the explorers are of course mapping out themselves.

On the road from Clayton to the next town of note, Alexandria, the motels are well spaced and the river is parked behind rows of caravans or trees, occasionally popping into view. The welcoming, old-fashioned arch at the entrance to Alexandria Bay is the kind favoured by many a small town along the upper St. Lawrence. Countless Americans who were children in the thirties associate passing under this arch with the beginning of summer holidays. The International Bridge that downloads Americans onto Wellesley Island and thence over the Canadian span into Ontario stands in distant silhouette over the town.

Alex, as Alexandria Bay is known, is built on a bumpy rock base, with boatyards and boathouses jammed into every inch of the snaking waterfront like books on a narrow shelf. On the short main street there are rhinestone amusements—glittering ways to shake money out of a stranger's pocket—and a floating hotel. Boats leave for Boldt Castle, it seems, every time I turn around, and I can see the folly from the end of Main Street, tourists swarming over it like ants on a hill. In the middle of Main Street, ensconced in the window of a dual-purpose art gallery and antique store, there's a new, sleek, full-sized rowing skiff, its various woods in a natural, varnished state. The price tag is six and a half thousand American dollars, and its creator, working to a classic design, has the sonorous name of Ringer.

Away across town, past the faded glories and neon entertainments of the busy side streets, I walk into the old Cornwall Brothers emporium. The store is the second on this site, the first having burnt down in 1866. A blockish stone building perched over the river, it is decked out as a combination folk museum, town archives, hangout for the local historical society, and seller of some things old, some things new. Several historical society types, people with pleasantly unpadded shoulders that echo the lines of the antique furniture, are discussing something in low, non-cellphone voices.

Through the large windows at the back I can see the Sunken Rock lighthouse, which has shone its light hereabouts for more than a hundred and fifty years, while the buildings back on the mainland fell down or were pulled out like teeth and replaced with synthetics. Just upstream from the lighthouse, in November

1974, the winter residents of Alex witnessed one of the river's most recent shipwrecks, when the *Roy A. Jodrey* struck a shoal. The boat was carrying over twenty tons of iron pellets, and it sank after a four-hour struggle in two hundred and fifty feet of water. It's still there.

Sitting in the middle of the worn parquet floor of Cornwall Brothers is an elegant wooden boat, painted white, that almost sank out of sight but didn't—the *Polywog*. According to the information affixed to it, the *Polywog* was built around the time Homer Dodge was born, and among the many boaters who used it were a young couple taking their honeymoon in 1905 along the Rideau Canal. Later in its life, the *Polywog* almost died in a local backyard, but it was rescued and restored by a gentleman in his nineties, one of those endearing people who hate to see objects die and are the bane of consumerism. This one has a dinky inboard "putt-putt" motor, a one-cylinder job with no carburetor. The only two skiffs I've seen in Alexandria today are like Homer Dodge's journeys, separated in age by a lifetime, one with a story to tell, the other waiting to start one.

Time grants beauty to anything made with the best of intentions and respect for the craft of it, and time has only served to make more beautiful the St. Lawrence skiffs that adorn museums and shop windows. A small rebirth of skiff building is taking place on both sides of the river around here. Craftspeople are blowing the dust off old moulds, and great-grandchildren are returning to the family tradition. No era is retrievable, but there is no reason why the new should entirely crowd out the old, as though all that went before were somehow less. There are designs that deserve to endure. The swish of skiff oars will never be loud enough to drown out the outboards, but happily, neither will it fall completely silent.

From Alexandria, I could carry on to Ogdensburg and

Massena on the remainder of the Seaway Trail—drop into
Larry's taxidermy studio and catch a few whopping fish stories,
or stare at Frederic Remington's beautiful, delicate oil paintings
of the river in his museum—but Canada calls and I'm starting
to feel a little gouty from all these confectionery boats. Taking
the bridge over to Wellesley Island, I pay the toll to get out of
America and smile in genuine innocence at the humourless
customs officer. Once on the adjacent Hill Island, Canadian
soil, I pull into the parking lot of the SkyDeck, an ugly, efficient lookout tower that rises four hundred feet like a vast
sword stabbed into the ground.

The open-air top of this giant bald eagle's aerie allows a spectacular three-hundred-and-sixty-degree view of the St. Lawrence
River valley, and almost the entire American stretch of the
St. Lawrence is visible with only a slight rotation of the head.
The dominant species from this height are the trees covering
the granitic flatlands that stretch away on either side of the
river. The St. Lawrence runs down the middle like a skipping
rope dropped in short grass, Lake Ontario a hazy mirage on the
right, the end of the islands in the far distance on the left, and
the stern of a big cargo ship slipping down the eastern horizon.
The region's beauty shines up from this height, a beauty so ele-
mental that the concerted efforts of two nations separated by
only a thin line of history have not yet managed to spoil it.

As I drink in the view, the woman next to me, an American, nudges my shoulder and points down to a field directly
below the tower. Three deer are grazing, one of them a fawn.
"Stateless and tax-free," the woman says, and the deer, as
though at a signal, all take one step forward.

20

ISLANDS IN THE STREAM

*It's a geographical novelty that everyone
who comes here has to be shown.*

"Actually, I was conceived on the river," Bud Andress told me
the first time we met, a fact that makes him part of a select
tribe. Bud is a big, loose-limbed, amphibious man who seems
involved in a slow, deliberate choreography set to his own
rhythm. He is a warden in Canada's smallest national park,
measured in acres of solid ground, the St. Lawrence Islands
National Park, which will be celebrating its centenary in 2004.
Bud lives on Hill Island, within sight of the Canadian span of
the International Bridge, and was trapped there for ten days
during the ice storm of 1998.

Bud is the great-grandson of George Andress of LaRue

Mills, the skiff builder, and several of his relatives, including Ed, Ray and Elmer Andress, were skiff builders too. Bud recalls being four years old and standing among the smell of fresh shavings and varnish in his grandfather Ray's workshop in Gananoque. Like other Canadian skiffs, an Andress boat was fuller at the ends than the streamlined American version.

To his chagrin, Bud does not own an Andress skiff. A couple of years ago a man who possessed not one but two Andress skiffs—one built by Bud's grandfather, the other by his great-grandfather—moved out of the islands. He took one of the skiffs with him and put the other up for auction. Bud heard about it a day too late. It sold for three thousand dollars, a price so low it provokes laughter. His quest to have an Andress skiff, to sail as it were in his own history, continues. "I do have a blue-point Siamese cat called Skiff," Bud will say, if anyone asks him about heirlooms.

There being no business to go into any more, Bud did not ascend into the family skiff-building tradition, but he does spend most of his days in a boat. It is part of his daily duties, and has been for twenty years, to move among beauty, in a boat equipped with a first-aid kit and stethoscope, a firefighting hose and a board for immobilizing trauma victims. Because nature and some segments of humanity have trouble sharing the same space, it is also part of his duties to deal with the effects of alcohol, overzealous anglers and outboard outlaws, with fines or a rare day in court. As Bud puts it, "There are occasional lapses in respect for my authority." That's a bad day for Bud, and for the disrespecter.

The day I spent on the upper St. Lawrence with Bud Andress was blanketed in the kind of sunshine that tricks you into believing the snow might not come this year. He sat as easily as a cowboy on a range horse at the controls of his inboard/outboard—a style of boat that locals call an I/O—and kept up a steady stream of facts and opinions that began as we pulled away from his front door.

We moved straight away to the International Rift, a miniature chasm between two islands. The rift is the closest Canada and the States get anywhere along their entire mutual border where they are separated by water. The gap itself is not wide, about the same as walking from the front of a bus to the back. It has been a favourite postcard subject for a century or more—the Grand Niche as opposed to the Grand Canyon.

Because it is so narrow, the current in the rift is strong. In fact, the previous month it had claimed the life of an American soldier. The young private, after a night out in Kingston's thriving bars, had been in the process of trying to smuggle two Canadian female runaways into the nearby American army base, Fort Drum. The joke among locals is that Fort Drum is in a state of readiness to invade Canada, if Quebec secedes and the country falls into civil war.

One of the girls made it safely across the rift. Then the soldier attempted the same route, and went under. The girl still on Canadian soil went for help, but the boy was gone, his life added to the annual statistic of people who die in the river. "Most of the people who drown in the river are the result of a boating accident or a spill while taking a leak. Alcohol is generally a factor. A lot of the guys we pull up still have their flies undone," Bud said.

As we paused between the two walls of stone and reflected on stupid ways to die, I remarked how peaceful it seemed. "This place is like the 401 highway in July, boats nose to tail," Bud said. "It's a geographical novelty that everyone who comes here has to be shown, and take a picture of." That day, by chance, we had the place to ourselves. I broke into a few bars of *O Canada* and set up a standing wave of echo between the rift walls, to which I added a snatch of *The Star-Spangled Banner* in the same key. The two tunes mingled in a jazz chord.

Coming out of the rift and into open water, boats from both nations mingle freely. The park was originally intended to serve as the jointly managed plaything of the two nations. The idea was much discussed in the 1890s, when there was a standing concern on both sides of the river—even back then—that the islands' resources, attractiveness and trees would go on the real estate chopping block and become for one, not for all. The rate at which the islands were being bought up also caused a general alarm, and local citizens and newspaper proprietors petitioned hard for arrested development.

The notion of a shared park had some powerful champions on both shores, but it was spiked by federal indifference and lawyers. The lawyers were worried about reciprocal labour agreements and the possibility of Canadians working in the U.S. The idea of a joint park was worried down to nothing, and so the Canadians, in 1904, went ahead on their own. The government purchased ten whole islands plus part of another for around ten thousand dollars, and dubbed it a park, which it still is. They quickly put up seven stone pavilions to mark their territory, in peaceful mimicry of the earlier British erection of forts, and three of the pavilions are still in use. For the same subsidized fees, Americans are now as free as Canadians to take up the park's docks and camping. The freedom of southerners to trample the park is a hook that sticks in the mouth of some Canadians, whose tax dollars go to maintain the landscape. Others are more global in outlook.

One of the world's problems is too many people, and that problem reached St. Lawrence National Park in the sixties, despite the fact that the number of whole or partial islands residing within the park had risen to twenty-one. Managing a modern park requires constant attention and occasional rethinking of its bedrock philosophy. The original idea behind Canadian parks was trying to preserve the primary resource of wilderness. The ideal park was to be a place that wildlife lived in and people visited, but exploitation is a relentless trait. The fear for park staff is that, step by step, things will come under the gun of developers, thrill-seekers, hunters and resource robber barons, and somewhere in the future people will thrive in areas where the wildlife have become guests.

Defining where the balance lies between human and natural rights is the big question for Bud, and for park wardens across the country. In his job Bud drives his boat along the dotted line between these two interests, and he makes a civilized job of it. (The problem, for obvious technical reasons, is not as acute in underwater parks like the one at the mouth of the Saguenay— at least not yet.) Even as we motored along, members of the St. Lawrence National Park staff were back at the low-key headquarters in Mallorytown staring into screens, making computer portraits of the park's personality, leaving no stone or salamander unturned. In this fashion they will uncover exactly what they are attempting to preserve, and the true effect of each wave of invasion can at least be assessed.

"Air boats, for instance. They worry me," Bud said, referring to those contraptions with a fan at the back that buzz like giant water bugs over southern bayous. We were slaloming through the Lake Fleet Islands: Bloodletter, Axeman, DumFounder and Deathdealer. Someone was in a bad mood the day they were christened. The dreaded air boats are set to come north into the St. Lawrence, and they can travel on the river, frozen or liquid, year-round. "Those things sound like an airplane that never takes off, and birds fly half a mile to get away from them," Bud said, a touch of sourness in his voice. "Where will all this lead to twenty years from now? There's a section of the public wants everything open to everybody all the time in here. Myself, I sometimes think the whole area, the resident fish and fowl, just need a chance to catch their breath."

A small island ahead was drenched in concrete. In contrast to some of its neighbours, no attempt had been made on this island to blend with the surroundings. The house, the encircling retaining wall, the dock—all were concrete, as though there had been a tiny nuclear accident here and the place had been Chernobyled with cement. A fire in the 1930s had burnt the original wood cottage to the ground, and the owner vowed it wouldn't happen again. The result was as directly at odds with the territory as humanly possible, a complete breakdown in aesthetics.

In a miniature inlet on Bostwick Island, near the bottom of the Admiralty group that lie due south of Gananoque, there is a vestige of the spiritual flavour of the islands, when God, who was assumed to be an outdoorsman at heart, was alive and well here. The inlet is called Half Moon Bay, although "Should have called it Crescent Bay, because it's more that shape," Bud said as we entered it. It's a narrow sabre of water, high-sided, with a ledge of land where the halyard would be. A hundred-year-old railing is nailed into the rock, to pull on and hold fast to from a boat. Bud let the I/O drift in here on suitably low revs and pointed out the big metal box up above, holding the church organ. Sunday ecumenical services have been held here in the months of July and August without a break since 1887. As the hour for vespers (the evening service) approached, the inlet would fill with skiffs, pressed in like a good day's catch of fish in a keep net, and at the granite pulpit the minister would give a sermon that carried over the bonnets and boats before him.

Five minutes heading north at good speed took us to the often misspelled town of Gananoque. A French surveyor going up the St. Lawrence in 1685 noted that the Native people, who spoke Onondaga, seemed to call the river that feeds into the St. Lawrence Ganonocouy, meaning "flint at the mountain." Joel Stone, who got the grant in 1787 to found a town at the mouth of the river, called it either Cadanoryhqua or Ganenoquay (easy for him to say). Since then it has appeared on maps with forty-two known variations of spelling. Whatever its name, this is where Bud's family made their boats, and where he was born and raised. In the small, classy museum and archives built on the site of the old waterfront railway station, past the obligatory St. Lawrence skiff in the doorway, there's a room on the second floor full of photographic clues to the Gilded Age of the Thousand Islands, some of them large enough to step into, like Alice's looking glass.

The town was once a fishing mecca on account of the record muskie hooked here. On the limestone wall of the old Cheevers Hotel, now the Stone Street Café, there's a whitewashed board pinned at eye height for passersby. Listed on the board are record-breaking muskie catches going back to 1955. Last time I looked, the latest entry was dated June 1993, when James Blair Junior from Cape Cod landed a fish weighing forty-five pounds.

For a decade now, a summer speedboat race called the Poker Run has dominated Gananoque for one day each year, when the town fills up with a lot of people who would have trouble spelling it. A class of vessel called "cigarette" boats—basically, advertising billboards shaped like arrowheads and capable of hitting one hundred and sixty miles an hour—starts from the Gananoque waterfront and charges around a circular route of one hundred and forty-three miles, collecting a playing card at selected stops. Needless to say, with the speed limit suspended for a day, it doesn't take them long to blast around the course, and the best poker hand wins. One hundred and fifty of these rockets come from all over to compete, and well over fifty thousand thrilled people stand and watch them go blurring past. As a ritual to the demigods of speed, it is perfect.

With Gananoque behind us and the sun directly overhead, it was time to eat. We dismounted at Gordon Island and set up at a picnic table freshly etched with the initials $\mathcal{RL}$. Beside the table there was a big, double pre-war stove, a hangout and feasting site for generations of fishing guides and anglers, "drinking," Bud said, "what they called Indian coffee. A pound of coffee, whipped up with seven or eight eggs like a batter, and pour that into a huge pot of boiling water. Back up to the boil. By the time you poured, the egg had coagulated and grabbed the grinds. It's the richest, best-smelling coffee you ever had. Just don't look in the bottom."

As we fed ourselves, the act of biting on meat prompted Bud to talk about his work with upper St. Lawrence bald eagles (who love to consume white-tailed deer). The eagles have become a passion of his, and his name sits with others at the top of several scientific papers. Around sixty bald eagles, Bud estimates, spend the winter in the Thousand Islands, although, come spring, they have declined to nest there—until this year. Bud recalled one eagle with a fine white head, showing her to be over five years old, flying past him in 1994 with several sticks in her mouth, but she later gave up. Now there is a nest with eggs in it, and his voice is a mixture of studious, solicitous and proud as he states this headline news.

The eagles are making a hesitant comeback after generations of laying eggs with shells so thin that they broke under their own weight, the end result of eating carcasses rich in DDT.

The erosion, through development, of the particular shape of tree they like to call home didn't help either. They were, in effect, evicted, but now, a little less distrustful, they are breeding. Ospreys too have been invited to move back in, with the erection of five nesting poles on five islands. Boaters moving slowly enough can watch the ospreys fold back their wings and plunge, as though trying to drop into a bottle, strike at a fish straying near the surface and lift off with a metallic perch skewered on a talon and fighting for release.

"I consider myself a conservationist by nature," Bud said, putting the lid back on his lunch box. "Where humankind has made a mistake, screwed up, I have no problem lending a hand to try and put things back right."

After we had eaten, Bud tended to park business while I sought out the place on the island where Native artifacts, some over five thousand years old, had appeared, flushed out of the banks of the island after a storm forced a high water in 1973. After the water relaxed, flint flakes, shells from the Atlantic that had gone into necklaces, even traces of worked copper from Lake Superior, were literally hanging out of the edge of the island. Discovered by a boater, they were reported to the wardens, and academics soon swooped on them. I took several cracks at getting through the undergrowth, much of which decided to stick to me, but I was beaten back and had to be content with reading the small pulpit that records the event and acknowledges the people responsible for the timepieces being there in the first place, the St. Lawrence Iroquois. Knowing that my footsteps overlaid theirs added an extra depth to the day; it extended by several thousand years the human timeline that seemed so crowded at this end and so sparse at theirs.

The way back to Bud's front door, along the south side of Grenadier Island, completed the long figure eight that we had made over the course of the day. Several times our path had been crossed by early-season tour boats, still crowded with sightseers. The boats bristled with lenses, snapshot hunters at their trade. The only things that retreated from our presence were several map turtles, their backs flat and patterned, who slid off a rock into the anonymity of the water, and some of the several hundred herons who nest in a line of dead trees on a point on Ironsides Island. Passing below the belly of Hill Island in the Lake of the Isles, Bud mentioned the explosion of another species infiltrating the region—golfers. "There's three courses on Wellesley now," he said, and pointed to an apparently thick line of trees on the island's northern edge. "If we were a sailing ship and you were aloft, you'd see that those trees are just a facade, like a movie western. There are two courses right behind."

A day looking at river life through Bud's eyes—at heart he is a naturalist, a bird man—or even through the eyes of a bald eagle had actually been an exercise in taste. Generations of Andresses had lived their lives out on this stretch of the river, and in Bud that database has come to an opinion: a thing is either for the river or against it, an enhancement or a detriment. It was all about the poetic and the financial again, with one oar each, trying to reach a compromise.

21

DEEP RIVER

*The architecture of the riverbed has been revealed
like a faded painting restored to full colour.*

Ten metres below the surface of the St. Lawrence River, I twist
my head around and look back to the place where I became
amphibious. Both my hands have tight hold of the thick
anchor chain, my plumb line downwards. The current is strong
here in the Brockville Narrows as it funnels past Sparrow
Island and the north shore. Were I to let go, I'd be propelled
downriver like a loose kite in the wind, and be forced to grab
for the rope waiting at the end of this "drift" dive. Over my
shoulder, three more divers come hand over hand down the
chain. Minutes earlier, on the island's rocky shore, they were
clumsy neoprene condoms bedecked in heavy underwater gear;

now they are Tai Chi graceful. I can see every detail of them, and behind them another androgynous diver, flippers crossing the threshold between air and water.

Facing down the chain and descending diagonally, I lip over a cliff, and there before me is the schooner we were making for, the *Lillie Parsons*. An American two-master, the *Lillie* came to her final rest, upside down, on August 5, 1877. A storm pushed her against the island's edge, causing five hundred tons of coal to shift and drag her down. The coal is still visible, like spilled guts, near the remains of the *Lillie's* windlass. Paired divers are moving in and out of the wreck in a choreographed fashion, pausing to read the labelled parts and examine a display tray of *Lillie's* artifacts, assembled by divers from an Ottawa organization called Save Our Shipwrecks. And everywhere, on every available surface, like a coat of paint, there are molluscs the size of a fingernail—zebra mussels.

It is because of these "zebs," as divers call them, that visibility is now so dramatically improved in the river. I can take in the entire wreck in one glance, whereas even five years ago I couldn't have seen my own eyelashes. Because of the zebra mussels, and the almost one hundred wrecks that reside on the bottom of the St. Lawrence between Cornwall and Kingston, recreational diving is the region's fastest-growing industry. Diving-related business has doubled each year for the last five years. A cohort of local charter vessels has emerged, skippered by men and women who spend a sizable portion of their adult lives in flippers, and who go to work downward into deep water, all the while developing a fund of stories to be fed like minnows to the tourists.

To be accurate, zebra mussels, which first arrived in Canada in the late 1980s in Lake St. Clair, via the ballast water of ships from the Caspian Sea, don't clean the water; they just clear it.

Dreissena polymorpha is a filter-feeder. By means of a two-way valve, it flushes out nutrients from the water and stores them in its fatty tissues. Water, scrubbed of particles and contaminants, goes back out the way it came in, adding a pinch of decontaminated sediment to the bottom. When the mussels die, the contaminants stored within them are released back into the water. They do all this very efficiently, in huge, dominating numbers.

As a side effect, the water in the upper St. Lawrence has gradually gained visibility, and the architecture of the riverbed has been revealed, like a faded painting being restored to full colour. Now, diving in among the fleet of wrecks littering the riverbed in the Thousand Islands—the ships that left but never arrived—is akin to flying. It's almost as though the river has been dammed at Wolfe Island and Brockville and then drained. Like birds, the divers flit among the scrapbook of Iroquois pots and rusting Ski-Doos, cannonballs and fishing lures, bones and bottles, occasionally clinging to the cliffs that are the sides of the islands to gaze in awe at this lost and now found world.

There are rumours hereabouts of vessels going down in the War of 1812 loaded with British payroll treasure—one, it is said, somewhere south of Wolfe Island. Several British warships were scuttled in Kingston harbour during the war, including the *Kingston* and the *Montréal*, and the magnificent *St. Lawrence*, the biggest sailing ship built on the Great Lakes. (The *St. Lawrence* saw exactly two years' service before committing hara-kiri. The hull was raised in 1833 and did duty as a wharf for a brewery.) As well as the huge, there are smaller curios to be found. In 1996, a diver from Montréal found a bottle from the late nineteenth century off Prescott, still corked and with the contents—bootleg liquor—still drinkable. The bottle bore the name of a company still in business in Syracuse. They were contacted and bought the bottle for eight hundred dollars, and now they show it off in their museum.

Since the outbreak of peace on the river, apart from skirmishes with smugglers and pirates (men like Bill Johnston, who sank the *Sir Robert Peel* off Wellesley Island in 1838, and is said to have buried some of his swag on an island near Alexandria Bay), the main enemies of shipping have been nature and man. Nature can claim to have sunk the majority with storms and fog, while man has done his fair share by means of human error or the habit of assigning geriatric ships to the muddy pasture of the river bottom. There are several graveyards of decommissioned wooden ships, most of them burnt and sunk in the upper river. One crematorium holding nineteen sailing ships is off Garden Island, the small, saddle-shaped spit of land near Wolfe Island's main harbour, where the Calvin family used to build their boats.

Wrecks draw divers like a fridge draws magnets, and one of the divers with the greatest attraction is Barbara Carson. She has been diving for over four decades and has visited—and in several cases relocated—most of the wrecks in the upper St. Lawrence and eastern Lake Ontario. "The first wreck I recall going on," she says, "was the schooner *Horace Taber*, which went down in 1921 in twenty-five feet of water off Simcoe Island. Visibility was three to five feet. After that I began talking to local fishermen to find out where the others were." In one year alone, 1963, Barbara Carson was the consistent half of several diving pairs that relocated the *City of Sheboygan*, the *William Jamieson* and the *Aloha*. When Jacques Cousteau, the inventor of the modern aqualung, sailed the *Calypso* up the St. Lawrence in 1980, he asked Carson to show him the whereabouts of the three-masted barque the *R. H. Rae*, sunk in August 1858, which Carson and her dive partner, Audrey Rushbrook, had found in 1976 but kept secret.

Ask her what she most loves to do and Carson, after allowing a couple of taciturn breaths to go by, replies, "Looking." By this she means both looking at and looking for "ships that have been lost." At a low estimate, Carson has accumulated five entire weeks of her adult life underwater, and she would no doubt site her home there if she could; every available inch of the riverside one she has now is devoted to water, from nautical knick-knacks to a fish mural to a hundred-year-old anchor parked on her lawn. For the veteran divers like Carson, the clearing of the water by the zebra mussels has been an eye-opener. She first explored many of these wrecks in the dark ages; now she is returning to them with her sight restored. "I was on a wreck recently called the *Keystorm*, which I first felt as much as saw many years ago. It's spectacular now."

Carson is a petite woman, which enables her to get through apertures on wrecks that others would get wedged in. She treats the calamities she visits with enormous respect. There are two schools of divers: those prepared to get to know a wreck, its place and relevance in the tale of the river, and those who dive and dash, who collect wrecks the way other people collect restaurants. A T-shirt available in dive shops in the upper St. Lawrence displays the names, outlines and dates of fourteen wrecks—most of which Barbara Carson was instrumental in relocating—which divers tick off as they visit them.

Discounting the two extremes, most divers swim between the shallow and the deep end, between the tourist and the traveller. An example such as Carson's is vital, broadcasting the need for diving with respect. The knowledge the wrecks have to offer is public property; if bits of it come to the surface, they should be professionally conserved and displayed, not plonked on a mantelpiece (like the one in Trois-Rivières that shows off the vertebra of a victim of the *Empress of Ireland* disaster). The wheel of the *R. H. Rae*, for instance, which Carson helped raise and have conserved at Queen's University, is now on splendid exhibit in a room devoted to diving in Kingston's Maritime Museum of the Great Lakes, which Carson and Rushbrook helped found.

The siren call of wrecks is strong both for the knowledgeable and the hasty, and all the wrecks in the St. Lawrence can expect an increase in traffic, even a rush hour at weekends. Their attraction is also their curse. Metal-hulled ships can withstand multiple visitations, but the older wooden vessels will suffer at the laying on of many hands, and some people also believe that the sheer weight of zebra mussels may force a slow-motion demolition on them. Over time, divers may go from seeing nothing to having nothing to see.

If there is a river any-where haunted by old ships and old adventurers, surely it must be the St. Lawrence.

—Blowden Davies, from a cruise brochure for "The Great White Fleet," 1935

Busy human hands will erode the wrecks, too, or even seek to blow them apart to get at the treasure beneath, as was almost the case with the *Empress of Ireland*. That is one dive I was not unhappy to refuse when offered the chance. In a rental store in Prescott, I met a man who had lost a friend on a dive down to the *Ireland*, and I recalled that the first people to dive to it, a few weeks after it went down, saw faces looking out from every porthole. The remains of the 1914 wreck still lie on their side in the lower St. Lawrence, three miles off Rimouski, a hundred and fifty feet down in cold, moving, salty water, a graveyard as populated as that of a small village.

Others have not shared my reticence. When the *Calypso II*, Jacques Cousteau's diving vessel, travelled the St. Lawrence in 1986, it had aboard Ronald Ferguson, young telegraph operator who had survived the sinking. He was there on deck when they brought up the glass from the captain's clock on the bridge. Eighty-five years after the tragic incident, two divers from Victoriaville, Quebec, announced three years after the fact that they had pried loose and taken the twenty-five brass letters making up the name of the ship. The first letter, an O, was found near the propeller while the divers were unearthing antique beer bottles that had tumbled from the aft bar. Next came the P of *Liverpool*. The idea that they might be in some weird TV game crossed their minds, and they set about seeing if they could retrieve all the letters. Hundreds of dives and two years later, when the R in *Ireland* turned up, they had bingo. The spellbinding achievement was revealed, the letters mounted on a panel and exhibited in April 1999 in their home-town, and later at the museum in Pointe-au-Père. One of the two divers said of the whole adventure, "We're happy to have put our hands on all the letters, because they are the most beautiful label that best represents this historical ocean liner." Sometimes, by hook or by crook, what goes down comes up.

The ships of history, in their ignorance, did not always go down in the most convenient places. Dive shops like to have a nice little wreck nearby, preferably a shore dive, as a starter for the novices. The solution to both these problems, and one that is being adopted around the world, is a sacrifice wreck, a vessel that has been deliberately sunk. Such artificial reefs, as they are called, can act as a decoy to take the load off delicate, irreplaceable submersibles, and as a bonus their position on the charts can be predetermined.

There are already two artificial reefs in the upper St. Lawrence, and plans are afloat for more. The ferry *Wolfe Island II*, which took generations of islanders to Kingston and back, was taken out of museum mothballs in September 1985 and

scuttled in a bay off Wolfe Island. Barbara Carson has dove it
many times as exercise, and it's a fine training dive. (There is
fun to be had conjugating the past tense of "to dive." Divers
often say "dove," "dived" and occasionally even "dave" in the
same sentence.)

The other instant reef in the upper St. Lawrence is directly
in front of the dive shop in Prescott, the owners of which had
to assume responsibility for it with the province of Ontario.
(The province owns anything embedded in the bottom of any
body of water within its territory.) In May 1999, a twenty-five-
foot yacht, dubbed the SY *Prescott*, was launched, if that is the
right word. ("SY" stands for Sunken Yacht, a new addition to
the taxonomy of ships.) Most of the town attended the ceremonies, and the local Anglican minister gave the blessing.
"We bless this vessel and pray that it will be a beneficial, artificial reef for the fish and other creatures who live in the depths
of the majestic St. Lawrence River. May it also be a safe wreck
for the pleasure of all divers who descend to its place of rest."
The SY *Prescott* went down without a fight, and as soon as the
all-clear was given, the line of divers perched like crows on the
dockside swooped into the water, each determined to be the
first upon her, a title that received several claimants.

Both these amusements pale alongside the plan proposed by a
school of divers, working with consultants, local merchants and
hospitality purveyors, to sink a decommissioned Canadian naval
destroyer in the waters near Brockville. Calling themselves
SARA, an acronym for St. Lawrence Artificial Reef Association,
the group hopes to catch the wave of divers with disposable
income entering the area and use the money to irrigate the local
tourist economy. The SARA committee estimate that their
stretch of the river, from Cardinal down to Gananoque, was
dived twenty-five thousand times in 1998. The sunken destroyer

will suck people in from a wide radius: put a compass point on Brockville, open it out to a day's drive and there is a catchment of forty million people, of whom a million are active divers, a third of them Canadian, all prepared to pay to have air tanks filled, to eat, sleep and gas up for the ride home, replacing the forwarding business of yore. And the diving season extends into October and November, when the heat-retaining water is warmer than the air above it and the weeds are in decline.

When the minister mentioned safety in his benediction for the SY *Prescott*, he rang a bell that Phil Wright has long heeded. Wright is a marine archaeologist of oceanic experience, a committed, philosophical diver currently engaged in mapping galleons off the coast of Cuba. Wright is as conversant with the St. Lawrence riverbed and what it has to tell as anyone ashore; he is regularly asked to identify and date artifacts other divers bring up. Since the idea of a drowned destroyer for the area first surfaced, he has been acting as an ex officio guidance counsellor for the SARA project. Wright's concerns are for both the divers and the things upon which they dive, because the increase in traffic will also increase the likelihood of irretrievable damage to both. (His fears were sadly justified when a diver was killed near Brockville in the summer of 2000.) There is a need for education, underwater traffic control and preparation for the worst, all of which Wright has experience in.

Wright and I went diving on his and many other people's favourite wreck in the Thousand Islands, the *Keystorm*. On October 12, 1912, the four-year-old, two-hundred-and-fifty-six-foot steamer *Keystorm*, carrying over two thousand tons of coal from Charlotte, New York, had just passed Alexandria Bay in fog as thick as mud. Deprived of clear vision, she dragged her hull over a shoal and inflicted a gash big enough to sink her in a matter of minutes. All the crew managed to save themselves, while below, the ship's bow reached bottom first and the stern continued to descend down to one hundred and fifteen feet. Then the redundant *Keystorm* rolled onto her starboard side, time's arrow pointing up at the unreachable surface.

Ten minutes due south of Mallorytown Landing, home of the conserved gunboat from the 1820s and an extended family of Canada geese, we tie up at the buoy marking the wreck. After some checks, Wright and I flip over the edge of the boat and pull ourselves down the marker rope into the clear deep. The *Keystorm*'s wheelhouse looms below. There is only one other diver in the vicinity, a foolish American diving alone. Most of the world is at work, and even the king-size pike dubbed Pete, the wreck's mascot, is elsewhere.

Putting a gloved hand on the zebra mussels that crust the wreck's flank, I push away until I can see the whole picture. This particular wreck is an industrial graveyard but not a human one; no one died here. It is both a sculpture and an underwater jungle gym fashioned by the watery hand of time, a ghost of technologies past, an artifact from a time when they did things differently.

This river began to flow again eight thousand years ago. This ship went down six months after the *Titanic*, in the same year Scott reached the South Pole, the year of the first parachute jump, the year the word "vitamin" joined the language. Since then, we who have already done much to alter and offend the river have found a way to stay submerged in it and begin our relentless task of rearranging nature. The past and the present flow into each other here, and the future is on its way, flapping its flippers, reaching for a credit card and a guide to the wrecks. The forces of the poetic and the financial, as ever, compete for our attention while we move in this luminous landscape of time and money.

Staying *inside* the river for an hour at a time, with amazing freedom of movement, is a heady mixture of obligatory vigilance and a very particular calm. It is the calm that envelops me as I float, suspended in time, in the flowing past of the St. Lawrence.

22

RIVERBOAT FANTASY

*As many as fifty ships could be sitting in the harbour then,
loading us with furs (above: Hotel Tadoussac).*

BEING AN ACCOUNT OF A TEN-DAY JOURNEY ALONG THE
ST. LAWRENCE RIVER AS A MEMBER OF THE CREW OF THE
CLASS C TALL SHIP, THE *MIST OF AVALON*.

THE FIRST DAY

At eight o'clock in the morning on Canada Day, the last of
both the century and the millennium, Skipper George Mainguy fired a powerfully noisy toy cannon from the mahogany
rail, the shot echoing against the cliffs and over into the Thousand Islands. The cannon, which fired nothing at all, consti-
tuted the ship's only means of defence if attacked by
descendants of Americans killed in 1812. There was waving

from several folks left behind on shore, and then the steady throb of the three-hundred-horsepower Caterpillar engine began to take the Mist of Avalon out into the stream, away from her home port of Ivy Lea.

The first time I laid eyes on the Mist of Avalon was two years earlier, sitting at the end of the marina in Ivy Lea. Ivy Lea is a barnacle of a one-road town just east of Gananoque. The few houses and docks that compose the place cling to a small, tilted shelf of rock. It's close enough to the International Bridge over to the States that the locals call it the Ivy Lea Bridge. There are more boats than cars in the town, whose name derives from the first postmaster, John Ivey, and not the vine.

To be accurate, I saw something that was going to become the Mist of Avalon. For the moment it was a long, high oak hull without masts, lying like a wolf in a flock of fibreglass chickens. On deck was a man wearing cut-off denim shorts and nothing else, sawing off a stump of wood rising out of the wide, sloping deck. He had long hair beginning to grey, which to me indicated a youth spent roaming the sixties. This was George Mainguy, who owned the marina, as his father had, and whose great-uncle was Admiral Edmund Rollo Mainguy, chief of naval staff in 1951. And this was George's boat, the Mist of Avalon.

The inevitable questions arose about the ship's statistics and origin. She started life as a fishing vessel, built of oak in the great Canadian year of 1967 in Nova Scotia. For twenty years she worked off the Grand Banks, filling her hold with cod, and then fish stocks took a dive. The owners, defeated, abandoned her at a Halifax pier for five years while the paint flaked away. In 1992, George bought her, had some stabilizing work done, and brought the renamed Mist of Avalon up the St. Lawrence to her new berth.

The next five years of George's life went into converting the *Avalon* into a fully rigged thing of beauty, a replica of a nineteenth-century schooner. ("Schooner" relates to a day in 1713 when a small, odd, two-masted vessel slid into the waters off Massachusetts with such elegance that her sponsor came up with a neologism to describe her glide: "Look," he enthused, "at how she schoons.") All that remained of the original fishing vessel was the hull, the forward bunks and the deck. Twelve tons of concrete had been poured into the old fish hold as ballast after it had been sandblasted clean, and skilled eccentrics such as a sailmaker from Kingston were located and given the challenge of making something no longer made. It was origami with wood and canvas, and the last thing to go aboard was the cat's-cradle rigging.

In 1997, the ship's bell was fitted to the pilothouse and rung; the *Avalon* was ready for sea. George had made a hole in time, reached in and pulled out a sailing ship from 1890. The *Avalon* was a replica, and a superb one. She could just as easily have been built in the Québec shipyards of the late nineteenth century. Then, she would have taken her place on the river alongside such famous schooners as *La Canadienne*, one of the founding vessels of the Canadian coast guard that schooned down on foreign fishing fleets in the lower St. Lawrence when they deliberately strayed into Canadian waters. Being made of oak, the *Avalon* was heavy enough to force aside a hundred tons of water, pushing down ten feet into the river to do so, and she was one hundred feet from the tip of the bowsprit (the mast that sticks out like a pointing finger at the front) to the stern waterline. These are roughly the dimensions of a blue whale.

The following spring—he's not one for the telephone, and his answering-machine message is so clumsy it's charming—George wrote to invite me to join the crew on a voyage to Halifax. I said yes before the envelope hit the ground. We would make our way down the north shore, dropping anchor at night and sleeping on board. How long it might take was up to the river, and as with all decent travel, arriving was to be the least of the journey.

I went aboard the night before the launch, and George's wife, Gisele, showed me to my bunk. It was at the very front, along with three others, two on the port and two starboard. A curtain separated us from the galley. Each bunk—a coffin with one side missing—was perched on the tapering side of the bow, like an exaggerated bookshelf. Directly in front of my head was the locker for the anchor chain, and ahead of that the prow of the ship. Lying in the bunk at a slight angle, I just fit in the space. By my right ear I could hear the St. Lawrence a foot away, lapping against the hull.

Feeling like the guest of honour at a wake, I looked at the bottom of the bunk above mine, six inches away, and noticed a scrapbook of initials and mathematics scribbled on the planks. I stared at them for a moment, puzzling about their meaning, then realized they were from the Avalon's former life as a fishing vessel. The little bunches of numbers were economics. One of the deckhands had used the planking as a notepad to work out his share of the profits for that trip: the poundage of fish caught, times the market value per pound, divided by the number of crew.

Climbing out of the galley on a vertical ladder, I took a walk around the ship, mainly to work out where to avoid banging my head. At one of the more favoured lump-inducing spots Gisele had hung a plastic seagull to prevent concussions. The big, brass, twelve-spoked wheel, the classic kind with the handholds resembling baluster knobs, was attached to the engine control housing, so that it was actually impossible to stand behind it. One struck the pose of the skipper, eyes gazing into the middle distance, from either side.

The mainmast, nearest the middle of the ship, rose ninety feet from the deck. The sibling mast—the foremast—was shorter by a body length and sat over the galley. Around the masts at the bottom were sewing baskets of ropes in tidy loops, plus pegs and hoops, all designed to get the sails up fast. The foremast supported sails ahead and behind it, three triangles ahead and a big parallelogram behind. The mainmast had one large, heavy parallelogram to contend with. Both masts were made of unsnappable steel, which made a bell-like sound when something loose slapped against it.

Wooden masts were once a Canadian specialty. Jack and red pines galore lined the shores like giant arrows, seemingly planted there for the express purpose of shipbuilders. The British, cut off by the Napoleonic Wars from Scandinavia, their usual warehouse for masts, were happy to plunder Canada's arboretum by the millions. But the wooden masts did have a tendency to snap, which modern steel resists.

My head overloaded with jibs and booms, I took a late-night swim in the St. Lawrence (to cries of "Writer overboard!") and squeezed into my bunk. Now, I thought, I know how toothpaste feels. For reading matter I had brought *Redburn* by Herman Melville published in 1849. The first real-life ship Melville worked on, in 1839, was called the *St. Lawrence*, a packet ship see-sawing between New York and Liverpool, and it was the tough time he had on board that summer that he fictionalized in *Redburn*.

Soon there came the sound of classic literature hitting a tired face.

I woke, at six in the morning on Canada Day, to the intoxicating smell of coffee. The bunk above mine was still empty, but the upper bunk opposite was now occupied. Mike, already loading his first pipe, had worked cargo ships for a couple of years in and out of the Great Lakes before going ashore as a teacher. He had sailed the *Avalon* the previous summer on her maiden voyage down the St. Lawrence and on to Bonavista, Newfoundland, where she rendezvoused with the *Matthew*, the reproduction of John Cabot's vessel of exploration that reached Terra Nova in 1497. That voyage, Mike said, over coffee strong enough to raise the dead, had been a fight. The weather attacked them almost the full length of the river and, stressed by the battering it took, the ship had revealed aspects of its character that needed adjusting.

Already up and clear-eyed were fellow crew members Doug, Joe and Lisa, the latter two a couple. Joe was born on an island in the St. Lawrence, the Île aux Coudres. He spoke English with a Newfoundland accent, having spent years there in the RCMP chasing smugglers and other malfeasants in boats. Lisa was his wife and sailing partner, having long ago gained her navigation papers. Doug lived on the riverfront near Iroquois and owned a construction company that built one of the river's landmarks, the SkyDeck tower on Hill Island, that enormous barber-pole affair topped with an observation platform like a pillbox hat.

The cannon fired, and we were off.

Still within sight of the dock, George ordered the sails up. As a crew we were not yet up to speed, and the canvas—actually a more durable synthetic called Dacron—went up raggedly. The two large sails were framed top and bottom by spars of wood—the gaff at the top, the boom at the bottom. As we pulled on ropes and the gaff rose, unfurling the sail away from the boom, physics demanded that the throat of the gaff, the end nearest the mast, stay below the end farthest from the mast. This we did not do, and I saw that being captain of a ship involved "face." I learned then to spot the slight blush that would come over George's forehead when something was clumsily done, though understanding and forgiveness blew just as quickly through him.

Overriding my clumsiness was the glory of being on a moving, fully rigged tall ship. Time's passing had lent a poetic veneer to a mode of travel that for millions had been uncomfortable and constricted. For me it felt as though, stalked by Time back on land, we had given it the slip on the schooner. Here was a reason for some people's enduring love of history: to study the past is to sidestep the present.

Because she drew ten feet of water, we were obliged to keep the *Avalon* in the deepwater channel that runs the length of the St. Lawrence. Ships coming into the river from Lake Ontario point their bow into the centre of the channel, which is marked like an airplane runway by pairs of bobbing buoys, green on the right, red on the left. Each buoy, whose well-being is the province of the coast guard, has a matching, pulsing light on top. (Ships employ the same system in their superstructure; you should see a red light on the right and a green one on the left if a ship is coming towards you.) In theory, all you do is keep your ship between the red and green buoys, and out you pop a few days later in the Gulf, with the paint and crew intact.

We threaded our way east in hardly any breeze, islands to the left of us, islands to the right. After an hour's pleasantness George put me in the deep end and let me take the brass wheel. An advisory panel was assembled at the picnic table by the wheel that acted as the de facto village green on the journey. The five people now seated there kept an eye on me, making five eyes in all, and a steady stream of instruction issued from the table. "The way you turn is the way it will go." "Oversteer. Spin the wheel more than you think you need to and then come back." "See if you can get a fix on your next two buoys on either side." "Which way do you veer when a ship approaches from the other direction?" "Wrong. Go to the left, to port." "Try that at night, when you find you're heading for some onshore street lights you thought were a pair of flashing buoys."

Near the Ironsides heron sanctuary, I was expounding my opinion that the heron, a creature designed in the art deco style, should be the official bird of the St. Lawrence River, when the *Maple Glen* of Canada Steamship Lines came around a bend, on its way to deliver iron ore from Sept-Îles to the Great Lakes. Already large, she appeared even larger and completely indifferent to the novice navigator who now had to avoid her. At the end of one long held breath, the big, silent ship was astern, the wake hardly rocking us. The same pressure it takes me to open a shirt button had caused a hundred tons to shift direction with a simple spin of a brass wheel. The art lies in gauging the lag between spin and reaction.

Soon enough, as a tanker registered in Monrovia glided past without a human soul in sight on its decks, we passed Brockville, the city that once boasted more millionaires than any other in Canada. Brockville was founded by a Loyalist born in Connecticut called Sherwood, a soldier turned surveyor who wrote an account of his first survey of the area in 1783 and called it, matter-of-factly, *Captain Sherwood's Journal from Montreal to Lake Ontario, noting the Quality of the Land from the West end of Lake St. Francis to the Bay of Kenty*. In his journal Sherwood noted that "I think there cannot be better land in America," which, as far as the soil was concerned, turned out to be a gross overstatement.

A gaggle of barges loaded with Loyalists duly headed up the St. Lawrence to occupy this overhyped Eden in May 1784, and Sherwood was made supervisor of land allotments. He supervised himself first and set aside six riverfront lots for his family, then went on to annoy the governor of the time, Lord Dorchester, with talk of holding elections for this and that, including the rank of governor. For his democratic aspirations Sherwood was cold-shouldered and reduced in civic stature. In 1798 he fell off one of two timber rafts he was taking down-river, at Trois-Rivières. He never came up.

Thereafter, Brockville did well for itself. It got its first passenger steamboat, the eponymous *Brockville*, in 1833, thus keeping up with the Joneses in neighbouring Prescott, which had already been running one for several years. The first train tunnel in British North America had to be built in the town to get Grand Trunk trains through a wedge of rock and down to the waterfront. If you were sick any time in the late nineteenth or early twentieth century, you most likely took a patent medicine pill made by one of two businesses based in Brockville. Comstock Brothers and the G. T. Fulford Company, one of the first multinationals, made their owners millionaires, and the Fulford mansion is now a museum and tea shop. Talk to someone from Brockville for more than ten minutes and the Fulford slogan "Pink Pills for Pale People" still comes up.

Brockville was also skiff-crazy. At twilight on any fine day in the late 1880s, hundreds of them were out on the river like hatching fireflies. The Brockville business register for 1880 lists five skiff companies. Connoisseurs went for a Sauvé Brothers skiff, the best made on the Canadian side of the river. One year a Sauvé skiff won a nine-mile race at the Lachine Regatta by two whole miles. By 1900, however, the trade had died and all the skiff builders had closed up shop.

Passing through the last three of the Thousand Islands, the Three Sisters, brought the *Avalon* into what the St. Lawrence Centre in Montréal still calls the International Rapids section on its maps, beginning at Prescott's Fort Wellington. We passed the massive concrete elevator at the edge of town and under another bridge, then the parade continued past the small town of Cardinal, where the river first broke out in rapids for those heading downstream.

The Native name for the Cardinal Rapids translates as "where the canoe is pushed upstream by a pole." The town was founded in 1790 by Captain Munro, a military Scot, then in his sixties. Like every single small outgrowth of humanity in Canada, Cardinal started from the twin nuclei of a gristmill and a sawmill, and the story goes that in order to reach the requisite number of townsfolk for incorporation—seven hundred and fifty—the town held a horse race on the day of the census and packed the place. The race tradition carried on, with competitions held on the ice of the canal in winter.

If you come into Cardinal by car, the first thing you notice is its curious, castrated, drained canal forced into disuse by the Seaway. When this canal, the town's second, was built in the late 1890s, it ran behind the town, making Cardinal an island. The first canal, known as the Galops from the French word for rapids, became the town swimming pool when the second was built.

One of the *Avalon's* crew, Doug, had lived in Cardinal for nine years in the 1960s, when the biggest thing in town was the century-old Canada Starch Company. His abiding memory of Cardinal was watching the Volkswagen boat go by two or three times each season. It was a huge, grey, car-stuffed tanker, five storeys high. As it passed the end of the street, it seemed as though a vast gate was rolling shut and then opening again.

Looming ahead of us now was a partially submerged section of the Great Wall of China. Or so it seemed. The seven-storey-high Iroquois Dam, joining Canada's Iroquois Point to Point Rockway in the United States, holds back the entire river and is fitted with thirty-two gates that dictate on a daily basis how much of the river gets into the man-made Lake St. Lawrence, which falls through the power dams at the other end and makes enough electricity to illuminate entire cities. Shipping sidesteps the dam to the north by using the eight-hundred-foot-long Iroquois Lock, which resembles a valley with perfectly smooth sides. Up above, as we were waiting to enter the lock, a small boy was doing some summer-holiday ship-spotting. He made a Jules Verneian entry in his notebook about the nineteenth-century schooner below him whose mast-tops were level with his pen, and he waved but did not say anything, in case the illusion should shatter.

Going through the Iroquois lock produced the odd sensa-tion of being an animal first captured and then released. Once inside, we were fettered by ropes in the lock, and the lockmas-ter appeared with a clipboard on a pole, to which we had to attach ten dollars before he would free us. He then inquired if we could move down and into the middle; the front locks had opened even before the back ones were shut. "That's not nec-essarily an option," George replied, the ship bobbing about beneath him like an apple in a barrel, and thus one of the catchphrases for the voyage was born.

"Where are you sleeping tonight?" the lockmaster asked politely.

"Upper Canada Village," came the answer, and it had a pleasant, antique ring to it.

Once through the Iroquois lock and past the site where the French made their last stand against the British, at Chimney Point in 1760, the *Avalon* was in Lost Villages territory. Morris-burg appeared on the portside, the village that had been only half gutted. I recalled the night in Morrisburg when I showed slides of old postcards of the villages taken fifty, a hundred years

ago from the same vantage point on the river we were at now.
The postcards displayed vanished homes and boathouses, and
islands now beneath the stream, and at least half the people in
the room that night had seen those houses and islands with
their own eyes. For an hour the older people stared at the
screen, looking through glasses at the contours of their youth.

After the show, a trim man in his late seventies told me a
story. When his turn came in 1957, he had taken Hydro's
money—market value of his Morrisburg house plus the fifteen-
percent bonus—and moved upriver to Kingston. His next-door
neighbour had had his home, which he was born in, moved to
Iroquois. The move had taken a day, and he had put a half-full
glass of water on the kitchen table; not a drop was spilt during
the relocation.

The two friends did not see each other for ten years, and
then the Kingston man came back for a visit. He entered the
new Iroquois, a place he did not know his way around, in the
dark, and followed directions till he found his friend's old
house at a new number, on a new street. They drank a few
beers at the kitchen table, as they had done in the old days.

When the out-of-town friend woke next morning in the
guest room, before the others were up, he made his way to the
front door, to grab a smoke on the porch. Opening the door, he
automatically expected to see the view his mind had enjoyed
formerly; instead, he was greeted with a vista of unfamiliarity,
and he had to close the door and sit for a moment, time dancing in his head.

The view outside the front door that morning was not as
busy as the Seaway builders had promised. Tourism will rise,
they told the relocated villagers in 1957, and fine parks, extensive bird sanctuaries and Upper Canada Village, an 1867 ham-
let staffed with time-warp actors and salvaged buildings from

the seven drowned villages, were added to the map as roadside honey pots. To be sure, the number of wild geese, black ducks, mallards, and green- and blue-winged teal visiting the area rose dramatically, but the tourist sanctuaries, after an initial flurry, have settled down to steady, mostly weekend migrations.

The head count in Morrisburg has not risen. The town planners of 1955 said that the number on the "Welcome to Historic Morrisburg" population board would rise from eighteen hundred to twelve thousand; they were out by a factor of ten thousand. Quite possibly the residents don't mind that—quality and quantity are not the same thing—and Charles Atlas, the muscleman who had sold new bodies to countless skinny kids in the fifties from the back of comic books, thought the town pleasant enough to retire there, where he amused the boys in the woodshed every now and then by straightening out horseshoes.

Head east out of Morrisburg on the relocated Highway 2 and you pass flaking signs pointing to boarded-up theme parks and desolate, denuded garages, entrepreneurial tombstones that broke their owners' backs. Even at Upper Canada Village, an educating amusement most visitors leave feeling their money was well spent, there have been ominous rumblings of adding a video arcade; and the gift store, with its tacky Made in Elsewhere trinkets drowning out the tastier, germane items, is a betrayal of the village's original intentions. The history business ain't what it used to be, and curators everywhere are unwrapping thirty-two-bit electronic bells and whistles to entertain the junior generation.

The northern riverbank gliding behind us had the look of an old landscape with low-budget new acres welded on. On a small loop off the highway past the former site of Moulinette, on a tear-shaped expanse of grass, I could see five old buildings collected together, almost like leftovers from a giant model railway. From the *Avalon* the squat structures reminded me of old men sitting chewing the fat on benches outside a general store. This is the erstwhile incomplete Museum of the Lost Villages, the labour of love of Françoise Laflamme.

Born in Wales, Ontario, the daughter of the village barber, Fran Laflamme was twenty-five when the Seaway claimed her hometown. She passed her working life as a nurse, librarian and schoolteacher in nearby Ingleside, but her passion for the lost streets of her youth never left her. In 1977 she founded the Lost Villages Historical Society and became its busiest ambassador, travelling Ontario with a slide show and tenderly amassing the segments of her museum: the old railway station from Moulinette, served until 1958 by the famous *Moccasin*, Canada's oldest steam train when it was withdrawn from service; the red brick SS #17 school from Roxborough township; the barbershop of Zina Hill, advertising a haircut for forty-five cents; the old-fashioned, Edith Wharton–style home that acts as Society headquarters; the tobacco and barber shop of Henry Laflamme, Fran's father, with its collection of cut-throat razors; and the Manson and LaPierre grocery store that once stood on Milles Roches's High Street and now sells Lost Villages T-shirts. Some people write books to revisit and lay to rest their childhoods; for Fran Laflamme, born Wales, Ontario, 1932, nothing less than a museum would do. (A year after we sailed by the Museum of the Lost Villages, Fran Laflamme died. Her last public appearance was at the renaming of Ault Park Road, the street that runs by her museum. It is now Fran Laflamme Drive.)

I suspect there are many places along the St. Lawrence

between Iroquois and Long Sault where lost villagers go to commune with their past. I'm not a lost villager (unless Ottawa counts as one), but there is a place not far from the Laflamme museum that captures my imagination. Ault Park is a plain, feral field fringed by a bike path and announced at the gate by a small wooden sign. A plaque offers a brief explanation that the town of Aultsville once lived just in front of this park. The park's only post-flood accoutrements are a derelict, unattractive building that once sold ice cream and a rusting child's swing at the water's edge. Otherwise the grass in the park grows thicker and wilder every summer, and there is rarely anyone there. The atmosphere is full of voices—or is it just the water lapping the rocky beach? The water is full of secrets, and staring it down will not force it to reveal them. Ontario songwriter Alex Sinclair has set to music the feeling the park gives off, in a song called simply "Aultsville."

> The engineers came in here with their glorious schemes
> and they ripped this whole town apart at the seams
> now the freighters glide by where the rapids used to run
> and the powerlines stretch toward the setting sun.

> There are tides that can't be denied
> so we moved to the high ground and let Hydro decide
> which of our villages wouldn't tally in their scales:
> Farron's Point, Dickinson's Landing, Aultsville and Wales,
> Milles Roches, Moulinette, Morrisburg, Aultsville and Wales.

On a sailing ship the mood of the sky becomes important, in a horoscopic sort of way. Sailors look to it for the future, to see the weather ahead or overtaking from behind. Then they prepare a list of tasks the impending weather will bring with it. As we searched for an anchorage off the back of Upper Canada Village, taking soundings with a weighted rope marked off in tens of feet, we looked up and saw a storm coming like a huge snake down the river, tongues of lightning at its front. The anchorage would need to be firm, the knots tight and the decks free of loose objects.

The sun set well on the St. Lawrence, and fireworks started behind us in Morrisburg and ahead in Cornwall to celebrate one hundred and thirty-two years since Confederation. At dinner, Gisele gave a Canada Day toast: "There are wooden ships and metal ships, there are new ships and old ships, but the best ships of all are friendships." Several toasts later, the day ended with many rousing off-key verses of Stan Rogers's song "Barrette's Privateers," about a Canadian sailor cruelly treated by the sea and war.

Sleep, when it came, was deep and dream-free.

The second Day

I awoke, like Scrooge on Christmas Eve, to the sound of rattling chains. The *Avalon* had tugged on her anchor and several links had paid out in the chain locker by my head. I climbed the vertical ladder that led out of the galley to the pitching deck, pushed open the wooden door and heard, felt and saw the storm all in the same moment. The slamming air was frothy with spray. The rigging whipped the booms and mast in a discordant horror-movie soundtrack. Lightning lit up the rooftops and the squat wooden lookout tower of Upper Canada Village, and it seemed as if time itself was being blown about as well as the ship. The anchor held and, drenched but pleased with the show, I went back to bed.

By sunrise the river had regained its composure, and we attempted to raise anchor. It was stuck fast, despite our trying every angle and manoeuvre short of a back flip. Eventually, as two men strained on the winch handles, it let go of the riverbed. The Avalon's anchor was of the classic design—two letter Js back to back—and one fluke had snapped off. It was crippled but still serviceable.

Underway again, the Stars and Stripes went up the mainmast as we veered to the American side. Crossing Lake St. Lawrence, the hundred-square-mile reservoir created in the flooding of the Seaway, we passed close to Sheek Island. The Seaway's excavations uncovered a treasure trove of archaeological gems there, and the island had undoubtedly been busy three and a half thousand years ago, because a tool box of Native artifacts had come to light, filled with knives, arrowheads, drills, adzes, sharpening stones, and tobacco pipes that had calmed the artisans as they patiently fashioned the rock. The pottery that emerged with the tools had designs on it that were Identikits of Siberian decoration of the same period.

In order to get out of Lake St. Lawrence we had to bypass the Long Sault dam and its companion edifice, the three-fifths-of-a-mile-long Moses-Saunders power station, with the international border running through the middle of it. A similar navigation problem faces the million young eels that arrive each fall at the Long Sault dam from the Sargasso Sea. An apparatus equivalent to a cat flap helps them overcome the dam. Once upon the other side, they head upriver for Lake Ontario and live a freshwater life for ten years. Then, in response to an internal message we don't yet understand, they go back down the St. Lawrence, through the eel door, and on to saltwater lives in the Sargasso Sea, where they spawn and eventually die.

Ships, being very large eels, use a double-door system to go around the dam obstacle: the Eisenhower and Snell locks. The locks sit at the beginning and halfway point of an eight-mile-long deepwater channel south of Barnhart Island that had to be dredged out during Seaway construction. Monster construction techniques were used to create the system, but the first person through the locks when they opened in July 1958 was a seventy-year-old canoeist from Massachusetts. We fit easily in the Eisenhower, rather like the floating marker in a thermometer. The eighty-five-foot-high doors at either end, just a bit smaller than the gates of hell, seemed to rise out of the water, as though we were being lowered forty feet into a roofless dungeon complete with dripping water. The sense of incarceration was sullied by the knowledge that cars were passing underneath us, in a tunnel built during the making of the Seaway.

In the three-mile gap between the two locks, the air hummed with electricity. A line of six electricity pylons stood either side of the river, with a battalion of identical pylons to the rear heading into Cornwall on the Canadian side and Massena on the American. The half-dozen pylons on the Canadian side looked as if they were waiting their turn to cross over, with half of the battalion lined up behind and the rest already across and marching towards Albany.

As we entered the second lock, the Snell, I noticed a sign saying CAUTION. DANGER OF BEING SWEPT OVER MOSES-SAUNDERS POWER DAM OR LONG SAULT SPILLING DAM WHEN SPILLWAY GATES ARE OPENED. Oh, really? But the rite of passage was as uneventful here as going through the Eisenhower. Together, the two locks had taken us ninety feet nearer sea level. When the forward gates of the Snell opened to let us leave, it must have been quite a sight for anyone on the other side, a tall ship gliding out like a model boat emerging from a bottle.

Slipping across the U.S.–Canada border for the last time and running up the Ontario flag, we chugged through the maze of islands that sit like stepping stones between Cornwall and Massena, the largest being Cornwall Island itself.

To mark the fortieth anniversary of the Seaway, three young Cornwallians studied the events that had so affected their parents' lives and put together a small, old-fashioned photo and text exhibit for the local museum, entitled *Seaway Story*. At the end of the handout accompanying the exhibit, the students asked this question: "Was the Seaway Power Project necessary?" The answer they gave, based on the replies they had received, was "No. In fact the project caused a lot of needless heartache to the 'Lost Villagers.' The project originally promised wealth, prosperity and an increased population to the area. It failed to provide any of these things." Certainly, that is true of Cornwall, although it did become a sufficient smuggling centre for cigarettes in the early 1990s that the mayor, who had declared verbal war on the smugglers, was shot at.

Robert Kitchen, a young man when he worked on the canallers in the 1950s, still lives in Cornwall, and many times during the year he visits the old Cornwall Canal, which he is campaigning to have turned into a recreation area. He has another project, too, to keep him busy. A few years ago Robert was loaned a set of diaries stretching from July 1855 to July 1902 and kept by a man named James Cameron, a farmer on a small island near Cornwall. As he worked his fields, Cameron took note of the traffic passing his domain, and he wrote it up at day's end. In 1885, for instance, Cameron noted several ships going by loaded with troops on their way to help put down the Riel Rebellion. Cameron's hand is not easy to read, and the spelling is archaic, but Robert is a dogged man, and he is transcribing it all, patiently assembling a portrait of five decades in the life of the St. Lawrence from the deteriorating, slightly water damaged books. The portrait will be published someday.

The deepwater channel buoys guided us past the Akwesasne Reserve, home to several thousand proud Mohawks, once the eastern doorkeepers of the Five Nations, and separate negotiators at the table when the Seaway was being designed. "Mohawk" is the name their neighbours and sometimes enemies gave them, much as Canadians call Americans "Yankees." Their own name for themselves is Kanien'kehake, meaning "people of the flint." The reserve (an ugly word that has undertones of internment; the Mohawks, like separatist Quebeckers, refer to themselves as a nation) lies in both U.S. and Canadian territory and encompasses all of Cornwall Island, St. Regis Island and an elongated chunk of the American mainland. A chain-link fence topped with razor wire defines the border, but the Mohawks tend to treat it as a figment of the colonial imagination.

Akwesasne—"where the partridge drums its wings"—is the second-largest reserve on the St. Lawrence (the biggest, by a long way, is Betsiamites, on the north shore near the end of the river), and just about everyone on it has a boat. The bingo halls and casinos within the territory deal in serious money, and the gas prices, which do not include tax, would make a European weep.

The summer before, the American pop band the Indigo Girls had staged a concert just for the inhabitants of Akwesasne, entitled "For the River." And in the small office of Sally Benedict, plans were already afoot for a conference to be held the following summer on the modern fur trade. Amazingly, this would be the first conference on the fur trade ever held on Native soil.

To date, the European invasion of Canada, over five hundred years, has reduced the territories of Saguenay, Canada and Hochelaga that Cartier sailed past to nine scattered reserves on the sides of the St. Lawrence. Officially, twelve thousand people live there, a reasonable attendance at a Montréal Expos baseball game these days, and they are allotted three hundred and forty square kilometres, an area half the size of St. Maurice National Park, just north of Trois-Rivières.

The drawing of borders is usually done with pen and paper at treaty time, and sometimes not everybody is paying close attention. That is how the town of St. Regis, which is in the United States, ended up with a tiny bit of Quebec stranded within it, when the border was fixed after the War of 1812. The line just cuts off the tip of St. Regis, and the only ways to reach these few houses and the water purification plant from Canada are by boat or by crossing the bridge, driving through New York State and then turning left towards the river. If you drive there, you arrive in a small town with small houses and big cars, then suddenly, with no mark in the road, the licence plates parked in the driveways change from "New York" to "Québec—Je Me Souviens."

Just north of the invisible border is a Canadian post office, and when I visited this orphan piece of Canadian real estate I mailed myself an old postcard of the river with the message "You are no longer here." The postcard arrived two days later bearing a rare postmark, having travelled through another country without requiring extra postage.

With St. Regis fifteen miles behind us, midway across Lac St-Francis the sails went up for the second time, and the territorial flag at the top of the mainmast was changed for the last time. We were in Quebec now, and would remain so until we reached the Gulf of St. Lawrence. Although the aqueous borders we had crossed were marked clearly on the map, there was of course no sign of them on the water, and beneath us the fish crossed freely. If Quebec were to separate, the invisible line on the water we had just crossed would become an international edge, a line between two countries, a notion that seemed a little silly on this sunny, peaceful day. The water was a mirror, and the ship's wake spooled out behind like a jet making a vapour trail, disappearing as though evaporating. It made the river seem like a giant blackboard wiping itself clean.

There was a time when sailing ships did not know exactly where they were, because there was no technology to give them an accurate longitude. Unable to draw a cross on a chart and declare "We are here" the best the navigator could manage was a circle marked "We are within this." After a precise method of fixing longitude was invented by master clockmaker John Harrison in the late eighteenth century, the quality of charts improved steadily until they became thin slices of virtual reality studded with information. "I have a set of charts for the St. Lawrence," Joe told me as we headed towards the lift bridge on the south side of Grande Île, "from the early 1900s, black and white, and I would happily frame one as a work of art. They are a family heirloom. But I wouldn't use them today. Things move in a river—new wrecks, shoals shift, storms rearrange things. And it still gets dark at night."

The history of charts is the digital story of long-distance travel, and plotting our position day after day often made me daydream about how the St. Lawrence has been trapped in an increasingly fine mesh net of coordinates. The Indians carried practical maps of these waters, of the eddies and shoals, in their heads, while Champlain's wonderful maps of the 1630s depicted the St. Lawrence as a worm hole in a strange fruit waiting to be plucked. James Cook's charts prepared for the siege of Québec were weapons, like computerized military guidance systems, and the charts on the *Avalon* were catalogues of danger. All of them were a version of the St. Lawrence, a way of seeing it that would one day end with a complete computer simulation, a virtual river without taste or feel. Nowadays there are electronic marvels available the size of a cellphone that can inform you of your position on the planet to within *fifteen feet*. Getting lost is becoming harder and harder.

So many pleasure boats were passing us heading towards the Thousand Islands—the majority with the letter D in their registration, showing they were from Montréal—that it felt as if we were going the wrong way to a party. Most of the drivers were young, half-naked, tattooed somewhere and laughing into a breeze of their own making as they opened up the engines in a burst of ego, sound system at thought-killing level and plenty of beer laid in. How the sons and daughters of the first settlers would envy them.

At the end of the lake we dipped down to the south shore, passed under the Valleyfield lift bridge and entered the Beauharnois Canal, the last of the canals to be remodelled in the Seaway's construction. The Beauharnois's two locks, the upper and lower, were hewn out of drill-killing limestone, so tough the workers had to resort to using a jet piercer—basically a rocket that produces an intense, focused flame—to heat it white-hot; then it was rapidly water-cooled, shattering it. (This canal got the Liberal party into hot water in 1931 when slush money paid to certain senators and to the Liberals' campaign fund surfaced. The Beauharnois Light, Heat and Power Company had made the payoff in return for the right to divert the old canal water and generate hydro with it. The scandal boiled for a while, but it didn't stop the Liberals winning the next election.)

At the end of the Beauharnois, with one lock (the lower) left to go, we came to a dead halt. Commercial traffic was heavy, and because the *Avalon* was classed as a recreational boat, we had to yield to the big-paying ships.

The afternoon stretched on to dinner, and beyond. Two young men in a D-boat alongside got out and practised their golf swings, then zinged a few white bullets over the water. When the fourth cargo ship of the day, the *Montréalais* out of Toronto, slid out of the lock, I asked the only person in sight on the ship, an equally bored young man moving a mop around the deck, what they were carrying. Sprinklers all along the vast deck were cooling it in the thirty-degree sun. "Iron ore ingots from Cape Breton," he said. "Heavy."

In the Seaway's first decade, forty belly-heavy ships a day would have passed this spot; now it is down to around ten. Seven hundred workers on the St. Lawrence Seaway have lost their jobs since 1990, and even at a cost to shippers of seventeen thousand dollars a trip, the St. Lawrence Seaway Authority has to ladle funds out of its own reserves to top up annual ten-million-dollar deficits. Add to that the breakup of Russia and the subsequent collapse of its money, as well as the European thanks-we'll-eat-it-here attitude, and you have a dramatic effect on grain shipments, which used to account for two-fifths of the stuff moving through the Seaway.

The previous year had shown an improvement, with steel imports hardening by two-thirds, grain shipments wilting only slightly and the début of a new broom of management, the Seaway Management Corporation. The latter is a Canadian entity which, to the annoyance of the Americans, includes businesses that use the waterway and can talk of cutting costs and removing duplication. Like pit-stop teams in a race, the Seaway is striving to get ships in and out of its locks faster. The Canadian government have also thrown out a lifeline, reducing charges for ice-breaking services by the coast guard, and there is even talk of jettisoning lock fees.

However, there is a deeper problem. Yet again, as in the past, the locks on the St. Lawrence are proving to be too small. There now exist even bigger tankers, mega-salties out on the ocean that are snookered by the Seaway system; they push down too deep and are too long. Meanwhile, the fleet working the Seaway is getting old, and less and less Canadian. Almost all the ships that can pass like camels through the eye of the Seaway are over ten years old. In 1996, for the first time since it opened, the number of ships bearing a maple leaf dropped below a hundred. Orders for new bulk tankers that are Seaway-friendly are as rare as requests for biplanes.

The economic solution is to do the obvious, and widen and deepen the locks and the channel. But 2000 is not 1950, and there are forces that will fight against that. The cost makes politicians, busy selling austerity as the new snake oil, shudder. Environmentalists, and residents with boats parked at the ends of their lawns, consider the tankers just one species of river user, one that has to operate in balance with the others. The civil servants in Quebec City whose job it is to promote trade on the St. Lawrence are valiant, underfunded, and anxious to forge the new kind of public–private partnerships that got, for example, the Chunnel built under the English Channel. But none of the Chunnel's investors have yet to see their money back, and attracting investors for a bigger, better Seaway will take a mighty magnet. Will there be ships a thousand feet long passing through these locks in the year 2525? Your guess is better than mine.

It was dark by the time we dropped forty-two feet in the lower lock to become level with Lac St-Louis. The huge Hydro-Québec power station on our right, one of the biggest in the world when it was built in 1958, was all lights and noise, sending power to a million televisions and computers. Tied up at the end of the lock's slipway, stiff with inactivity and bored with a day of little forward motion, we voted for an early night. Then a shout came from outside. Two of the power station's security guards could not allow it, this docking, and they gave us the standard Québécois shrug, the one conveying a wish to be kind that is thwarted by impersonal regulations. The only thing was to push on through the dark hours for Montréal. Resigned to a long night, we pulled away into the dusk of Lac St-Louis, the surface still as glacial stone, towards the distant lights of skyscrapers.

The habitation on the grey shores consisted of standard-issue Quebec villages, clustered around spired churches. I went and stood by the bowsprit, a favourite spot for crew who wanted a semblance of solitude. Spending night and day together on a sailing ship is an exercise in proximity, necessitating tongue-biting and accommodation to others' moods. Privacy goes out the porthole, so there is respect for someone snatching some time in a bubble in their bunk, or by the bowsprit. As the deepening dark stole the details from the shore, it was easy to imagine myself a deckhand on a schooner from a century ago.

The Third Day

Although it wasn't my turn, I stayed on deck for the midnight-to-four-in-the-morning watch as we travelled through the bottleneck out of Lac St-Louis, down an eight-mile overland canal and into the La Prairie Basin, a crescent of water shaped like a bowl stood on a forty-five-degree angle. The nose of Île de Montréal sticks into the bowl, and where the contents would spill out are the Lachine Rapids, just after the reduced Kahnawake reserve. It was trimmed when part of the reserve's waterfront was expropriated in 1958 and blasted away to make the deepwater channel, framed on the north by an extended dyke that provided us with tame, straight water. The dyking and blasting were held up for several weeks during the Seaway's construction while six Mohawks held out for what they considered decent compensation for the loss of their homes. They got it.

On the other side of the dyke, in a darkness that made it seem as though we were sailing through space, I could hear but not see the rapids. By day they remain formidable, with only the occasional loose tree sailing through them since the *Rapids Prince* made her final voyage. I can't find any record of a canoeist shooting the rapids solo since John Smith did it in mid-June 1934, at the age of twenty-four. Smith, an ex-whaler, set out in a determined and, it has to be said, off-course state of mind to canoe from Peterborough, Ontario, to Peterborough, England. He made it through all the St. Lawrence rapids, certainly the last person to do that, and even into the stormy Gulf, but his journey ended when first his shredded canoe, then a tin holding his diary, and finally his body washed up on the shore of Newfoundland at River of Ponds.

The darkness seemed to amplify the sounds of the river as the south shore became more and more industrial and the lights of Montréal began to overwhelm the stars. The town of La Prairie was asleep, the traffic lights playing catch and release with no one at all. It was from here that, on July 21, 1836, just six years after the first railroad opened in the coalfields of northern England, the first railway journey in Canada was made by the engine Dorchester, financed in part by John Molson.

At two in the morning we came upon the eerie sight of a floodlit tanker being emptied by rolling cranes, one-armed dinosaurs reaching in and pulling out containers like innards, then neatly stacking them up. Another ship nearby was silently retching out a hill of red powder down a tube.

An hour later the sun rose ahead of us. Red sky in the morning, sailor's warning. The windows of Montréal's skyscrapers caught the ruddy light for a few minutes, then returned to grey anonymity.

To arrive at Montréal by ship is a most Canadian thing to do, and the city was just awakening as we tiptoed past the old site of Expo '67, the frame of the Geodome so solemn and useless now. In that very Canadian year, one of those points in its history when Canada cut another strand of the rigging binding it to Britain, the voyageur canoes were back in town. On Labour Day, a dozen twenty-five-foot canoes shot the whitewater at Lachine and came to rest at Expo '67 on Île Ste-Hélène, the island directly in front of Montréal's old port district. The twelve facsimile birchbark canoes, maple leaf insignia on their prows, had travelled three thousand five hundred miles down the old fur trade route from Rocky Mountain House in Alberta. The trip had taken thirteen weeks, for an average of forty miles a day.

The Lady of the Harbour statue atop Notre-Dame-de-Bonsecours chapel welcomed us with open arms, as she has all ships since 1893. A church dedicated to the protection of sailors has stood here since 1657, and a huge fleet of model ships hangs in the nave, put there by grateful sailors over the last century and a quarter. We tied up against a restored wharf at the exact end of the Lachine Canal, where there was pungent evidence on the concrete steps of someone having slept there rough the night before.

The Lachine Canal, like its senior partner the Coteau-du-Lac, is out of the loop now, its lock gates still as the swing doors on an abandoned saloon. But it is being slowly reawakened, starting at the as yet undiscovered pleasures of the Lachine waterfront, and proceeding along paved paths that run beside the glorious art deco Atwater Market to the old port, a distance of seven miles. Mountain bikers and in-line skaters with their perfect tans populate the canal banks like tropical fish in an airy aquarium, and the brick, castlelike warehouses that once hummed with import and export are either already converted into condos—a habit catching on in ports around the world that have lost their purpose—or waiting their turn. There are moves afoot to open the canal itself to the rippling sport of kayaking and the burgeoning number of Montrealers who own powerboats, and indeed a canal without boats upon it looks underdressed. Government signs along the banks state that thirty million dollars is to be put into the renovations—considerably more than it cost to build it.

As the St. Lawrence river moves toward the sea, the current slackens as it goes. The river has become so wide and deep that its movement is hardly felt although its volume is far greater than that of the waters foaming at Lachine. So it is with the history of Montreal, indeed to some degree with the history of any city as it grows from early settlement to metropolitan life. Its history merges more and more into the wider history of the nation.

—Stephen Leacock, Montreal, Seaport and City, 1942

Ashore, the jazz festival was on, offering free music in the streets, and Montréal was in a good mood. Place Jacques-Cartier, the inclined, triple-wide boulevard that runs from the town hall to the old dock buildings, was a corral stuffed with aimless, happy people. The port itself, which for many years after 1851 (when it was first dredged) was the busiest in Canada, its piers never tranquil, was now packed with whiter-than-white recreational boats, like so many fish piled in a shop window. Several of them were big enough to have manservants. Woodheads refer disparagingly to fibreglass pleasure boats as "tupperware," and they do not sail so much as drive. Of the old port, the one that appeared in so many postcards bristling with masts, there was not a trace.

The Fourth Day

Three a.m., and another storm had rolled in, twice as aggressive as the one two nights before. The tupperware was bobbing about in the basin as if attacked from below. Tridents of lightning struck close by in pairs and triplets, lighting us up as though the gods were taking snapshots. The ship was trying slowly to turn, the bowsprit tracing an arc of one hundred and eighty degrees back towards the river, tearing loose a piece of the dock.

There was not enough room for the *Avalon* to make the turn; the bowsprit would hit the side wall of the basin and break off like an icicle. We cast off the hookups to the electricity and fresh water, which were starting to stretch. Just as the bowsprit was due to snap, George started the engine and backed up. Everyone froze and looked forward. The bowsprit swung like a clock finger running backwards past midnight, just a light "click," and an hour later we were docked against unyielding concrete, in a tight space between a millionaire's yacht from New York and a booze cruise ship that made a nightly run down the river. The storm was later graded a hurricane, and a killer; a boy had been crushed beneath a dismembered branch. Come dawn, there was only sunshine and the deckhands on the bigger powerboats straightening the deck chairs.

The weather report for the next leg of the journey said, "Montréal to Trois-Rivières. Wind west by northwest, ten to fifteen knots. Possibility of thunderstorms."

"They always say that," Joe said. "It's CYA: cover your ass." Four more crew had come on: the married business couple, Guy and Nicole; Christopher, a recently graduated marine architect; and Charles, a travelling purchaser of sites for cell-phone relay towers. The latter two were co-owners of a used sailboat that they were busy resuscitating, and Charles was from an old Québécois shipbuilding family.

The loading and unloading of ships went on for several miles on our port side as we left Montréal, followed by a massive refinery. On the third deck of the static container vessel *Canmar Fortune*, a dozen well-dressed ladies and gentlemen waved to us as she was loaded. In eight days they would be in Felixstowe and know a great deal more about each other.

Once past the hard-working town of Sorel, we were in Lac St-Pierre, a twenty-mile-wide bulge between there and Trois-Rivières. The Europeans, flaunting geographical correctness, named it for how it appeared to them. It is in fact extremely shallow, two thousand times as wide as its average depth (as is sometimes said, erroneously, of Canadian history). In spring the lake floods right under the highway along the north shore and into the fields on the other side. I've driven this stretch of road in April as though driving on a dike, and gone past two men in a punt wearing camouflage jackets and fishing the shallows for pike no more than fifty feet from my passenger seat.

René Béland makes his living as a guide on Lac St-Pierre in a rumpled, blue, wide-hipped boat. An aesthetic, slightly haunted-looking man with a fine head of greying hair, René has a degree in anthropology from Laval University and regards looking at books and looking at nature as equal opportunities to learn. He is both a naturalist and a hunter's guide, and in any given week René will arrange for as many cameras as guns to be pointed at the wildlife. A few weeks before sailing on the *Avalon*, I got René to show me the lake's inhabitants going about their ways of life and death.

René and I were equally shallow in each other's mother tongue, but he was used to the problem and had with him a book of photographs and sketches of the local fish and fowl. When we came upon a fence of thin branches standing up out of the water, ten of them about six feet apart, he flipped past herons and snapping turtles till he came to a drawing of an eel—*anguilla rostrata* in Latin, *anguille* in French—that returns to the sea through here in September and October. Netting arranged in Vs between the poles ushered the eels into submerged cages at night, when they preferred to travel. When I mimed eating a wriggling eel and then gagging, René just smiled sympathetically. Using sign language and a sort of franglais, he informed me of the commercial fishery that still works Lac St-Pierre, taking out several hundred tonnes of brown bullhead, yellow perch and sturgeon as well as the eels.

Half a mile offshore, two small, funny-shaped dots sat on the water, black buoys possibly marking a shoal. René located a photograph of a mallard (*canard sauvage*) and pointed, but as we got closer I saw they were human heads. Duck hunters. Because Lac St-Pierre is so shallow, René explained in charades, the men were able to stand in a submerged hide with a slightly raised rim, stepping up onto a box to shoot when a duck flew by. They were dropped off there and would be collected later. The silhouette of their hunting caps gave them a misleading duck bill.

Suddenly, with great speed, one of them rose up to his waist as though pushed from below, the gun butt went into his shoulder, and *bang!* I tracked the line of fire to a duck doing a death roll in mid-air, then falling straight to the water as though suddenly seized by a gravity beam. One of the *chasseurs* resented our coming so close and popped up again like a trick dolphin, shooing us away with his hands; the Québécois swear words *hostie* and *tabarnac* could be heard. A couple of minutes later the hunters were once again just two wobbling dots on the water, no bigger than the full stop at the end of this sentence.

In the half-dozen reed-grass islands clogging the western end of Lac St-Pierre, stretched out by centuries of prevailing current, it was easy to imagine we were in a northern bayou. A fallen log might be a basking crocodile, and several of the cottages, reachable only by boat, were akin to Louisiana catfish-hunter homes, up on stilts. If we had pulled in at a shack and bought a gallon of moonshine while chained dogs begged for the chance to bite us, it would not have surprised me.

Later in the day, I helped René load some plywood, canned goods, a box of men's magazines and stacks of soft drinks into the boat. An older, worn-looking man joined us and lay on top of the heap. He rolled a cigarette one-handed and, with considerable reluctance but having no way of avoiding me, explained in patient French that he had once been a river pilot and that now he worked on the dredger we were making for. He flicked the ash of his cigarette in the direction of a squat, dark piece of machinery sitting in the middle of the lake.

Dredging is the maritime equivalent of ironing—a chore that temporarily smoothes things out but soon needs doing again. Dredgers made possible the great ports of the ancient world, like Alexandria, Carthage and Ostia, and they do the same for the Seaway. At any given moment a dredger somewhere is scooping

up some part of the bottom of the St. Lawrence channel, throw-
ing it into a floating skip to be dumped elsewhere, and restoring
the Seaway to the crucial depth of twenty-seven feet. The silt is
sucked up by hydraulics, torn up by an endless elevator with
teeth, and grabbed by a huge bucket rigged to a dipping arm. It
is a dirty, Sisyphian task not too distant from oil rigging. It is
done by men who will trade boredom on a slowly moving factory floor for good money, and the commercial Seaway would
literally grind to a halt if their work ceased.

A trio of young men emerged as René brought us alongside
the dredger in tipsy-turvy water. The endless elevator brought
up a few more noisy buckets of mud, and the ex-pilot paused on
the edge of our boat, judging his step, then hopped back into
his routine. He dropped a book from his pocket when he
jumped, and I handed it to him. It was a much-thumbed book
of lyrical French poetry by the lifelong Montrealer Émile Nelligan, who died in 1941 after spending sixteen years in hospital. Nelligan, who once took an extended sea voyage, would
have been pleased to find himself on a Conradian scow so near
his hometown. "Merci," the old man said, without making eye
contact, and René drove us back to shore in rough water.

Now, two months later, the *Avalon* passed the same dredger
a little farther downriver. I looked for the man with the book,
but no one appeared on deck.

In the middle of this great pancake of a lake, George produced a white Dacron condom fit for a giant. From it he pulled
a new gaff topsail, made in Kingston. (Sails have great names.
The three uppermost sails on the mainmast of a square-rigged
ship are called cloudbreaker, skyscraper and moonraker.) "Perfect conditions to try it," he said. "There's a light offshore
wind." Sail in his teeth, George monkeyed seventy feet up the
mast to attach it.

Installed, the new sail caught the breeze and puffed out like one of Dizzy Gillespie's cheeks. Doug, at the wheel, began calling out the speed until it peaked at just over ten knots, by which time the wind had taken over and was providing more thrust than the engine. One hundred tons and eleven people being moved through a viscous medium by something none of us could see. The cargo ship behind us, the *Jean Laprise* out of Toronto, which was slowly overhauling us, came on the radio. "She's beautiful ship, her," the captain said in a static-filled voice, and no one argued with him.

In a short time we were under the bridge and racing towards Trois-Rivières—and at that moment another nineteenth-century topsail schooner appeared coming the other way, black and gold with a suit of sails that could have used a good bleaching. She was flying the American flag and bore the name *Pride of Baltimore*, returning home via Lake Champlain, Lake George, down the Hudson and round into Chesapeake Bay. We fired our toy cannon at them, and they replied with a loud car horn. There was a round of camera action followed by big American waves, with the hand held high over the head.

Docking at Trois-Rivières's new concrete wharf was, by comparison with crowded Vieux-Montréal, like parking a car on a village main street. The waterfront, like Kingston's, has been tinkered with and made cruder, more blockish. There is the inevitable large, bland hotel blocking the view of the river and casting a long shadow behind it, and the sloping main street, once-removed from and parallel to the water, is struggling, but it has retained, like Valleyfield, a fifties feel to it, with old-style fonts forming the shop names. Parc Portuaire, in the centre of the old town, has a dock for pleasure craft and excursion boats, including one, the *Jacques Cartier*, that offers a couple of hours on the river.

Cartier, on his second voyage, anchored off Trois-Rivières on the seventh of October, 1536, "opposite a stream which enters the river from the north and at the mouth of which lies four small islands covered with trees." Cartier was being conservative; there are in fact six islands, and the stream was the Rivière St-Maurice. If you take the Boulevard des Forges out of Trois-Rivières, past the large church that is a small-scale replica of Westminster Abbey, and follow the St-Maurice, you eventually come to a museum dedicated to the first large-scale iron foundry in North America, which fired up in 1730 and later built the engine for the *Accommodation*, first steamboat on the St. Lawrence.

Only two other ships were tied up with us at the Trois-Rivières wharf, one a replica of an older ship and the other very modern. The older one, the *Canadian Empress*, was a Mark Twain–ish affair, a bright white imitation of a steamer en route from Kingston to Québec, with a complement of cruising passengers drawn from the senior classes. Ahead of that was a member of the coast guard fleet, a working boat compared with the elegant tourist tub.

The coast guard ship was busy mapping the bottom of this stretch of the river via a complicated arrangement that swung out at right angles to the sides, rather like masts that went horizontal rather than vertical. Spaced out along them, hanging below, were white objects like shiny plastic rugby balls. These were echo sounders, and they were relaying a sonic picture of the riverbed. The ship was proceeding upriver, feeding data into a computer that would eventually be transformed into a new chart.

Land maps cover the top of the landscape, whereas river charts map the bottom. The first survey of the hidden depths of the St. Lawrence was undertaken in 1830 by a Captain

Bayfield, whose crew spent fifteen months lowering and raising a weighted rope, taking soundings in fathoms. Bayfield's charts were considered state-of-the-art; and now they are regarded as works of art.

There was one other boat near us, lying on its side on the docks, chained up. There is a race across the river at Trois-Rivières every winter, in *canots de glace*—iceboats. Before there were metal-hulled ferries and massive arched bridges, the postal service delivered letters to people on the opposite shore of the St. Lawrence in rowboats. In winter, the intervening ice floats and edge ice were overcome by using the *canot de glace*, which had a severely sloped prow that could belly-flop far onto the ice. The boat was then dragged to the next patch of water. The there-and-back race at Trois-Rivières is a re-creation of this exhausting part-time job. Several towns along the St. Lawrence have a *bal de neige*, winter festival, that includes a *canot de glace* race, and teams start training for the races as soon as there is ice in the river.

"I first swallowed a big bit of the St. Lawrence when I was fourteen, in 1949." Jean-Guy Beaumier is telling me the story of the first boat he built, an ambitious but awkward trimaran, fashioned with his father's tools. Now in his sixties, Jean-Guy is the only maker of canoes in Trois-Rivières, once the home of dozens of builders of the great voyageur craft. I was glad of the chance to visit him in his workshop.

Jean-Guy's homemade trimaran floated for a short while on its maiden voyage, then sank right in the path of the six o'clock cross-river ferry. Jean-Guy went down with his ship, avoided the ferry, trod water for half an hour, and then, with a cargo ship bearing down indifferently upon him, swam to a buoy and hung on. "The ship see me, and they phone the ferry. The ferry picked me up, and I was home in time for the nightly prayers at seven on the radio."

There was a gap of eleven years before Jean-Guy attempted his next boat. He had aspirations of becoming an Olympic canoeist, a dream that did not come true, but he did win the Canadian championships in the thousand-metre singles at the Rideau Canoe Club in 1952, and came third in a North American cup race at Bangor Park in Toronto. "I was skinny then, but the man who won was six feet and four inches, a foot and two inches above me. If he do sixty strokes a minute on one knee, I have to do eighty to beat him. I couldn't." Realizing he needed an Olympic-style, cedar-strip canoe designed to fit his particulars, Jean-Guy became an autodidact. He borrowed one, took it apart, made a small model, then his own full-size one. After some prodigious displays in long-distance canoeing, including covering a joint-wrecking one hundred and twenty-five miles on the same knee, Jean-Guy retired from racing in the early seventies.

In an old two-room schoolhouse in Cap-de-la-Madeleine, where he had grown up, Jean-Guy founded Les Canoes Beaumier. In his first year, 1972, Jean-Guy's reputation landed him a contract to build, in six months, a hundred canoes and kayaks for the Quebec Games. For the next twenty-two years the schoolhouse turned out an average of fifty Beaumiers a year. Canoe clubs around the country boast of their Beaumiers, and canoeists on the nearby Lac Simon reserve favour them. Fibreglass racing kayaks have now become his stock-in-trade, and Jean-Guy hasn't made anything in wood in ten years. Five years ago, when he turned sixty, Jean-Guy sold the schoolhouse and set up shop in a corner of the fibreglass and metalworking factory run by his son.

Jean-Guy, a quiet-spoken man, stroked the short length of a wooden kayak only as tall as himself as he looked back on fifty years of river work. "It's for my granddaughter, Kayla," he said, with a firm sense of family continuity in the sport, although he has recently sold the business. Two more years as a living database for the new owners, an ex-Olympic canoeist from Hungary and his wife, then Jean-Guy will "go sit on the porch of my house at Cap-de-la-Madeleine and look across the river to Trois-Rivières. At the end of the week, an hour or two in a canoe."

Perhaps destined to be the last indigenous canoe builder in a guild three centuries old, Jean-Guy stroked the handiwork on his granddaughter's kayak with a well-used hand. It was a voyageur's hand, one that might easily have dropped over the side of a freshly made canoe on its way upriver to Montréal for the start of the fur season a dozen generations ago, and scooped up some of the clean, cold water of the St. Lawrence in a pewter canoe cup.

Trois-Rivières marks the beginning of the fluvial estuary portion of the river—the tidal zone. Here there is a hint of salt in the water. The tide was going out, and as the evening wore on, the *Avalon* appeared to be sliding down the dock wall, inch by inch, as though measuring the fall of darkness. Lights came on in several of the rooms in the monolithic hotel, and our crew divided up, half voting to explore the nightlife, half staying out on deck under the stars to splice the main brace, not with rum but with single malt whiskey.

As we sipped, Christopher, the marine architect, explained the physics of seasickness, which had not affected anyone on this trip. (The word *nausea* comes from the Greek word for *ship*.) There is, he said, a freak frequency of judder that can get established on a ship ploughing through certain wavelengths, and no stomach can resist it, no matter how seasoned. A modern Norwegian ferry had recently hit it, and everyone lost their lunch, even the captain.

The night-on-the-town crew returned, reporting that the cafés on main street were full, people sitting out, the depression the town was suffering forgotten on a starry summer's eve. An hour later I discovered that two of my bunk mates snored, in different keys. Not even this, after four days of fresh air, could keep me awake.

The Fifth Day

The river is a natural canal along the stretch between Trois-Rivières and Québec, steepsided on the south shore, villages on top only just big enough to cover both sides of the road, an occasional wharf and small beach when the chance comes at the cliff bottom. The Canadian giant Modest Mailhot was born at one such clifftop village, St-Pierre-les-Becquets, in 1763. He stood seven feet four inches and weighed over six hundred pounds, and his shoe is on exhibit at the Laval University museum. On the edge of the village, there is a rock the size of a Volkswagen Beetle, which Mailhot was able to roll. Try it sometime.

By mid-afternoon, with Cap-de-la-Madeleine several hours behind us, we were approaching the Duhamels. (The St. Lawrence has a series of "Caps" stretching from Madeleine to Cap-des-Méchins at the far end of the river; these dovetail with a complementary series of "Pointes" from Pointe-des-Cascades to Pointe-des-Monts.) The Duhamels are not a family of islands or a nasty set of shoals, but a married couple,

Delphus and Monique. They are known to every sailor on the St. Lawrence who has passed their aerie on the clifftops just outside the topiary-laden village of Deschaillons-sur-St-Laurent, on the south shore. Known not by sight, but by sound.

Most days, as each ship comes within range of the Duhamel residence any time just after breakfast until sundown, the couple take up their stations by the impressive flagpole at the cliff edge; the pole is visible, with binoculars, a mile east and west by someone standing on the bridge of a ship. Once the nationality of the approaching vessel is known, husband and wife go into action with marital precision. From two large white weather-proof chests that flank the base of the flagpole, lids are lifted, drawers are pulled out, and a flag and a cassette appear. These are then loaded, one onto the pole ropes, the other into a stereo machine. The flag corresponds to the ship's home country, while the cassette bears a recording of its national anthem. The ship draws level, the flag rises and Monsieur Duhamel, a retired carpet store owner with the demeanour of an off-duty, clean-shaven Santa Claus, presses *Play*.

There is a pause as some blank tape winds on, then a noise issues from the speakers that is immense, bird-stunning, worthy of a rock festival. It is melodic thunder coming from a speaker the size of a garden shed. With military precision the flag reaches the top of the pole just as the last gigantic note cannons down to the ship and past it like a sonic wind echoing along the river. The ship replies with a grateful blast on its horn, long and low, a peashooter compared with the bazooka that has been aimed at it.

"A thousand ships a year pass here, I would say," Dolphus reckons. (I have seen a figure as high as ten thousand; split the difference and call it six.) "Undoubtedly, the anthem I play the most is the Philippines; most sailors are from there. Then

Indian, then Chinese, then the Russians. The captains are German, Greek, Indian." In all, the Duhamels say, they have collected one hundred and fifty separate anthems, of which they have played eighty. Monsieur will not admit to having a favourite, although "the new Croatian one is very nice. I've played that around twenty-five times. Northern countries have beautiful anthems, and the new Asian ones have a tendency to be military."

How on earth did all this start? "My uncle was a captain of this river. He gave me his charts, some of them from 1907, and I marked on them three places I would like to live. I had no wish to go to become a seaman, but I wanted to be by the river. This place, Cap-Charles, was one of the places I marked. You are looking at the dream of a young man come true."

That put Monsieur Duhamel in sight of the ships, but this business of the big hello came a little later. It started with soap powder. In the powder box was a giveaway map of the world, which went up on the wall. Then Dolphus took the first inno-cent step. "Why not on this map, I said to my wife, show the kids where the ships that pass in front of us are from?" Some ports, like Paco Gradee in Ghana, were not easy to find, but the pins accumulated like ants on a picnic cloth. From there it was but one step to writing in the names of the ships, and then a bigger one to actually saluting them. "Canada and Quebec only the first year," Dolphus told me, "then we branched out." That was thirty-five years ago. Sailors from all over the world know of the Duhamels. Most of them have never spoken to him, though, because by law he can only listen to the ship-to-shore radio—he cannot reply. Dolphus and Monique, united in their habit, are a beacon of respect that sailors on the St. Lawrence look forward to, a snap of the fingers in a life of boredom. And no neighbour has yet complained.

So it was that at fifteen minutes to eleven that morning we heard *O Canada* boom out from the clifftop, followed by *The Maple Leaf Forever*, as the flag rose up the pole. A message of thanks went out from our radio, and a moment later three other flags were run up. We had to consult the chart to discover the letter signified by each pattern, there being a different flag for each letter of the alphabet. U - R - W. You Are Welcome.

Ice fishing is a very Canadian thing, and on the stretch of the St. Lawrence we were in now, it is an epidemic. The undisputed capital of ice fishing is the small north shore village of Ste-Anne-de-la-Pérade, directly opposite the Duhamels' loudspeakers. In mid-December, *pêcheurs*—anglers—arrive from all over Quebec, collect their huts from the fields where they have been stored during the warmer months, and set them on the ice in the mouth of the Rivière Ste-Anne. The huts, painted in a rainbow of colours, number over a thousand, each sheltering between four and twenty people. By the opening of the season on the twenty-sixth of December there are far more huts than homes in the town; they constitute a village unto themselves, connected by roads and with electricity brought to them on poles.

The object of all this rapid settlement is a small fish popularly known as *petit poisson des chenaux*. In English they are nicknamed tommy cod. In the fall, a bell goes off in the fishes' brains, and they move—some estimates say a billion of them—from the salt water of the lower St. Lawrence and the Gulf into the fresh water of the tributaries past Québec. Because of its sandy bottom and Perrier-like water, which suits their spawning technique, the fish have developed a fondness for the Rivière Ste-Anne, and anglers have developed an equal fondness for hauling them out of it, to the startling tune of several million fish a year. When the full fever is on both fish and fishers, it is possible for the occupants of one medium-sized

chalet to keep re-baiting their hooks with shrimp and pork
liver, two hooks to a line, and yank a thousand fish onto the
cabin floor between sunrise and sunset. Meanwhile, the commercial fishers on the ice at the edge of the St. Lawrence, who
get first crack at the fish, extract them by the netload through
bigger holes, pile the fish on the ice and then scatter them with
shovels to freeze and die. By the end of the season on the fifteenth of February, five million *poissons de Noël* will not make
it to the spawning ground four miles up the Ste-Anne, but millions more will.

Just before we reached Québec, Gisele appeared beside me at
the rail and pointed at the town before us, a classic affair with a
river mouth in a valley inhabited on both slopes, and a wooden
railway bridge linking the two sides. A large grey stone building
sat on a hilltop—the old nunnery. "That is where I was a
younger woman," she said. "Cap-Rouge. My father worked in
that place when it was a nunnery, maintaining the grounds, and
we had a small farm. I rode many times with him on the tractor,
and we swung out below that bridge on a rope when we swam."
I left her to carry on looking at her memories as the tide pulled
us towards Québec, under the grand old bridge.

To sail into Québec is to walk in the footprints of history.
The walled city is almost a history factory, as evidenced by the
two cruise ships in port busy disgorging their clients armed
with cameras primed to capture some history and take it home.
Québec is one of those towns that exists in two tenses simultaneously, past and present, and makes part of its living from selling the way it used to make a living. Where there is now a
coast guard station, with a helicopter sunbathing beside it and
the *Sir John Franklin* parked and awaiting assignment up north,
I could envisage the half-finished sailing ship *Québec*, abandoned after the unsuccessful defence of the town in 1759. I

could see evidence of that, too, simply by lifting my eyes forty-five degrees to the Citadel. (Taking the long view, Québec was hardly conquered at all. It retains much of eighteenth-century French civil law and religion, and ninety-five percent of its inhabitants are French-speaking.) The French version of the Canadian national anthem was written here in 1880, before the English version, and it attests to the St. Lawrence as the mother river of French Canada. "Sous l'oeil de Dieu, près du fleuve, géant, le Canadien grandit en espérant," the second verse says; "Under God's gaze, by the giant river, the Canadien grows in hope."

Up in the control room of the marine traffic centre, our arrival was duly noted, entered on a card and filed in a rack under "Recreational Vessel." The tide was in our favour and carried us to the old port, through a narrow lock and into a basin already full of ships. The one alongside ours had been there a while. Its last time out was as part of the 1998 *Titanic* expedition, when it had been a floating canteen and supply ship; now it had a large FOR HIRE sign. Blocking our eastern view was an enormous grain elevator, and taller still was an oil rig in dock for repair, the biggest nautical object ever to come into Québec harbour. Sitting here, out of context, it was completely impressive, one of those man-made objects so large and complex that it seemed to have been forged by a race of giants with advanced engineering degrees.

The lower town of Québec, just across the small bridge over the lock by which we had come in, was charm itself. I roamed the street of cafés and second-hand stores for postcards—I was a confirmed St. Lawrence deltiologist now—and kept seeing paraphernalia from sailing and steamships, brass-housed compasses, folk-art models of their ships made by retired sailors, ships in bottles, even a box of belaying pins.

As I strolled through the bygone artifacts, I noticed I'd developed a sailor's roll, a feeling that you are fine but the world is having problems staying level. The sensation disappeared the moment I returned to the ship. I had scored several postcards, including one from 1905; the message on the back, written by an American, read, "Everyone speaks French here!" George was not so lucky, having missed out on a bag of rare reefing irons, implements for getting caulking out from between deck planks.

That night we assembled down below deck with Gisele's family, a crowd ranging from babies to grandmothers, swapped songs in each other's language, and drank the same wine and beer. It was the best of times, *nos meilleurs moments.*

The sixth Day

George was already on deck fussing, anxious to get back on sea, but the tide would not be running our way till noon. At Trois-Rivières the tidal rise was no more than a bump, from ankle to knee, but here at Québec the mean tide, averaged out over the year, is ten feet. The strongest tide, in the spring, just after a new or full moon, can raise the water the height of a man on a stepladder.

Departure was further delayed by a wind that kept us holed up in the basin like a toy boat in a bath, but after a few passes at it, George had us through the lock, and chugging past the cranes and giant sheds of the Davie shipyards across from the port of Québec.

Davieship have had a checkered career since the opening of the Seaway. That same year they built what was at the time the biggest Canadian ship ever, with the politically confused name of *Federal Monarch*. Within months the *Monarch*'s title was ousted by the *Emérillion*, weighing in at almost forty-two thousand tons. A boat like that could enter the Seaway from Lake Ontario on Monday morning and have dinner in the Gulf on Friday afternoon.

The post-Seaway golden years continued for another decade, the yard turning out tugs, trawlers, tankers, ferries and frigates. The highlights were the outfitting of the Canadian navy's only aircraft carrier, the *Bonaventure*, and the manufacture of the *Eskimo*, sturdily constructed to service the remote Arctic villages created to maintain the DEW Line. The *Eskimo* was sturdy enough to set the annual record for deepest penetration of the river in winter, reaching Trois-Rivières on the fourth of January, 1960.

Then, in the early seventies, the reach of the Davie managers exceeded their grasp and an order for two Greek ships sapped the yard's money and morale, almost bankrupting them. Since then there have been ownership shuffles, and requests for bailouts and user-friendly loans, but they were still at work when we sailed by, almost two centuries after Davie built his first ship. A crane in the shipyard swung towards us as we passed; perhaps the schooner stirred something in its memory.

It's possible to pass either side of the Île d'Orléans—via the north channel, with the huge eyebrow of the bridge built in 1938 connecting the island to the mainland (and putting the ferry out of business), or via the south channel. We went south, past the site of the island's old shipbuilders. At three in the afternoon the sails went up, the engine was turned off for the first time and the *Avalon* leant over. There was a snap as everything locked into place, and the only sound was the hiss of the water moving quickly along the side. I walked, Buster

Keaton–fashion, down to the rail nearest the water, and had only to reach over to touch the river and splash it on my face. An old saying has it that time spent at sea is not deducted from a person's life, and sailing this glorious made it believable. "This," George said, "is as good as it gets." And so it was—for forty-five minutes, until the wind dropped and the engine was fired up again, north of Grosse-Île. From this side the island appeared uninhabited, only the top few feet of the monument to the Irish who died in 1847 showing above a hill. The monument was erected in the shape of a Celtic cross by the Ancient Order of Hibernians, and inscribed in French, Gaelic and English (with noticeable differences between the English and Gaelic regarding the reasons for the exodus from Ireland). The gathering on the day it opened in 1909 included survivors of the terrible summer of 1847.

The island's benighted history did not end when the quarantine station closed. After the germ warfare station finished its business in 1956, an agricultural station moved in and began studying animal diseases. In 1965 it became a quarantine station again, for large animals such as Charolais bulls coming into Canada, who were detained and checked over for infectious diseases; that closed in the late seventies. (Nowadays, imported bulls arrive in 747 airplanes as germ-free embryos.)

Since 1984, Grosse-Île, quite rightly, has been a historic site in the capable hands of Parks Canada. The second-class quarantine hotel now houses a café for visitors, with the former outlines of the rooms marked on the floor. Research by historians has produced a growing number of worthwhile publications, and all the renovations, save for a governmental display of multiculturalism in the old bakery, are honestly done. There is one brilliant stroke, in the old embarkation hall, where the rows of disinfection showers stand ready for a fresh batch of immigrants. In the waiting room on the second floor, projected onto the back wall from an enclosed box near the front, in a slightly green sepia, are slides made from photographs taken here on the island or from family albums, one fading down after fifteen seconds or so as the other comes up. They hit the wall life-size, the families stern-faced and posed, with almost no expression. Ahead lies the uncertain future, and all of them, except one or two babes in arms, are dead now, their adventures lived out, all equal in the sight of time.

Perusing with binoculars the south shore past Grosse-Île, I could make out the skyline of L'Islet over the top of the low Île aux Oies (Goose Island). This was the town that produced all those hard-sailing Berniers, including Joseph-Elzéar, who died here on Boxing Day, 1934, holding his wife's hand and staring at the Madonna, the Star of the Sea, on his wall. He lived a fourscore, Melvillian life, making over two hundred and fifty voyages under sail for a total of half a million miles at sea, delivering forty-six new sailing ships from Québec to their British owners, carrying the mails along the remote north shore during the Great War. He lives on in the town's maritime museum.

A famous picture of the legendary Joseph-Elzéar came to mind, depicting him standing proudly beside a huge polar bear he had shot in Arctic waters. The very dead bear was spread on the deck like a giant's rug, and Joseph-Elzéar has a proud look about him. I imagined this sea-hardened man, who knocked out several of his crew when they were drunk, here on the *Avalon*. What would he have made of us? In Joseph-Elzéar's day, once the anchor was weighed on the St. Lawrence, with each foot that the gap between wharf and vessel widened, the captain became more and more almighty, holder of the power and the possible glory, wrangler of the winds and broker of rags or riches. George governed in a more modest way, and did not have the option of leg irons.

The chemical industry had not yet set up its stall in Bernier's day, and our synthetic ropes, sails and modern varnishes would undoubtedly have gained his approval as a means of reducing the chores relating to hemp, canvas and shipworm. Ship-to shore-radio was not around until the end of Bernier's life, and in his day captains manufactured their own weather reports from experience. It struck me that farming and sea-captaining are similar professions in that both use a wide set of skills, one is always in the hands of the weather no matter how sophisticated the technology becomes, the help is usually low-paid and itinerant, it runs in families, and big business buys out the little guy whenever it can.

Some things have not changed. Our captain, as our course took us past the high mountains to the north, the slopes scored with ski runs, was doing his rope chores. Though synthetic, the ends still frayed, and they did it so realistically that it was only now that I learned they weren't hemp. That versatile plant would have been the first crop cultivated by many of the farmers on the south shore of this part of the river. It grows like Jack's beanstalk, and the fibre can be spun into clothing as well as rope. Every town on the river where sailing ships were built had a rope walk, a narrow, quarter-mile-long building for braiding the long strands together, then tarring it to make it waterproof.

On his left hand, the one with a piece of the thumb missing, George had a sailor's palm, an inch-wide-leather-and-metal prophylactic device for pushing a large needle through rope.

Within the hour I had picked up the skill of whipping a rope end, but I hadn't mastered it. There were so many skills like this along the river that had been swallowed by time, and a whole language associated with sailing that has become extinct—terms like "reeving a Burton" and "clearing a foul hawse."

The north shore rose and fell beside us in a series of cliffs and bays, the grey line of the highway snaking through it in tight bends and impossible gradients. This is the Charlevoix district, and because of its natural beauty the area has a pulse of artistic activity. There is a studio on every hilltop, and the small towns in between—Baie-St-Paul, St-Joseph-de-la-Rive, La Malbaie—trade in arts and crafts. Writers, poets, singers, painters and filmmakers repay the places and people they smuggle into their works by making them glow on the map, and that has certainly happened in Charlevoix. Gradually, the artists of the St. Lawrence have created a fictional river that runs alongside the real one, a parallel dimension that resembles it but is stocked with imaginary people and perspectives. Gabrielle Roy, author of *The Tin Flute*, summered and wrote in Petite-Rivière-St-François, and on the south shore there is Kamouraska, the town made famous in book and film by the French Canadian, very private Anne Hébert.

The Île aux Coudres was coming up, and Lisa and Joe had taken the wheel to guide us through the narrow gap between island and shore. A day left over from October had settled on the river, casting the cliff face of the island in a sombre mood. The Île aux Coudres claims the distinction of being the first island in the St. Lawrence to be stepped on by a European, when Cartier disembarked there in September 1535. A huge wooden cross marked Cartier's landing spot until 1788, when, beyond repair, it was removed.

Joe was born on Île aux Coudres, an island famous for its sailors and ships. *Goélettes* (schooners) and *chaloupes*—rowboats that were used to unload schooners and work in among logs—were made here. The island was a major centre for goélette manufacture when Joe's grandfather came of age to get a job, but that had died away, and there are only one or two in regular service on the river now.

Docking at Île aux Coudres was no longer possible. Joe, pointing to the old harbour, said, "She's silted up now. The only place to dock is reserved for the ferry." A modern, ugly warehouse sits next to the ferry wharf where a company has recently started building tugs designed to spin on their own axis like figure skaters. The warehouse has its own self-contained launching ramp, and once or twice a year the big doors open and a gleaming tug poises at the top, receives a blessing, bleeds wine down its flank and slips into the river.

A small crowd of people with similar features, Joe's family, were lined up at the end of the dock, his sister waving hard, his father raising his hand slowly, just once. Then they piled into their cars, chased us on the high road for half the length of the island, piled out and waved us out of sight.

I was noting all this when Joe said, "Here, let me borrow that," and drew a series of dots on the page in a spiral. It represented, he explained, a system for catching belugas, used on the island before beluga hunting became illegal. Each dot represented a pole six feet from its neighbour. The white whales entered at the front of the spiral at high tide, and swam in ever decreasing circles until they reached the centre, where they could not turn. When the tide went out, they were stranded and slaughtered.

Dusk fell, the river widened and the shore darkened to a horizontal constellation of street lights traffic lights, and the lamps of home and workplace. Finding the next buoy in the confusion of illumination became a chore; I tried it and had us making straight for a set of traffic lights. The penalty was only ten lashes, the skin hardly broken.

One by one the stars came out, like pinpoints of marine phosphorescence on a bottomless black ocean. An amazingly large moon rose over the hard-working town of Rivière-du-Loup on the opposite shore. In addition to its moonrises, the town is famous for its sunsets, one of the things about it that attracted Sir John A. Macdonald, Canada's first prime minister, to keep a summer farm cottage there in the 1870s, when it was still a growing village. His first cottage was often used as a retreat, as when he fled Montréal in 1873 after a scandal—involving himself, Sir Hugh Allan, large sums of money and a very substantial railway contract—pushed him back to the bottle. Les Rochers, the Macdonalds' second cottage at Rivière-du-Loup, was where he installed his encephalitic daughter, Mary, every summer on the recommendation of his doctors, the lower St. Lawrence salty air being considered remedial.

The Eighth Day

Sometime past midnight, Doug spun the wheel hard left, and a ninety-degree turn to port at the Prince Shoal lighthouse put us in the channel leading to Tadoussac. The Montagnais, gathering here to trade in the summer, had canoed this channel for centuries without a chart. The northern hunters traded with the southern Native farmers, and later all of them traded with the Europeans—Cartier in 1535 and Champlain in 1603, when he attended a victory celebration by the Algonquins and Montagnais after a skirmish upriver against the Iroquois had gone well.

The French put the first trading post here in 1599 (the foundations were discovered in 1941), and eleven of sixteen potential colonists died here in the winter of 1600, abandoned by their employers, who had scuttled back to France. The five survivors were taken in by the Montagnais. The European God pitched his tent here in 1615, and during a brief half-century of glory before the fort at Québec usurped it, Tadoussac was a busy place. As many as fifty ships could be sitting in the harbour then, loading up with furs. In 1661 the Iroquois decided the place needed a fresh start and burnt it to the ground.

The massive deluge of fresh water pouring out of the Rivière Saguenay pushed against us, slowing us down to a sea slug's pace. The sun came up and jumped several feet into the sky before we reached the harbour. This is the geographical edge of the upper estuary, and on a calm day a line of foam develops across the river where St. Lawrence salt water butts up against Saguenay fresh. Both flavours are part of a marine park that has whales available for spotting by the quarter of a million people who visit each summer. Tourists with their breakfasts still undigested were zinging out of Tadoussac in rubber Zodiacs, while the public address systems of small cruise ships chanted the words *baleines* and *whales* like a mantra. The whales, with the help of a lawyer, could sue for workplace harassment. They had got their own back the previous summer when a Norwegian cruise ship changed course to let the passengers have a whale photo op and then ran aground. The ship was towed back to Québec and the passengers took a train home.

Tadoussac is an overstuffed summer resort, and thanks to tourism, as many as fifty boats may once again jam the small bay. Today the harbour was a parking lot with not a berth to be had, so, as the steamships of the great white fleet once did, we took a side trip up the Saguenay. The sides of the river quickly rose in granite, too steep to permit a home. The water beneath us was deep enough to hold the CN Tower or the Empire State Building with nothing to show above the surface. After two hours, however, it was all spectacularly the same, so we turned back, passing a family of belugas, nine of them in a line, moving upriver along the edge of the cliffs. The eight white backs and one greyer young one broke the surface in turn.

There was still no place to tie up back in Tadoussac, but the coast guard had docked for the day. After Joe skipped over and had a word with them, we lashed up against their boat on the proviso that we might have to unhitch if they got a distress call, as they had every day that week. I walked the town, added a few pieces to the jigsaw puzzle in the lounge of the Hotel Tadoussac and walked down the beach to chat to the marine biologist Robert Michaud, head scientist at the interpretation centre devoted to the marine park.

Michaud, when he was not administrating, studied and regularly visited a local family of belugas, as well as tracking the movements of the twenty-five fin whales fitted with radio location packs. The pod of white whales followed a regular route and could be expected to be at a certain place at a certain time. The week before we spoke, Michaud said, the belugas had not turned up because a Sea-Doo had started tracing its inane circles on the same stretch of the river they visited. The belugas, being intelligent creatures, would not go there.

The Ninth Day

The next morning, the day of my departure from the adventure, I packed in no great hurry and wrote my name and sailing dates on the wooden scratch pad on the roof of my bunk. The

rule of thumb that it takes a day's sailing to cover the same distance a car can accomplish in an hour on shore had held true. I
had seen the river in a way that many had, once upon a time,
but that very few would in the times to come.

On top of my bag I put Melville's story of his first sailing voyage, which I had finished the night before. The last sentence
read, "But yet I, Wellington Redburn, chance to survive, after
having passed through far more perilous scenes than any narrated
in this, My First Voyage—which here I end." I fashioned my
goodbyes to the returning crew, all of us making sincere gestures
of reunion. Some others would also leave here while the rest carried on into the Gulf of St. Lawrence, where many more opportunities awaited to ride the waves using only the sails. The
Avalon would not dock again on the St. Lawrence River this trip,
so I intended to continue to the end of my journey by car and
ferry. I told George that our ongoing cribbage game would have
to await an outcome, said thank you as hard as I could to him
and Gisele, and walked over the deck of the coast guard ship in a
light drizzle to dry land, while the crew made preparations for a
sea voyage that would take them hundreds of miles farther east.

An hour or so later, after visiting a small maritime museum
run by offshoot members of the Molson family and talking to
some Native people camped on the beach in a replica of a
teepee, making dream catchers and belts to sell, I was ready to
leave. Already my sailor's roll was almost gone, and I walked to
the edge of the water and looked out into the thin fog that had
settled in for the day. The *Avalon* was disappearing into it, just
her stern visible. I waved to the ship and to the river, both of
which had my deep respect, and vowed to sail again the history
of the St. Lawrence.

There was a small piece of string in the sand nearby. I picked
it up and with a brief flurry of hands tied a perfect bowline knot.

23

MANY RIVERS TO CROSS

*The pilots spent their days with one foot on
the shore and the other on a boat.*

The line for the ferry across the river at Les Escoumins, half an
hour past Tadoussac, is long. I leave the car, sit on the dock and
look out at the St. Lawrence, hoping for the sudden lift of a massive blue tail or the black crescent moon of a minke whale's
back. A bruised maple leaf goes past me, spinning as though trying not to land on the coal dark river. Then I hear that high,
lonesome sound overhead—Canada brant geese leaving for the
southern warmth, their bellies full of spilled harvest seeds. In a
few short weeks the ice will return and much of the river, twenty
miles wide here and wider yet to the east in the fluvial estuary,
will hibernate. In this crisp light the river is more fjord-like than

ever, for that is what the St. Lawrence really is: a fjord stuck onto a river—lake at one end, ocean at the other—which is why the French call it a *fleuve* and not a *rivière*.

It is a rough crossing. A motorbike tied to the deck loosens and dances as we bounce on the waves, until one of the crew goes out as though competing in a rodeo and hog-ties it. We dock at Trois-Pistoles, with its huge, medieval-looking church of Notre-Dame-des-Neiges, regilded and refaced in the fifties by artisans from France and Italy who left their symbols, a boot and a flower, on the columns. The house of God was oversized for the village, even a Quebec village where daily life used to be proportional to the bulk of the church and the height of its spire. On the feast of Corpus Christi the entire population would march down to the river in procession, where there were statues of Our Lady of Fatima, there to decorate and pray. Some of the statues are still there.

The well-known Québécois writer Victor-Lévy Beaulieu lives in Trois-Pistoles and publishes books there. He was born in the town the day the Japanese surrendered to end World War II, and his family migrated to the big city of Montréal in the fifties, as so many lower river people did then. Breaking the grasp of tight-collared village life along the river was not easy for rural Quebeckers, and until the Quiet Revolution in the sixties most people died within a day's travel of where they were born.

Back in the days of sail, young men could take to the sea to free themselves of the unseen fence, heading for Nantucket and the whalers, where they might find work alongside Maliseet Indians from the St. Lawrence and Mi'kmaq from Nova Scotia. But Victor-Lévy Beaulieu returned to Trois-Pistoles in his forties when, as Jung said, we begin the inner life. The lower river welcomed him back, inspired his pen, and in the early nineties he assembled a collection of poems, old and new, about the St. Lawrence, *Les gens du fleuve* (*People of the River*.) In the introduction he writes of the indelible spell the river casts on a young mind. "I've never learnt to swim," he says, "nor have I ever set foot in a boat. Water both fascinates and repels me. I like to have it in front of me but not under me. Maybe this is because my childhood was filled with tales of shipwrecks on the open sea, huge storms, and sailors swallowed up forever by the waters of the river."

Out of Trois-Pistoles and back on the highway, I lose sight of the river, my view of it snookered by a very even line of hills. Through an attractive gap in the ridge, I turn off to visit the provincial park at Bic, there to dip my feet in salty water. The park in late afternoon feels like it's at the ocean's edge, an unexplored country waiting for its first footfall, the far side of the river lost to sight. Rocks the colour of honeycomb undulate into the water, as though poured from a giant's pail. I gatecrash one of the empty houses that is still there from when the park was appropriated, and wonder why I have such a beautiful place to myself, with such a glorious sunset building up, when a late-season battalion of mosquitoes hits. They make the most of an unexpected, bloody fuel supply and I am running as though chased by a bear when I get back to the car, my feet still dry.

I push on for Rimouski and come into it in less than an hour, at twilight, a level of illumination that suits it. The town was founded by a man called Lepage in 1696. By 1758 it had seventy-two inhabitants, just over a thousand a century later, and now it's the biggest conurbation along the stretch of shore between Rivière-du-Loup and Matane. The Île St-Barnabé that sits just offshore is a long pencil mark with cottage lights. Rimouski is pretty tonight, although its hindquarters are as blandly ugly as any other urban mass devoted to the car. The riverside esplanade runs like an eyelash on the downtown. The seawall lights are on, a handful of strolling Rimouskians taking in the salt and carbon monoxide evening air, and with the window down I can hear a boat chugging by. The big doors of the cathedral face the river as though they might open and a lifeboat come sliding out instead of a congregation. In the large fire that wiped out most of the eastern half of the town in 1950, on a night the town now calls *la nuit rouge* (the red night), the flames did not dare proceed past the cathedral walls.

The next day I walk the halls and intriguing rooms of Rimouski's Institut maritime du Québec, a building where they have been making sailors since 1944, and an institution that operated long before that in other structures now gone. In the late 1600s, the intendant of New France, Jean Talon, wrote, "The Canadian youth are improving their knowledge. They take to schools for sciences, arts handicrafts and especially navigation and if this movement is sustained there is every reason to hope that the country will produce mariners, fishermen and skilled workmen." They did, and continue to do so here at the Institute, and the graduates are among the most travelled people in the world.

Among the Institute's wonders are a nightmarish, sixty-foot-deep chamber in the floor of the swimming pool for trainee divers, and a planetarium that can simulate the night sky on any day in history, including the night the *Empress of Ireland* went down.

If you look diligently in the newspapers of the towns along the St. Lawrence, you will occasionally see an advert for a river pilot in the Jobs Vacant section. Apply, and if you have a certificate from the Institute at Rimouski, six or seven years' experience on the high seas, and were born on the river, you might get the job. Some years there will be no vacancies; others, three might come up. It's a case of waiting for any one of the one hundred and ninety pilots who hold St. Lawrence licences to retire, men like Michel Pouliot, who has worked the beat between Les Escoumins and Québec for over thirty years. (The river is divided into piloting sections all the way along.) Through all those years Pouliot has stuck to the pilots' golden rule: things happen when you least expect them. Fog, a gust of wind, drifting ice, a sudden summer mist, a sneak snowfall—any of these can seize the day and ruin it.

Michel Pouliot has never had the misfortune to ground a vessel, although ten years into his career the engine broke down on a vessel he had just boarded at Les Escoumins. Right after that a gale started to blow, and it continued to blow for twelve hours while the ship drifted wherever the wind took it. It eventually halted just off the reefs at Tadoussac. A happier day came in 1981, when he took the *Queen Elizabeth II* into Québec, the first time she visited there.

A little way east of Rimouski is one of the highlights—literally—in the history of the St. Lawrence pilots, the lighthouse at Pointe-au-Père. There is a dramatic painting of this structure by the Group of Seven artist Lawren Harris, done in 1930 when it was still operational. The sky is much the same this day as in the picture, whitish-grey clouds sitting over the swooping lines of the red-and-white edifice, a cross between a barber's pole and a giant ice cream.

The lighthouse is a tourist trap now, flanked by a restaurant and a shop selling riverine trinkets and *Empress of Ireland* memorabilia. Stuck to the side of the cash register, out of sight of customers, I spot a 1-800 number. Staff are to call it if they suspect someone of pilfering the wreck of the *Empress*, an act that was made illegal after a businessman from Gaspé declared his intention of blasting away the wreck to get at the million dollars' worth of nickel he believed was underneath. This was a twist of greed so odious that the provincial government passed a bill in the legislature to stop him.

Close to the lighthouse is a wetlands bird sanctuary, a court-yard for over a hundred different species. I spy, with my untrained eye, over twenty, including the arresting sight of a dozen herons walking in line, as though in organized search for a young one gone missing. There is plenty of life in the wetlands, but the rest of the point, which includes a fenced-off oceanographic institute with a modern power-generating windmill, seems sullen.

Things were once much busier at Pointe-au-Père. Among their other salvationist duties, lighthouse keepers at Father Point, as the English called it, were expected to chauffeur river pilots out to ships that had safely crossed the Atlantic and needed nursing through the considerable dangers of the St. Lawrence. John McWilliams, who kept lookout for a quarter of a century until 1905, was such a keeper. McWilliams passed his working days in the tower with one eye to the east, searching for the dot on the horizon that would grow bigger, a steamship that he was always the first on the river to behold. Then, as the law required, he would shuttle a pilot out to the side of the ship, whatever the weather. Over the years the sides of those ships grew taller and moved ever more quickly, and his sailboat became relatively smaller. He managed to hold on to his life, and those of the pilots in the boat with him, although the river came for him many times.

John McWilliams was himself a pilot, a member of that respected fraternity of the St. Lawrence that goes back as far as 1635, when the Frenchman Abraham Martin was appointed to the post for the entire river. As the annual trickle of sailing ships grew into a steady flow and piloting became a career option on the river, freelancers began competing with one another, sailing out alongside incoming boats and offering themselves to the captains for money. Some companies, like the Allan Line with its seventy-six ships, had their own company pilots, and it was Allan who had the lighthouse built at Pointe-au-Père.

The for-hire pilots spent their days with one foot on the shore and the other on a boat, looking for a plume of smoke to chase after like squeegee kids. A contemporary account, written in 1817, of freelance pilots foraging for a contract comes to us from the diary of Reverend Bell.

> The pilots have their numbers painted, in large figures, upon their sails, as well as boats. They cannot lawfully come much lower down than Father Point, and should take the first vessel they meet, whether large or small. But they sometimes run much lower down, looking for a large vessel, as they are paid, (a guinea I was told) per foot, for whatever water she draws. This man had left the island of Orleans nine days before, and run all the way, two hundred and seventy miles, in an open boat manned by himself and his son. They went on shore at night and sailed all day. They had run seventy-five miles this morning before we fell in with them.

It was chancy, hard work, but the ranks of the St. Lawrence pilots swelled, and the competition led to danger as the men ventured farther and farther out into the Gulf to be first to reach a ship and get a job. To the brave, the spoils—or death.

The British, three years after taking over navigational control of the St. Lawrence, designated Bic as the official station for pilots downstream of Québec and, with the typical English urge for tidiness, began regulating the pilots under a branch outpost of London's Trinity House. Pilots are by nature independent men, more used to guiding than being guided, and in 1860 they founded the Corporation des pilotes pour le havre de Québec et au-dessous, thus putting themselves in charge of themselves. The corporation had three schooners built to work out of the Bic station and bought Allan's Pointe-au-Père lighthouse, which burnt down in 1867 and was rebuilt. Five years later a pilot station went in at Pointe-au-Père. It became the primary station in 1905, and a small steamship, the *Eureka*, was made available. The station then also boasted a compressed-air foghorn called a diaphone, a Canadian invention, an almighty thing with a mouth three feet wide that deafened passing seagulls. People on the other side, thirty miles away, claimed to hear it.

In 1909, the piloting situation grew less dangerous with the arrival of Marconi's waves. Now it was possible for ships to communicate from far away with the station and order up a pilot in advance. In the same year a brand new lighthouse was built, twice as tall as the old one, with more dramatic lines.

In 1959, the pilot station closed and Les Escoumins, the town on the north shore where I caught the ferry, took over. The Seaway channel runs along the north shore in that piece of the river, so it made sense to have the pilots there. Ships can make their own way in the nice wide river east of Les Escoumins, but they must take on a pilot there if they are entering the river or drop the last one off if they are leaving.

The Pointe-au-Père lighthouse eventually went automatic, its outbuildings fell into disrepair and the dock got a DANGER! notice as it crumbled. But the buildings got a second wind in 1980, and now, thanks to the wreck of the *Empress*, tourists' money is used to keep the historical site in repair, although the ships shun it.

The voyage to river's end continues as I pull away from the lighthouse, and soon I am in Matane, a town much concerned with shipping. There are six working cargo ships sitting in the basin, and several more lined up alongside the dry dock like cars in for a "qwik lube." Two shipyards are still laying hulls here—one of them built the jet ferry that belts across the river from Rimouski to Forestville in one hour—and the streetscapes are harsh. This is a working town, with all its windows facing the river. The inhabitants' lives are bookended by the harbour at one end of town and the paper mill at the other.

The last ferry to traverse the St. Lawrence operates from Matane, chugging over in two hours. As it has already left for the day, I check into a motel called the Pinguoin, with a six-foot wooden penguin on a pole as graphic backup for its name. The owner has a slight limp, which gives him a penguin's gait, the one seamen unconsciously mimic. When I ask him if he has perhaps been to sea, he replies yes, he has done his time; it was that or the mill, and the mill was in the same place every day. He tries an old joke on me when I inquire if he has lived here all his life. "*Pas encore,*" he says. Not yet.

A squeegee kid wearing a Florida Panthers T-shirt is working the lineup of cars waiting for the ferry the next day, and in between squeaky strokes he tells me of the whole week two years ago when the ferry couldn't cross because of ice buildup. A coast guard icebreaker had to come and "unstick" things, the first time in living memory—meaning his, which is relatively short—that has happened. Where, he says as he finishes up, is global warming when you need it?

I have a choice of ferries. I can go to either Godbout or Baie-Comeau, and I sit in the car and weigh their virtues. Baie-Comeau is farther upriver than Godbout but takes about the same time to reach from Matane. Godbout is smaller, no more than a T comprising two streets, and far less industrial. Baie-Comeau is essentially one big factory, Reynolds and Donohue the main game in town, built up to city size in the 1920s by a Chicago newspaper baron called McCormick, who had been taking wood out of the area since 1913 to make paper for his *Tribune* and *New York Daily News*.

I decide to eschew the Viking town—I've been there before—for the fresh delights of Godbout.

The ship that takes me there, the *Camille-Marceux*, built in Montréal in 1974, is afflicted with many of the vices of modern ferry travel. Inside, a man is doing a karaoke kind of thing, singing to pre-recorded tapes. He takes a swing at "What Now My Love" and I go on deck, past the Loterie Vidéo games, where I am greeted with constant Muzak from which there is no escape but suicide. There are small billboards for tourist attractions hanging from the inside of the ship's rails.

I try to ignore all this pecuniary and peculiar distraction and look out over the water, first on the starboard side, towards Anticosti Island—the famous smuggling depot during Prohibition for some of Canada's finest families—and the rest of the world. A small fishing vessel, low in the water, is coming in. I give them my seasoned wave and the deckhand waves a fish back at me. Strolling over to the port side, I am almost immediately rewarded with a whale sighting, a small minke. Its back appears like a thick stitch of black thread, then it hears the Muzak and dives down deep.

The greasy spoon in Godbout is busy with the seasoned stomachs of the ferry arrivals, and I share a table with Agent Laroche, the very fit, taciturn policeman whose beat includes Godbout and three hundred other square miles down as far as Les Escoumins. Today he is in his car, but he is just as likely to be in a boat patrolling a salmon river or on a Ski-Doo. He is, actually, Quebec President of the Canadian Ski-Doo Society and one of the driving forces behind the Trans-Canada Ski-Doo Trail, which took him forty-two days to traverse. "Tourism, mines and salmon," he says, wiping his plate with his bread. The holy trinity of the lower north shore.

The ghost of Napoléon Comeau, one of the most famous residents of this part of the north shore, is all over the town. Napoléon Comeau was born in the spring of 1848 at Îlets-Jérémie (an hour by car east of Godbout), the son of a Hudson's Bay man who had married the adopted daughter of the founder of the nationalist *Le Canadien* newspaper. The Comeaus shifted their lives from remote post to remote post, and Napoléon attended school only for one cramped year in Trois-Rivières, long enough to learn to read and write in English. Back in the wilderness, with his mother and then the Indians as his professors, he became a famous field scientist, his desk in Godbout littered with pieces of the natural world. A plaque on the main street announced that he died in Godbout on November 17, 1923, leaving behind a powerful set of notches on his fishing rod and rifle and his byline on a compendium of nature writings, including the classic *Life and Sport on the Lower St. Lawrence and Gulf*, in which he proves that the north shore is a place where men are men and the salmon are nervous.

Comeau pops up again when I visit a cozy museum of northern Native artifacts in a house once owned by one of his sons. It is now the home of the Greniers, the mayor of Godbout and his wife, both of them practising artists. The artifacts in the house are from their time up north setting up independent artists' co-ops, and now they teach art to classes of people from all over the country in a studio at the back of the house. Several people are working away there on sketches of river and mountains, and then two Montagnais come in clutching bits of paper, and the mayor falls into amicable discussion with them. While they chat, one of the women in the museum tells me of the time in 1951 when a blue whale washed up on the shore and nothing could move it. It was eventually cut up and hauled away. "I remember the huge blueness of it," she says, "and how we would sit in the shade of it on the beach." Godbout is that kind of town, and I know I am leaving many a story behind as I climb up the one road out of town and head for river's end.

The turnoff to Pointe-des-Monts is a road perched on a sandy plateau, a vast beach of dunes and sword grass beside a sea hundreds of feet below it. To my left the Gulf of St. Lawrence, its northern, ragged edge curving away, accepts the never-ending output of the river. I can see a glint of Les Méchins straight across on the far side, and a line of hills like a stripe of putty stuck to the glassy surface. The road winds down to river level and a scattering of log holiday chalets, each enjoying an imposing view off the porch and a degree of isolation from the domestic affairs of the rest of the river. Several small, rocky coves lead to a car park and a wooden pedestrian bridge connecting to a treeless island. Adorning the island is a home, a handful of outbuildings including a visitor's centre, and a lighthouse.

Walking across a small plot of wind-bent grass, I step onto a slab of rock with a squat cannon on it, once used to catch the attention of passing shipping. Beside the cannon is a metal pulpit, and the plaque on it tells me I am at the "point of separation" of the Gulf of St. Lawrence and the St. Lawrence River. Journey's end. Then I turn and ascend the lighthouse, anxious for a higher view.

The lighthouse, stuck like a map pin to the end of the north shore, is a museum. For very little money you can take an enthusiastic history lesson from the two women guides from Godbout, the curators of the tower's story.

Given the safety record of the river in the opening chapters of its navigation, it is no surprise that in 1829 an Admiral Ogelin called for better charts and some lighthouses. The art of lighthouse building and anchoring had recently been brought to a new level by the Stevenson family—the same one that later included the storyteller Robert Louis—along Scotland's treacherous coast, and their technological advances were exported throughout the colonies. On September 20, 1830, the light at Pointe-des-Monts was lit for the first time, by James Wallace, the lucky candidate from a list of eleven.

Wallace, as was his duty, kept a diary that he called his *Journal of Occurrences* in which he paid obsessive attention to the weather and how much oil the lamp had consumed; his target was two gallons and a pint a night. A good day was described in the journal as "light air," the meteorology at midnight was noted, and in a separate column he recorded the way the wind was blowing. Every now and then Wallace made a rescue report, detailing how much food the survivors that had rowed or been washed to his shore ate before leaving him. (The roll call of the shipwrecked who have appeared at Pointe-des-Monts is as long as a schooner's keel. In the mid-1990s a wreck was discovered just offshore dating from Admiral Phips's disastrous expedition of 1690, the one that claimed nine hundred lives in a single afternoon.)

The family that followed Wallace, the Bédards, had two adopted children, one of whom, Luce, married Antoine Comeau, another of the ubiquitous Comeau clan. The Bédards had a dozen children, who set about populating that stretch of the river with the eagerness of missionaries. The Bédard dynasty lasted twenty-two years at Pointe-des-Monts, and they lived in the tower, each successive layer of it a different room with a different function, and with curved walls slightly smaller in circumference than the room below, rather like living inside an overly grand wedding cake. The tower's backbone is a spiralling set of narrowing stone steps, like a DNA spiral, each set of steps from one floor to the next less worn than the one below. Some nights in the depth of winter, the Bédards all slept in one bed to keep warm. Nevertheless, when Zoël Bédard died in March 1867, his wife wanted to carry on. Her request was refused on the grounds that "men are always more efficient."

Paul Pouliot, a man unattached, then moved in for the five-year stretch that saw steamships become the majority over sail on the river. Like the keepers before him, he used the traditional method to decide the moment for lighting up: extend the arm straight ahead from the shoulder, turn the hand vertical, and lower it till the bottom finger rests on the horizon. If the sun is sitting on the top finger (each finger representing fifteen minutes) then it is an hour to sundown, so proceed to the lamp and ignite it. It was during Pouliot's tenure that the invention of the telegraph system arrived in the world of communications, although he was long gone by the time the lines reached the tower in 1883.

As sometimes happens with lighthouses, a factor perhaps of the lack of nearby employment, another family dynasty of keepers then established itself. From 1872 all the way to 1954, someone with the surname Fafard was in charge of this gateway to and from the St. Lawrence. The Fafards were like an ancestral throwback, creatures that had left the water for land but could not move far from it. The Fafard lineage began with Louis-Ferdinand, who passed the torch to his fourth son, Victor, in 1889, whose daughter, Elioza, became quite a famous journalist in Montréal and wrote a short book about her life at Pointe-des-Monts. Victor enjoyed his lofty position for thirty-seven years, then handed it over to his son Georges—who was born in the tower—in 1926. Georges saw the light through till 1954 when, eager for a change of scene, perhaps somewhere more inhabited, he transferred to the lighthouse at Métis-sur-Mer and worked out his time there. Ten years after Georges's departure, semi-automation arrived, and by 1978 the Pointe-des-Monts light could manage by itself and had no need of an attendant.

The museum provides some extracts from the journals of daily life the various Fafards kept, like the day the family sat down to a Sunday dinner of fresh roast eagle, shot shortly before it was served by one of Georges's daughters. The journals speak of the Montagnais who came to visit and to hunt the *loup marine* (sea wolf), the seal. One Montagnais woman, Angélique Michel, appears many times in the journals. She died in 1904 at the age of one hundred and six, and had known every lighthouse keeper since the tower was built. A few years after her death, the Innu stopped appearing.

A small entry by Louis-Ferdinand in January 1886 mentions one of the St. Lawrence's great survival stories, the night Napoléon Comeau and three other men inadvertently crossed the icy river and cheated death. Comeau's nightmare was a seal hunt gone wrong. Going to the aid of two brothers in danger of being sealed off from shore by slush ice, Comeau's canoe was itself denied a return to Pointe-des-Monts. The only way to avoid becoming frozen in was to go forward, and thirty hours later four men (Comeau's elder brother was with him) staggered up to a farmhouse on the south shore, having dragged their canoes most of the way. They had slept part of the night behind a windbreak fashioned from the two canoes on an ice floe in mid-river, and Napoléon had shot down three ducks, which they had eaten raw, warming the meat and themselves by putting slices under their armpits. Comeau's "I'm alive!" telegraph message to the lighthouse at Pointe-des-Monts was not believed—no one could have made that journey—but later, as the truth emerged, the story was promoted into legend. Reading Comeau's own telling of it in his autobiography makes the book itself feel frozen.

I work my way slowly up the tower through all this history, rubbing away a few more molecules of stone step with my boots, then bend to go through the door at the top of the lighthouse and into the light. The view is a feast. The arc of the Gulf stretches away on my left shoulder, lines of rock like fingers testing the water. I imagine someone standing at the top of the Tibbet's Point lighthouse eight hundred miles to the west of me at Cape Vincent, New York State, looking simultaneously towards me.

In the distance, just along the Gulf coast, I can see Trinity Bay, where Joseph-Elzéar Bernier, in 1877, went ashore with a party of sailors and a judge, and uncovered the skeleton of a whale one hundred feet above the level of the Gulf. The local fishermen knew of the whale but had not bothered to disturb it. Bernier and the judge each took a massive vertebra with them, and Bernier's souvenir served as a stool in his house. The judge's bit of backbone fell into the water while being loaded, and perhaps it is there still.

Behind the rush of wind slapping the waves against the rocks below, I hear the echo of history coming down the river, ships' horns and sailors' voices, the swish of the paddle, the tumble of the rapids, the gunfire and the storms. Just at that moment there isn't a ship in sight, and all seems as it once was, when the river enjoyed a state of grace, before it was scarred with the wake of canoes that grew into cargo vessels as long as a city block. I look down at the restless water for the small green bottle I launched at Long Point, but it hasn't arrived—at least not yet.

*A
great river, after all, is more than
a personality in its own right. It is a vital link
with a people's past, and also it is mystery. The eternal
river is always a new river yet forever the same; just as men
are new in each generation but forever the same, and always
must relearn what the others learned before them.*

—Hugh MacLennan, *Rivers of Canada: The St. Lawrence*, 1974

Acknowledgements

A ship without a crew, especially one as experienced and willing as the one on this voyage, does not arrive. My thanks to the following for helping me reach safe harbour:

John Almstedt for calling in.
Bud Andress for the great day out.
Jean-Guy Beaumier for paddling upstream.
René Béland for the bayou sojourn.
Brian and Louis for the musical interludes.
JoEllen Brydon for the rapid story.
Trayton Cheesman for the clipping.
The good folks of Clayton.
George and Gisele for hoisting me aloft. Ahoy there.
David Gerstel for the support, I'll wear it always.
Ken Ginn, for *hasta la visa*.
Phil Goyette for the tales of the riverbank.
Don and Ree Graham for the various views.
Gwen Guth for the Moodies.
Jeff and Louise for the space/time continuum.
Joe and Lisa for the sharing.
Jackie Kaiser for the course correction.
Jean Lavigne for *le grand tour*.
Hugues Morrissette for his generosity above and beyond.
John Parry for vigilance overseas.
Pierre Auger for the liner notes.
PJ Robertson for the quotes and votes.

ACKNOWLEDGEMENTS

Alan Sinclair for being lyrical.
John Sweet for knowing good is in the details.
The taxpayers of Canada, via the Canada Council.
Phil Wright for taking me down,

and, toujours, Liette for the loving spoonfuls.

INDEX

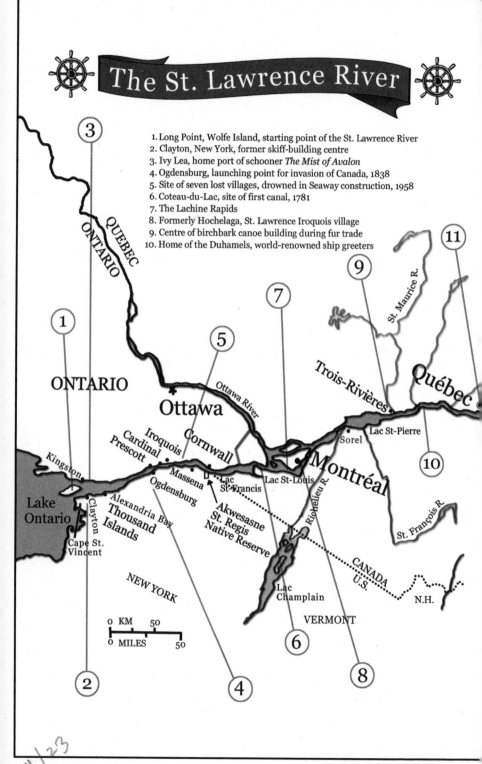

The St. Lawrence River

1. Long Point, Wolfe Island, starting point of the St. Lawrence River
2. Clayton, New York, former skiff-building centre
3. Ivy Lea, home port of schooner *The Mist of Avalon*
4. Ogdensburg, launching point for invasion of Canada, 1838
5. Site of seven lost villages, drowned in Seaway construction, 1958
6. Coteau-du-Lac, site of first canal, 1781
7. The Lachine Rapids
8. Formerly Hochelaga, St. Lawrence Iroquois village
9. Centre of birchbark canoe building during fur trade
10. Home of the Duhamels, world-renowned ship greeters

QUÉBEC
ONTARIO

ONTARIO

Ottawa

Ottawa River

Trois-Rivières

Québec

St. Maurice R.

Kingston

Iroquois
Cardinal
Prescott

Cornwall

Sorel

Lac St-Pierre

Lake
Ontario

Massena
Ogdensburg

Lac
St-Francis

Lac St-Louis

Montréal

Alexandria Bay

Akwesasne
St. Regis
Native Reserve

Richelieu R.

St. François R.

Clayton

Thousand
Islands

Cape St.
Vincent

NEW YORK

Lac
Champlain

CANADA
U.S.

N.H.

VERMONT

0 KM   50
0 MILES   50

4/23